THE NEW TIMES COOK BOOK

THE NEW TIMES
COOK BOOK

SHONA CRAWFORD POOLE

WILLOW BOOKS
Collins
8 Grafton Street, London
1983

Willow Books
William Collins Sons & Co Ltd
London · Glasgow · Sydney
Auckland · Toronto · Johannesburg

First published in Great Britain 1983

Illustrations by Stephen Johnson

Poole, Shona Crawford
The new times cook book
1. Cookery
I. Title
641.5   TX717

ISBN 0 00 218056 1

Filmset by Rowland Phototypesetting Ltd, Bury St Edmunds, Suffolk

Printed in Great Britain by William Collins Sons & Co Ltd, Glasgow

To Margaret Allen

Contents

Introduction

An anthology or collection tends, like the painter's one-man show, to be a patchwork of material made at different times and in response to stimuli which are now long forgotten. Newspaper journalism is inevitably here today and gone tomorrow, ephemeral in the true sense of the word, so it is immensely pleasing to have an opportunity to gather the recipes that I have liked best in four years of writing the weekly cookery column in *The Times*. Friends are amused to find me cooking dinner from cuttings of old articles and notes for new ones stuck up on the kitchen wall, but it proves that I for one need this book because it is the only one which has all my favourite recipes in it.

Making this kind of collection does have its dangers though. It quickly shows up biases of taste and style which are much more difficult to spot when the dishes are described two or three at a time. I cannot help noticing too late in the day how the acquisition of a food processor has encouraged a cavalier attitude to the work involved in making purées, or how often cream appears, even if optionally, in my soups. Other patterns emerge too, like a taste for nuts. Hopefully, most of these repetitions will be pleasing.

Insatiable curiosity about old and new recipes, about how and why they have evolved, makes the research endlessly interesting. Books are a source of ideas of course, but the greatest stimulus of all is other people's cooking. Occasionally, because opportunities to sample the work of great chefs are infrequent, it is a dish created in a master's kitchen which inspires an attempt to recreate it in my own. Sometimes such recipes will be simplicity itself, relying for their impact on an unexpected combination of tastes or textures. More often though they will demand plenty of time, some skill and ingredients which are not necessarily cheap. Not everyone has enough interest, let alone time to make tricky fish terrines and the like. These are dishes for the adventurous and cooks whose greatest treat is cooking something special just for the fun of it. But I do believe that I have explained such dishes fully enough for everyone to be able to cook them with confidence.

Most recipe ideas have come from meals enjoyed in simpler restaurants at home and abroad, and at the tables of friends. I first tasted galantine of duck, that *trompe l'oeil* creation where a boned bird is stuffed with pâté and reassembled to look as properly duck-like as possible, at a summer party given by Sheila Hutchins of the *Daily Express*. And it was Pamela Vandyke Price, former wine correspondent of *The Times*, who introduced me to the easy and interesting Mediterranean salad of orange slices with black olives and onion.

In the mix of recipes gathered over the years from my mother, friends, reading and travelling, are a few that may be sufficiently different from anyone else's creations to rate as original. I know that it was Chef Anton Mosimann's delicate smoked salmon mousse which inspired me to attempt an equally light and creamy confection based on Parma ham. So far, I have not come across anything at all similar, but there are times when one's inventions can prove disappointingly unoriginal. I was not, I learned later, the first person to think of adding ground cinnamon to the pastry for an apple pie.

The only real disadvantage of writing about food is that it seems to inhibit people from cooking for you. It is as if they thought, mistakenly of course, that one must be terribly fussy. Chefs, who like cookery writers clearly enjoy food enormously, ruefully admit to the same discrimination. I tried to put someone at ease once with a tortuous analogy about Yehudi Menuhin appreciating any kind of music more than someone like me because he understands so much more about it. But that only suggested, even more intimidatingly, that I might be a red-hot connoisseur, or that my cooking could be compared in the same breath with his violin playing, which, except by felicitous chance, it cannot. So now I keep it simple and say only that I like food, which is why I cook and write about it.

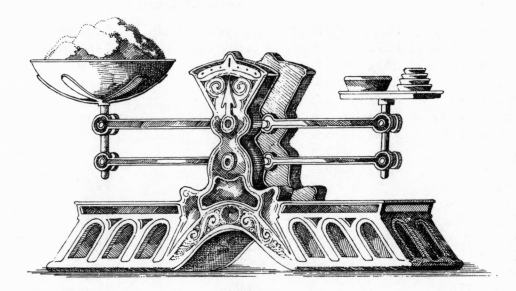

Measures

More or less, but how exactly?

Underlined, italicised, or printed in bold capitals, the words *more or less, but seldom exactly* should be stamped on recipes as insistently as cigarette packet health warnings.

The point is easy enough to take when it concerns seasonings. How else would you add salt, except to taste? But how soft is a slack dough, how thick is a thin batter, or firm a meringue when it is stiff, but on no account dry? Experience tells you of course. And recipes try to. But when one brand of flour will mop up more or less liquid depending on the humidity of the place it has been stored, and other makes are ground more or less finely from harder or softer blends of wheat, it is not difficult to see why my dough needs three tablespoons of water and yours needs four.

If apparently standard ingredients are infuriatingly variable, cooking times are more elusive still. Your gentle simmer is unlikely to match mine outside a laboratory, and my electric oven undoubtedly has tricks which differ from those of any gas cooker, never mind a solid fuel stove. Quite aside from hot spots or cold spots to which many an oven is prone, numerous other factors affect baking times. The thickness and heat-conducting properties of the tins or dishes used makes more difference than sometimes seems reasonable. Chilled food obviously takes longer to bake than ingredients already at room temperature. The larger the quantity the greater the difference, and so on.

Hence all those seemingly hedging *abouts* in cooking times, advice on tapping loaves for that well-baked hollow sound, and jabbing cakes with skewers which must come out clean.

That said, a tablespoon is an accurate measure of volume. It holds 15 ml or ½ fluid ounce and when dealing with dry ingredients, a tablespoon is level. The same goes for a teaspoon which measures 5 ml. A dessertspoon is no measure at all, and neither is that battered silver serving spoon with a bent handle.

The charts which follow show the metric and imperial equivalents used throughout this book.

Weights

15 g =	½ oz	1 kg	=	2 lb 3 oz
20 g =	¾ oz	1.35 kg	=	3 lb
30 g =	1 oz	1.8 kg	=	4 lb
55 g =	2 oz	2.3 kg	=	5 lb
85 g =	3 oz	2.7 kg	=	6 lb
100 g =	3½ oz	3.2 kg	=	7 lb
110 g =	4 oz	3.4 kg	=	8 lb
140 g =	5 oz	4 kg	=	9 lb
170 g =	6 oz	4.5 kg	=	10 lb
200 g =	7 oz			
225 g =	8 oz			
255 g =	9 oz			
285 g =	10 oz			
310 g =	11 oz			
340 g =	12 oz			
370 g =	13 oz			
400 g =	14 oz			
425 g =	15 oz			
450 g =	1 lb			
500 g =	1 lb 2 oz			
570 g =	1¼ lb			
680 g =	1½ lb			
900 g =	2 lb			

Liquid Measures

1 teaspoon (5 ml)	= 1 teaspoon
1 tablespoon (15 ml)	= 1 tablespoon
120 ml	= 4 fl oz
150 ml	= ¼ pint
175 ml	= 6 fl oz
200 ml	= ⅓ pint
250 ml	= 8 fl oz
300 ml	= ½ pint
350 ml	= 12 fl oz
400 ml	= 14 fl oz
450 ml	= ¾ pint
500 ml	= 18 fl oz
600 ml	= 1 pint
750 ml	= 1¼ pints
900 ml	= 1½ pints
1 litre	= 1¾ pints
1.2 litres	= 2 pints
1.25 litres	= 2¼ pints
1.5 litres	= 2½ pints
1.6 litres	= 2¾ pints
1.75 litres	= 3 pints
2 litres	= 3½ pints
2.25 litres	= 4 pints
2.5 litres	= 4½ pints
2.75 litres	= 5 pints

Oven Temperatures

very cool	(110°C/225°F, gas mark ¼) (120°C/250°F, gas mark ½)	moderately hot	(190°C/375°F, gas mark 5) (200°C/400°F, gas mark 6)
cool	(140°C/275°F, gas mark 1) (150°C/300°F, gas mark 2)	hot	(220°C/425°F, gas mark 7) (230°C/450°F, gas mark 8)
moderate	(160°C/325°F, gas mark 3) (180°C/350°F, gas mark 4)	very hot	(240°C/475°F, gas mark 9) (250°C/500°F, gas mark 9)

Dimensions of cutters, tins, etc.

3 mm	= ⅛ in	15 cm	=	6 in
7 mm	= ¼ in	18 cm	=	7 in
1.25 cm	= ½ in	20 cm	=	8 in
2 cm	= ¾ in	23 cm	=	9 in
2.5 cm	= 1 in	25 cm	=	10 in
5 cm	= 2 in	28 cm	=	11 in
6.5 cm	= 2½ in	30 cm	=	12 in
7.5 cm	= 3 in			

Capacity of pans, bowls, tins, etc.

300 ml = ½ pint		1 litre	= 2 pints
450 ml = ¾ pint		1.25 litres	= 2½ pints
600 ml = 1 pint		1.5 litres	= 3 pints
900 ml = 1½ pints		2.5 litres	= 5 pints
		3.5 litres	= 7 pints

1

A Soup for all Seasons

Almost anything edible can be made into soup and pretty well everything edible is. Soup and bread in one form or another have sustained much of humanity since fire and cooking pots were first combined. Even before pots, animals were boiled after a fashion by pushing a slain beast into a flooded trench and heaving hot stones in round it. There must have been worse than a hair or two in the mud produced by this primitive exercise in culinary science.

The arrival of pots and kettles that could be set over fires made possible various combinations of cereals, pulses, roots and leaves with the flesh of all manner of creatures. And the soups we serve now are no more than deliberate and sometimes refined versions of the peasant pottages made down the centuries by people who cooked only what they could grow or garner. This is one reason it is not hard to deduce from a list of ingredients where many a classic soup hails from. Could *bouillabaisse* be anything other than a fishermen's soup or from any sea but the Mediterranean? Could *borscht* be from anywhere but eastern Europe, or *minestrone* other than an Italian invention?

There are some soups the mere thought of which conjures a wisp of imaginary steam. London particular, as thick with split peas as the famous fog which its name commemorates, is unthinkable in any state but scalding hot. At the other extreme are the chilled soups of warm summer evenings. Who would dream of serving cucumber and yogurt soup anything but iced? In between are the soups for all seasons, all-weather soups so well adapted to our capricious climate that the decision to serve them piping or iced can be postponed until after the table is laid. Vichyssoise is probably the best known recipe in this category, cream of Stilton soup one of the best, and watercress the simplest.

Taking stock, as one must in any discussion on the subject of soup, raises the question of whether to keep a stockpot, to feed it with careful economy on bones and trimmings, and boil it daily. I confess that I do not and that a perpetual stockpot is an ideal of good housekeeping as impractical in my life as baking all my own bread. Some cookery books have a sneaky way of implying that stock cubes will never do, though their instructions for making stock often demand enough meat to feed a family for days.

My own views on the subject are strongly middle of the road. If the choice is between home-made soup using a cube or no home-made soup, then it is no contest. The cube wins. It is when the choice is between a very nice soup and the best possible soup that home-made stocks really come into their own. Subtly flavoured iced soups made with real chicken stock that sets to a shivering jelly when chilled are a good example of the case in favour of taking pains.

When stock cubes are unavoidable, as they sometimes must be for reasons of time, expense or the availability of ingredients, the trick is not to add the same taste on every occasion. Ring the changes between brands and look out for kosher and vegetarian varieties. It often pays to think twice about adding a cube at all. Water in which vegetables have cooked, or straight from the tap can be a better choice. Tins of consommé are an invaluable standby for chilled soups.

Tap water is all that is required for *franglais fish soupe* which came about through trying to make in London a fish soup that tasted something like, preferably very like the fishy, fox-coloured nectar of Corsica and the Côte d'Azur. I dare say that a decent approximation of *bouillabaisse* is possible so far north, but my sights were set on an even-textured *soupe de poissons* thickened with small particles of fish – a soup that leaves you with the breath of a St Julien road mender in August because it is served with *rouille*, corrosively garlicked mayonnaise rusted with cayenne. Powerful stuff all this, but there is more if the *soupe* is to be supped in all its splendour. There must be thick croûtons of dried French bread and, optionally, freshly grated Parmesan.

I swotted up on the bony Mediterranean rock fish such soups demand. Angry sounding *rascasses* and *wrasses* were recommended but the fishmonger did not have them. He had met this *soupe* problem before though and pointed out two sorts of gurnard: one pinkish, the other greyish. I am not sure exactly which kinds. Drawings of fish with all their fins erect and fanned never seem to match the folded reality on a marble slab. So I took one of each, plus a piece of monkfish, a chunk each of conger and rock eel, and a small red mullet. They were not a particularly pretty sight, but cleaned and chopped into big, rough chunks and slices, they looked likely enough ingredients for a Marseillaise recipe for fish soup.

It was a good soup, there is no denying that, but it was not the right soup. It was not the rough, tough, boisterous soup of waterfront dives and natty jetties. Three additions put it right. First, and inevitably, a generous slug of pastis. Then I tipped in a paste of raw red peppers (the sweet kind) mixed with olive oil and breadcrumbs. This had been a version of *rouille* that turned out not to be the variety I was trying to make. Finally, it was a couple of inches of tomato paste that did the trick.

It was a winner. Everyone had seconds or thirds. Nobody finished the next course. Cheese and pudding were quite forgotten and songs were sung.

Franglais Fish Soupe

SERVES 6–8

*2 kg (4–4¹/₂ lb) fish, including
   conger eel and 1 or 2 whole fish*
120 ml (4 fl oz) olive oil
*2 leeks, white part only, finely
   sliced*
1 large onion, finely chopped
*1 small bulb Florentine fennel,
   finely sliced*
2 cloves garlic, finely chopped
*2 ripe red peppers, deseeded and
   finely chopped*
*225 g (8 oz) tomatoes, roughly
   chopped*
*bouquet garni of parsley, thyme,
   bay and orange zest*
*salt and freshly ground black
   pepper*
*pinch of saffron, soaked 5 minutes
   in 2 tablespoons boiling water*
*55 g (2 oz) fresh white
   breadcrumbs*
2 tablespoons tomato paste
6 tablespoons pastis

Wash and gut the fish and cut into large pieces. Scrape the scales off any fish which has very large ones, but keep the heads, tails and fins on the fish pieces.

Heat the oil in a large, heavy-based pot and add the leeks and onion. Cook on a medium heat until the onion is tender, but not browned. Add the fennel, garlic, peppers, tomatoes and fish, together with about 2.75 litres (5 pints) of water. Bring quickly to the boil, adding the herbs, salt, pepper, saffron, breadcrumbs and tomato paste. Cook the soup, uncovered, at a soft, rolling boil for about 30 minutes.

The easiest way to render this awesome brew into a smooth, bone-free soup is to work it through a *mouli légumes* fitted with its finest disc. This allows all the fish flesh to be pushed through, and really does eliminate the bones. Alternative methods are to process or liquidise the mixture, then sieve it, or to press it through a sieve with a wooden spoon.

Whichever method you choose, discard the bones, etc., and reheat the soup. Adjust the seasoning and add the pastis just before serving with *rouille*, croûtons and freshly grated Parmesan cheese.

Rouille

MAKES 150 ml (¼ pint)

2–6 cloves garlic, crushed
2 egg yolks
2 teaspoons cayenne pepper
¹/₂ teaspoon salt
150 ml (¹/₄ pint) fruity olive oil

Like mayonnaise, *rouille* is most quickly and simply made in a food processor. Put the garlic, egg yolks, cayenne and salt in the bowl and process for a few seconds before adding the oil in a thin steady stream while the machine is running.

Alternatively make the sauce in a pestle or bowl, pounding the garlic, egg yolks, cayenne and salt to a smooth paste before working in the oil, drop by drop, until the mixture forms a thick, glossy sauce.

Should the *rouille* separate because the oil is being added too quickly, put a fresh egg yolk into a clean pestle or bowl, and slowly work in the separated sauce, a little at a time, until a stable emulsion is formed. Then add the remaining oil.

For the croûtons try, if possible, to use real French bread. A slim *baguette* is ideal for cutting into 1.25 cm (½ in) thick slices which can be very lightly brushed with olive oil and dried for 10 minutes in a preheated moderate oven (180°C/350°F, gas mark 4). They should be dry and barely coloured, not too hard or too golden.

Prawn chowder is quickly made and almost a meal in itself. There is no need to thaw frozen prawns before adding them to the soup.

Prawn Chowder

SERVES 4–6

15 g (½ oz) butter
3 rashers streaky bacon, finely chopped
225 g (8 oz) onion, finely chopped
450 g (1 lb) potatoes, peeled and diced
300 ml (½ pint) chicken stock
600 ml (1 pint) milk
1 bay leaf
freshly ground black pepper
225 g (8 oz) peeled prawns
150 ml (¼ pint) single cream or natural yogurt
salt
2 tablespoons finely chopped parsley

Melt the butter in a large pan and add the bacon. Cook gently until the bacon fat begins to run. Add the onion and fry gently together, without allowing the mixture to brown, until the onion is soft.

Add the potatoes, stock, milk and bay leaf and bring almost to the boil. Reduce the heat, season with the pepper, cover the pan and simmer until the potatoes are soft and beginning to break up.

Fish out the bay leaf. Add the prawns and cream or yogurt and heat gently until the prawns are hot, without allowing the soup to boil. Add more pepper and salt to taste. Just before serving, stir in the parsley.

An extra bonus of serving lobster at home is that the shells can be boiled up again to make a bisque. Here is a simple one.

Lobster Bisque

SERVES 4–6

2–4 lobster shells
1.2 litres (2 pints) lobster cooking liquid, or water
salt and freshly ground black pepper
30 g (1 oz) butter
1 tablespoon plain flour
150 ml (¼ pint) single cream
2 tablespoons cognac (optional)

Pound the lobster shells into tiny pieces and put them in a pan with the stock or water, salt and pepper. Bring the liquid to the boil, cover the pan and simmer for about two hours. Strain the liquid through a sieve lined with a double layer of muslin or a tea cloth.

Rinse out the pan and melt the butter in it. When the butter froths, stir in the flour and cook the *roux* for a moment or two before gradually adding the strained stock, stirring constantly. Cook the soup for a further five minutes. Remove from the heat and add the cream and cognac. Serve immediately.

The Scandinavians seem to do the most miraculous things with the most ordinary of fish. Their pickled herrings are justly renowned, and the humble mackerel is made much of. If fresh dill is not easy to come by use fennel (buy a bulb of Florentine fennel with plenty of feathery green leaves on it) or parsley.

Mackerel Soup

SERVES 6

680 g (1½ lb) mackerel, cleaned
30 g (1 oz) fresh dill or parsley, or ½ a small fennel bulb with all its leaves
150 ml (¼ pint) single cream
juice of 1 lemon
salt and freshly ground black pepper
2 egg yolks

Cut off the fish heads, rinse the fish in cold water and cut them in 2.5 cm (1 in) slices. Put the fish in a pan with 1.75 litres (3 pints) of water. Reserve a tablespoon of finely chopped dill, parsley or fennel leaves for the garnish and add the remainder, coarsely chopped, to the pan. Bring to the boil, reduce the heat, cover the pan and simmer for about 10 minutes.

Strain the stock into a clean saucepan and stir in half the cream and all the lemon juice. Remove and discard the skin and bones of the fish and return the flesh to the pan. Season well with salt and pepper. Bring the soup to the boil and remove it from the heat immediately.

Mix the remaining cream with the egg yolks and stir into the soup to thicken it. Do not boil after the egg has been added. Serve immediately, sprinkled with the remaining herbs and without reheating.

This soup which I found in Marcella Hazan's *Classic Italian Cookbook* is a robust dish of mussels cooked briefly in tomato and garlic. No liquid is added and the mussels release the juices from their shells to form the soup. To prepare fresh mussels scrub them very thoroughly in cold water with a stiff brush and pull or cut off the tuft of beard clenched by each one. Throw away any with broken shells, and any which do not snap shut when tapped.

The recipe calls for Italian wholemeal bread which is not widely available, so substitute another kind, or leave out the toasted bread and serve hot crusty rolls or bread separately.

Mussel Soup

SERVES 4

2 cloves garlic, peeled and chopped
6 tablespoons olive oil
1 tablespoon coarsely chopped parsley
225 g (8 oz) tin of Italian tomatoes, drained and chopped
⅛ teaspoon chopped or powdered chilli
900 g (2 lb) fresh mussels, cleaned and scrubbed
4 slices Italian wholemeal bread (pane integrale), toasted and (optional) rubbed with garlic

Choose a casserole large enough to contain the mussels later. Sauté the garlic in the oil on a moderate heat until it has coloured lightly. Add the parsley, stir once or twice, then add the tomatoes and chilli. Cook, uncovered, at a gentle simmer for about 25 minutes, or until the tomatoes and oil separate.

Add the mussels, cover the casserole, increase the heat to high and cook until the mussels open their shells – this will take about three to five minutes. To cook all the mussels evenly, grasp the casserole with both hands, holding the lid down tight, and shake it sharply two or three times.

Put a slice of toasted bread in each soup dish and ladle the mussels, with all their sauce, over the bread. Serve piping hot.

Vichyssoise, the famous American leek and potato soup, is usually rich in cream. To make a lighter, less expensive version, which is excellent in its own right when served chilled, substitute natural yogurt for the cream. If you want a white soup use only the white parts of the leeks, otherwise use the whole vegetable.

Vichyssoise

SERVES 4–6

45 g (1¹/₂ oz) butter
680 g (1¹/₂ lb) leeks, roughly
*   chopped*
450 g (1 lb) potatoes, peeled and
*   roughly chopped*
900 ml (1¹/₂ pints) chicken stock
salt and freshly ground black
*   pepper*
freshly grated nutmeg
300 ml (¹/₂ pint) single or double
*   cream, or natural yogurt*
2 tablespoons finely chopped chives

Melt the butter in a large pan and add the leeks. Cover the pan and allow the leeks to sweat on a gentle heat until they are soft, but not browned. Add the potatoes, stock, salt, pepper and nutmeg and bring the soup to the boil. Reduce the heat, cover the pan and simmer gently until the potatoes are soft.

Pass the soup through a *mouli légumes* fitted with its fine disc, or press it through a sieve. If you use a blender or food processor you will still have to sieve out the stringy bits of leek, and there is always the danger of ending up with the curious wallpaper-paste consistency caused by over-processing potato.

Add two-thirds of the cream to the puréed soup and reheat. Serve hot with a swirl of cream and some of the chives on each serving.

To serve vichyssoise cold, chill the purée and stir in the cream or yogurt. Top each bowl with a sprinkling of the chives.

Cream of Stilton Soup

SERVES 6

55 g (2 oz) butter
30 g (1 oz) plain flour
600 ml (1 pint) milk
600 ml (1 pint) chicken or veal
*   stock*
150 ml (¹/₄ pint) dry sherry
150 ml (¹/₄ pint) double cream
225 g (8 oz) Stilton cheese, crumbled
salt and cayenne pepper
2 tablespoons flaked almonds,
*   lightly toasted*

Melt the butter in a large, heavy saucepan and stir in the flour. Cook the *roux* on a gentle heat for a minute or two without allowing it to colour. Add the milk gradually, stirring constantly, to make a smooth sauce. Cook the sauce gently for about five minutes before adding the stock, sherry and cream. Bring almost to the boil and stir in the cheese. Remove the soup from the heat as soon as the cheese has melted and season to taste with salt and cayenne. Serve this soup hot or chilled with a few flakes of toasted almond floating on each bowl.

18

Watercress soup is one of my favourites, and I make it with the slightly smokey flavoured stock which results from boiling a knuckle end of gammon. Chicken stock is more usual though.

Watercress Soup

SERVES 4–6

2 bunches of watercress
900 ml (1 1/2 pints) gammon or
    chicken stock, fat free
1 clove garlic, peeled
300 ml (1/2 pint) single cream
2 egg yolks
salt and freshly ground black
    pepper
a few sprigs of watercress to garnish

Wash the watercress thoroughly and discard any roots and badly damaged or yellow leaves. Chop the leaves and stalks roughly and put them in a pan with four table-spoons of the stock. Cover the pan and sweat the water-cress on a low heat for about five minutes before adding the remaining stock and whole clove of garlic. Bring the soup to the boil, then reduce the heat, cover the pan and simmer for about 20 minutes.

Fish out and discard the garlic. Purée the soup by passing it through a *mouli légumes*, or pressing it through a coarse sieve. Alternatively, use a food processor or blender.

Return the purée to a clean pan. Mix half the cream with the egg yolks and stir this liaison into the soup. Heat gently, stirring constantly and without allowing the soup to boil, until it has thickened a little. Season to taste with salt and pepper, remembering that chilled soup needs to be more highly seasoned than hot.

Serve the soup hot, or chilled, with a swirl of the remaining cream and a sprig of watercress in each bowl.

To peel tomatoes for the gazpacho and iced tomato soup recipes, drop them into boiling water for 30 seconds, then run them under the cold tap and the skins will slip off easily.

Iced Tomato Soup

SERVES 4

900 g (2 lb) ripe tomatoes
300 ml (1/2 pint) crème fraîche (see
    page 227), sour cream or
    natural yogurt
300 ml (1/2 pint) dry white wine,
    or half and half wine and water
1 tablespoon fresh lemon thyme
    leaves
salt and cayenne pepper
a few sprigs of lemon thyme to
    garnish

Peel and deseed the tomatoes. Purée the flesh, by passing it through a sieve or *mouli légumes*, or in a food processor or blender. Stir in the cream or yogurt, wine and lemon thyme. Season to taste with salt and cayenne. Chill well before serving with a sprig of lemon thyme in each bowl.

There are as many ways of making gazpacho as there are people who make it. Stock is called for in some recipes, and the proportions of vegetables used vary enormously. Sometimes it is a raw tomato soup flavoured lightly with onion, garlic, cucumber and sweet peppers. Sometimes it may include olives, or be green with onions, cucumbers, and peppers. Not all recipes start with a garlic and bread paste, and the finished soup may be rough, or smooth. The only attribute that every gazpacho must have is the fresh taste of good raw materials.

Gazpacho

SERVES 4–6

1 clove garlic, peeled
30 g (1 oz) fresh white
   breadcrumbs
2 tablespoons red wine vinegar
2 tablespoons fruity olive oil
450 g (1 lb) ripe tomatoes, peeled,
   deseeded and finely chopped
1 cucumber, peeled, deseeded and
   finely chopped
110 g (4 oz) spring onions, thinly
   sliced
110 g (4 oz) sweet red pepper,
   deseeded and finely chopped
2 tablespoons chopped fresh herbs:
   basil, marjoram or parsley
300 ml (½ pint), or more, iced
   water
½–1 teaspoon Tabasco sauce
salt and freshly ground black
   pepper
4 thick slices white bread, cubed
   and fried in olive oil

Using a pestle and mortar, food processor or blender, reduce the garlic, breadcrumbs, vinegar and oil to a smooth paste. Transfer the mixture to a bowl and stir in the tomatoes, cucumber, spring onions, red pepper and herbs. Add the iced water and Tabasco sauce and season to taste with salt and pepper. Alternatively, purée half the soup in a food processor or blender and mix it back into the remaining coarser mixture.

Chill the gazpacho well before serving with a bowl of freshly fried croûtons.

Do try making chilled cucumber soup with fresh ginger. It adds a really refreshing tang to this traditional summer cooler.

Chilled Cucumber Soup

SERVES 4–6

1 clove garlic, peeled
small piece of green ginger (same
   size as garlic clove), peeled
600 ml (1 pint) natural yogurt
1 cucumber, peeled, deseeded and
   finely chopped
450 ml (¾ pint) iced water
salt
½ teaspoon Tabasco sauce
150 ml (¼ pint) crème fraîche (see
   page 227) or double cream
1 tablespoon chopped chives or
   mint to garnish

Using a garlic press or pestle and mortar, reduce the garlic and ginger to a smooth paste, and mix it with the yogurt. Add half the cucumber and blend until smooth in a blender or food processor. Stir in the remaining cucumber and the water, and season with salt and the Tabasco sauce. Chill well before serving with a swirl of cream and a pinch of the chives or mint in each bowl.

Almost any combination of avocado, chicken stock, and cream or natural yogurt, makes a good soup to serve chilled. The proportions can be varied and additional flavourings added on a taste-and-see basis. Spice it up with Tabasco sauce or cayenne pepper. Try whole or ground cumin seeds for a milder spicy taste. Add finely chopped onion and cucumber for variations of texture; fresh basil or coriander leaves for flavour.

Chilled Avocado Soup

SERVES 4

2 ripe avocados
1 clove garlic, crushed
1 sprig of fresh basil
900 ml (1½ pints) chicken stock
salt and freshly ground black pepper or cayenne
150 ml (¼ pint) single cream

Peel the avocados, discard the stones and purée the flesh with the garlic and basil. A food processor or blender achieves this in seconds, but pushing everything through a sieve does not take much longer. Blend in the stock, salt and black pepper or cayenne to taste, and the cream. Chill well and check the seasoning again just before serving.

Always *pull* the stalks off artichokes. Cutting them off leaves tough fibres in the base of the vegetable which are wrenched out with the stalk.

Chilled Cream of Artichoke Soup

SERVES 4

salt
4 large globe artichokes
900 ml (1½ pints) light chicken stock
150 ml (¼ pint) double cream, lightly whipped
4 tablespoons chopped fresh chervil or parsley
freshly ground black pepper

Half-fill a large saucepan with water, add a tablespoon of salt and bring to the boil. Wash the artichokes, pull off the stalks and drop them into the boiling water. Boil them briskly, uncovered, for about 40 minutes, or until the outer leaves can be pulled off easily.

Drain the artichokes, heads down, and when they are cool enough to handle, pull off the leaves and carefully remove and discard the chokes. Scrape flesh off the larger leaves and roughly chop the hearts.

Mix the flesh from the artichoke leaves and hearts with the stock and purée the mixture by pressing it through a sieve, passing it through a *mouli légumes*, or processing it in a blender. Chill the soup before stirring in the cream and chervil or parsley. Season to taste with salt and pepper. Serve well chilled.

Walnut soup is the one iced soup I often serve in winter. It makes a fitting prelude to roast game.

Chilled Walnut Soup

SERVES 4–6

2 tablespoons olive oil
1 large onion, finely chopped
55 g (2 oz) shelled walnuts
900 ml (1½ pints) chicken stock
300 ml (½ pint) single cream, or
    half and half single cream and
    natural yogurt
salt and pepper

Heat the oil in a large pan, add the onion and cook gently until it is soft, but not browned. Add the walnuts and fry them with the onion for a minute or two before adding the stock. Bring to the boil, reduce the heat, cover the pan and simmer for about 10 minutes. Cool the soup.

Purée the mixture by pressing it through a sieve, or blend until smooth, then strain. Add the cream or cream and yogurt, season with salt and pepper and mix well. Chill thoroughly and check the seasoning again when the mixture is very cold. Stir well just before serving.

The excellence of this soup depends on the quantity of asparagus and the quality of the chicken stock. Asparagus that is too thick or too thin for top grading is often sold loose and quite cheaply.

Chilled Asparagus Soup

SERVES 6–8

680 g (1½ lb) asparagus
1 onion, finely chopped
300 ml (½ pint) water
900 ml (1½ pints) chicken stock,
    skimmed of fat
salt and cayenne pepper
150 ml (¼ pint) double cream

Cut off the asparagus tips and reserve them. Chop the stalks into short lengths and put them in a pan with the onion and water. Bring to the boil, cover the pan and simmer until the asparagus is very tender. Purée the vegetables with the liquid, then strain the purée.

Mix the purée with the stock and season to taste with salt and cayenne. Bring the soup to the boil and add the reserved asparagus tips. Simmer them gently in the soup until they are just tender. Cool the soup, then chill it well. Stir in the cream just before serving.

Lady Boreham requested recipes to use up her bolting lettuces. Happy to oblige, I cooked up a column of lettuce recipes. This was one of them.

Chilled Lettuce Soup

SERVES 6

3 large lettuces (any sort will do)
2 tablespoons peanut oil
2 large onions, finely chopped
2 cloves garlic, finely chopped
1.25 litres (2¼ pints) good chicken
  stock
150 ml (¼ pint) double cream
2 egg yolks
salt and freshly ground black
  pepper
2 tablespoons finely chopped chives

Trim the lettuces of any damaged leaves and wash them by dunking them head first in several changes of cold water. Shred them coarsely, discarding the central core if there is one.

Heat the oil in a large saucepan and add the onions and garlic. Cook on a low heat until the onion is tender, but not browned. Add the lettuce, cover the pan and cook until the lettuce has wilted. Add the stock and bring to the boil. Reduce the heat and simmer gently for about 15 minutes.

Sieve the soup, or blend or process it briefly, and return it to the pan. Beat together the cream and egg yolks and stir them into the soup. Cook on a low heat, stirring constantly, until the soup thickens a little. Do not boil or it may separate. Season to taste with salt and pepper. Chill well before serving with a sprinkling of the chives on each bowl.

Back to hot soups, and to begin with a traditional soup made with stock from the carcass and slivers of meat from a roast chicken.

Chicken Soup with Rice

SERVES 4

55 g (2 oz) butter
2 chicken livers, roughly chopped
1 large onion, finely chopped
900 ml (1½ pints) chicken stock
110 g (4 oz) long grain rice
110 g (4 oz) cooked chicken, diced
salt and freshly ground black
  pepper
4 tablespoons chopped parsley

Melt the butter in a large pan until it foams, then add the chicken livers and cook until they are just firm and each piece is still a little pink in the middle. Remove the chicken livers and set them aside. Add the onion to the pan and fry until it is soft, but not browned. Add the stock and bring to the boil. Throw in the rice, cover the pan and simmer for 20 minutes, or until the rice is very tender. Add the chicken and chicken livers and season to taste with salt and plenty of pepper. Reheat and stir in the parsley at the last moment, giving it just enough time to soften before serving.

London Particular

110 g (4 oz) smoked streaky bacon,
    diced
1 large onion, peeled and chopped
2 carrots, peeled and chopped
450 g (1 lb) dried split peas, soaked
    overnight in cold water to cover
2.25 litres (4 pints) vegetable or
    chicken stock
salt and freshly ground black
    pepper
1 teaspoon Worcestershire sauce
6 tablespoons croûtons (made by
    frying small cubes of stale bread
    in hot oil until golden)

Put the bacon in a large, heavy-based saucepan and cook on a gentle heat until the fat runs out. Add the onion and carrots and cook gently until the fat has been absorbed.

Drain the peas and add to the pan with the stock. Bring to the boil, season lightly with salt and pepper, cover the pan and simmer for about two hours, or until the peas are mushy.

Pass through a sieve or *mouli légumes*, taste and adjust the seasoning. Add the Worcestershire sauce and reheat. Serve topped with the croûtons.

People who vow that they never touch spinach have been caught enjoying this delicious soup.

Cream of Spinach Soup

SERVES 6–8

100 g (3½ oz) butter
55 g (2 oz) plain flour
600 ml (1 pint) milk
2 medium onions, finely chopped
900 g (2 lb) fresh spinach, or 450 g
    (1 lb) frozen leaf or chopped
    spinach, thawed
1 clove garlic, finely chopped
1.2 litres (2 pints) light chicken
    stock
salt and freshly ground black
    pepper
freshly grated nutmeg
4 egg yolks
300 ml (½ pint) single cream

Melt 55 g (2 oz) of the butter in a saucepan and stir in the flour. Stir the *roux* on a moderate heat for a minute or two without allowing it to colour. Gradually add the milk, stirring constantly, until the sauce is thick and smooth. Continue to cook it for two or three minutes, then set it aside.

Melt the remaining butter in a large pan and add the onions. Cook on a low heat until the onion is soft, but not browned. Add the washed fresh spinach or thawed frozen spinach and the garlic. Cover the pan tightly and shake it over a moderate heat for about five minutes, or until the spinach is tender. Add the reserved sauce and mix it with the spinach.

Purée the spinach mixture. The best and easiest way is to pass it through a *mouli légumes* using the medium disc. Alternatively, rub it through a coarse sieve, or whizz it in a blender or food processor and then sieve all, or part of the purée.

Return the purée to the pan, stir in the stock and bring almost to the boil. Season to taste with salt, pepper and nutmeg.

Just before serving, beat the egg yolks into the cream and stir this liaison into the soup. Taking care that the soup does not boil, stir it on a low heat until it has thickened a little more.

Serve it just as it is, or with croûtons of fried bread, or with a swirl of cream or sour cream in each bowl.

Open field mushrooms have much more flavour than dainty buttons and these are the kind to pick or buy for soup.

Cream of Mushroom Soup

SERVES 4

30 g (1 oz) butter
1 large onion, finely chopped
450 g (1 lb) mushrooms, sliced
1 litre (1¾ pints) game, duck or chicken stock
salt and freshly ground black pepper
1 tablespoon soy sauce
150 ml (¼ pint) double cream

Melt the butter in a heavy saucepan, add the onion and fry until it is soft, but not browned. Add the mushrooms, cover the pan and sweat the mushrooms until they are tender and have released their juices. Add the stock, season with salt, pepper and soy sauce and bring to the boil. Cover again and cook gently for about 20 minutes.

Purée the mixture by passing it through a sieve or *mouli légumes*, or processing it briefly in a blender or food processor. Return the soup to the pan and stir in the cream. Check the seasoning and reheat to just below boiling point. Serve immediately.

Cream of Flageolet Soup

SERVES 6

170 g (6 oz) dried flageolet beans
55 g (2 oz) butter
1 large onion, finely chopped
1 leek, finely chopped
1.2 litres (2 pints) chicken stock
salt and freshly ground black pepper
150 ml (¼ pint) single cream
2 tablespoons chopped chives or spring onion tops

Rinse the beans and soak them in cold water for at least four hours, or overnight.

Melt the butter in a heavy pan, add the onion and leek and cook gently on a low heat until they are soft, but not browned. Drain and rinse the beans and add them to the pan with the stock. Bring to the boil, cover the pan and simmer for about one hour, or until the beans are tender.

Purée the soup in a food processor or blender, or by passing it through a sieve or *mouli légumes*. Rinse the pan and return the soup to it. Season to taste with salt and pepper and reheat.

Serve the soup very hot with a swirl of cream and a sprinkling of the chives or spring onion tops in each bowl.

This is the most splendid of carrot soups. Unlike potatoes which quickly turn to glue in a food processor, carrots are transformed to a silky purée.

Curried Cream of Carrot Soup

SERVES 4

40 g (1½ oz) butter, or 3
  tablespoons sunflower or peanut
  oil
110 g (4 oz) onion, chopped
450 g (1 lb) scraped carrots, sliced
1 eating apple, peeled, cored and
  chopped
2 cloves garlic, crushed
2 teaspoons curry paste or powder
900 ml (1½ pints) chicken stock
salt and freshly ground black
  pepper
150 ml (¼ pint) double cream

Heat the butter or oil in a large saucepan and add the onion, carrots, apple and garlic. Cover the pan and sweat the vegetables on a low heat for about 30 minutes without allowing them to brown. Stir in the curry paste or powder and cook for a minute or two before adding the stock. Bring to the boil, season to taste with salt and pepper, cover the pan and simmer until the carrots are very tender. Sieve or liquidise the soup and return it to a clean pan. Stir in the cream, check the seasoning and reheat. Serve the soup very hot. A few flakes of toasted almond or slivers of fried apple make a festive garnish for this soup.

2

Warm Introductions

The trouble with cocktail parties is that they are too useful. Having people round for drinks is still the most economical formula for meeting social obligations incurred throughout the year. Invitations may be engraved, or over the hedge; numbers, six to several score; dress, cocktail hats or gardening jumpers; drink, dry martinis, champagne, plonk or punch. It is party time. Brave smiles and something to nibble must be offered.

Ask anyone what kind of food they prefer not to be offered at cocktail parties and the list will include disco-coloured onions steeped in battery acid, less than crisp crisps and crisps flavoured with anything more than straight salt; plain peanuts, chunks of mousetrap and pineapple impaled on a grapefruit, stringy celery filled with unseasoned cream cheese, chopped chipolatas sizzling, but in their own fat, soggy crackers topped with this and that, and fancy open sandwiches glazed with aspic to withstand the central heating.

Cost is plainly no guide to the acceptability of cocktail canapés. Expensive caterers produce silvered trays of gourmet morsels which are undoubtedly mouthwatering when assembled at ten in the morning, but are boringly flabby by seven at night. Harrassed hostesses who do for themselves face exactly the same problem: the dilemma of advance preparation versus last-minute panic with blobs of *crème de fois gras* on the front of a new frock.

Experienced survivors of the cocktail party circuits report numerous delicacies which stand repetition. Smoked salmon sandwiches, daintily cut from brown bread and well seasoned with black pepper and lemon juice are universally acceptable, just so long as they are fresh and not curling at the edges. Chicken livers wrapped in bacon and hot from the oven go down well, as do plumped prunes (stoned of course) given the same treatment. Freshly roasted almonds with plenty of salt are always popular. So are the bought varieties, and cashews, hazels and more exotic nuts. Olives are a matter of taste but crisps, plain and fresh, are seldom ignored.

For something a little different and not too demanding of time or money, the classic reference books provide a wealth of ideas which plastic food wrap and freezers make a great deal more practical now than they once were. The only real rules are that what should be hot is hot, what should be crisp is crisp, and that with standing room only, nothing should be bigger than bite-sized.

Many of the cocktail snacks at the beginning of this chapter – finger foods in the repellent terminology of the catering trade – are as good or better eaten at table. There is something especially welcoming about the simplest of hot dishes that cold food, however elaborate, can never quite match. When I have enough time at the right time, I very often use it to make a hot first course.

For frying deep-fried foods, peanut oil is almost flavourless and stands up well to high temperatures. Sunflower oil is another excellent choice. The taste for corn oil is one I no longer like, and olive oil is unsuitable for many recipes because it cannot be heated to sufficiently high temperatures without breaking down. Pure lard can be substituted for oil in any of the following recipes.

Beignets soufflé, deep fried puffs of choux pastry flavoured with cheese, are relatively simple, pretty impressive and absolutely delicious. They are at their best when first made, but can be frozen after frying and reheated, without thawing, for five minutes in a hot oven (230°C/450°F, gas mark 8).

Beignets Soufflé

MAKES ABOUT 30

150 ml (¹/4 pint) water
45 g (1¹/2 oz) butter
70 g (2¹/2 oz) plain flour
³/4 teaspoon salt
¹/2 teaspoon cayenne pepper
2 whole eggs and 1 yolk
100 g (3¹/2 oz) Gruyère cheese, cut into tiny dice
oil for deep frying

Put the water in a small, heavy pan with the butter and bring to the boil. Sift the flour, salt and cayenne into a bowl. Remove the pan from the heat, add the seasoned flour, all at once, and mix well. Return to the heat and stir until the paste leaves the sides of the pan.

Remove from the heat and allow to cool slightly before beating in the eggs and yolk, one at a time. Stir in the cheese.

Using two teaspoons, mould half-teaspoonfuls of the paste into balls and deep fry (see page 229) at 190°C/375°F for six to eight minutes, turning them over at about half time. At this temperature a 2.5 cm (1 in) cube of day-old bread will brown in 60 seconds and the paste will swell, more than doubling its size, into golden puffs. Drain and serve very hot.

Serve deep-fried pillows of Camembert as a cocktail snack or with a few pretty leaves of dressed salad.

Croquettes of Camembert

MAKES ABOUT 30

55 g (2 oz) cornflour
120 ml (4 fl oz) milk
255 g (9 oz) Camembert cheese, diced and crust removed
55 g (2 oz) butter, cut into small dice
1 teaspoon salt
½ teaspoon cayenne pepper
pinch of nutmeg
2 eggs, beaten
dry breadcrumbs to coat
oil for deep frying

Put the cornflour in a small, heavy pan and stir in the milk. Add the cheese, butter, salt, cayenne and nutmeg.

Heat the mixture slowly, stirring constantly, and cook until it is really thick and comes away from the sides of the pan. (There is a stage when it looks like scrambled egg. Fear not and keep stirring.) Spread the mixture on a buttered tray and leave it to cool.

When the cheese has cooled and solidified, cut it into 1.25 cm (½ in) cubes and dip them first in the beaten egg and then in the breadcrumbs. Repeat the egg and breadcrumb procedure to give each cube two coats.

Chill the prepared croquettes for at least 30 minutes before deep frying, or freeze them for cooking at the last moment. There is no need to thaw frozen croquettes before frying.

Deep fry (see page 229) the croquettes for three to five minutes at 190°C/375°F. At this temperature a 2.5 cm (1 in) cube of day-old bread will brown in about 60 seconds, and the cheese mixture will melt inside its coat of golden crumbs. If the oil is not hot enough the cheese will leak out. Drain the croquettes on absorbent paper and serve immediately.

Fritters of ricotta cheese resembling small, savoury doughnuts are an Easter-time treat in Italy. In Tuscany they are most often served together with vegetable fritters, spinach and broccoli, but they are just as nice on their own as a first course, or with drinks.

Frittura de Ricotta Pasqualina

SERVES 4–6

225 g (8 oz) ricotta cheese
85 g (3 oz) plain flour
1 teaspoon baking powder
1 large egg
salt and freshly ground black pepper
1 teaspoon finely grated lemon zest
3 tablespoons grappa or rough brandy
oil for deep frying

Put all the ingredients in a bowl and mix them thoroughly together. Cover the mixture and set it aside for about one hour.

Deep fry (see page 229) the fritters, a few at a time, at about 190°C/375°F. At this temperature a 2.5 cm (1 in) cube of day-old bread will brown in about 60 seconds. Drop small teaspoonfuls of the mixture into the hot oil and fry them for about one minute, or until the flour is cooked and the fritters are golden brown. Sprinkle them with salt and serve very hot.

Martabak are a sort of Indonesian sandwich in which a spicy meat filling is held between two layers of fine fried dough. Chinese and some other supermarkets stock *wun tun* dough in packets of ready-rolled and cut squares. These will freeze. Lemon grass can be difficult to find. Finely grated fresh lemon zest tastes different but good.

Martabak

MAKES ABOUT 20

40 sheets wun tun *dough about 7 cm (3 in) square*

For the filling:
olive oil
1 or 2 large onions, finely sliced
2 cloves garlic, crushed
1 teaspoon ground coriander
½ teaspoon ground cumin
½ teaspoon ground ginger
½ teaspoon chilli powder or freshly ground black pepper
½ teaspoon ground turmeric
1 teaspoon powdered lemon grass, or 1 stick fresh lemon grass, sliced very thin
450 g (1 lb) cooked lamb or beef (roasted or boiled), minced
2 or 3 eggs
55 g (2 oz) chopped spring onions or chives
15 g (½ oz) chopped flat-leafed parsley, or ordinary parsley
salt

Put one tablespoon of the oil in a wok or frying pan, add the onion and garlic and fry until they are soft. Add the coriander, cumin, ginger, chilli or pepper, turmeric and lemon grass. Stir-fry for 30 seconds, then add the meat. Mix well and continue stirring for one or two minutes. Leave this mixture to cool before you break the eggs into it and add the spring onions or chives and the parsley. Mix well again and season to taste with salt.

Working on a floured board, put one heaped tablespoon of filling on a square of dough. Then put another square on top and seal the edges roughly.

As each *martabak* is filled, drop it into a frying pan with two tablespoons of well-heated olive oil renewed from time to time as necessary. Flatten the *martabak* with a spatula for a few seconds, so that the thin casing will be moist and will not be fried crisp. Fry for one minute or a little more, on each side, turning only once.

Martabak freeze successfully. To serve from the freezer, thaw thoroughly; put the *martabak* in an ovenproof dish, cover and heat in the oven (180°C/350°F, gas mark 4) for 20 minutes.

Prawn and sesame toast, a popular appetiser in Chinese restaurants, is another hot fork or fingers snack or starter.

Prawn and Sesame Toast

MAKES 20 PIECES

450 g (1 lb) prawns, cooked and shelled
1 tablespoon finely chopped parsley
1 teaspoon sherry or vodka
1 teaspoon salt
1 teaspoon cornflour

Finely chop or mince the prawns and put them in a bowl. Add the parsley, sherry or vodka, salt, cornflour and ginger, and mix well together. In another bowl, whisk the egg white until it is stiff, but not dry. Fold the meringue into the prawn mixture and beat until the paste leaves the sides of the bowl.

½ teaspoon finely chopped fresh
  ginger root, or ground ginger
1 egg white
20 crustless fingers of day-old
  bread about 7.5 × 2.5 cm ×
  7 mm thick (3 × 1 in × ¼ in
  thick)
2 eggs, beaten
55 g (2 oz) sesame seeds
oil for deep frying

Divide the prawn paste between the bread fingers and spread it in an even layer to the edges. Coat the prawn layer with the beaten egg, sprinkle with the sesame seeds and lightly press them in.

Heat the oil to about 190°C/375°F. At this temperature a 2.5 cm (1 in) cube of day-old bread will fry to a golden brown in about 60 seconds. Deep fry the prawn and sesame toasts, a few at a time, for two or three minutes. Drain them well on absorbent kitchen paper and serve hot or warm.

They may be fried in advance, cooled and reheated in a warm oven, or frozen and reheated without thawing in a preheated moderately hot oven (200°C/400°F, gas mark 6) for 10–20 minutes depending on how many are in the oven at one time.

Fresh uncooked scampi or giant prawns are the ideal ingredients for spiced scampi fritters but frozen ones often have to do. If neither can be found, use chunks of fresh, firm-fleshed fish. Monkfish is excellent.

SERVES 4–6

Spiced Scampi Fritters

450 g (1 lb) raw shelled scampi
1 clove garlic, peeled
2.5 cm (1 in) cube of fresh green
  ginger, peeled
4 tablespoons lemon juice
1 tablespoon soy sauce
½ teaspoon cayenne pepper or
  ground chilli
1 recipe fritter batter (see page 229)
oil for deep frying

If the scampi are frozen, thaw and dry them thoroughly.

Crush the garlic and ginger in a garlic press and mix with the lemon juice, soy sauce and cayenne or chilli. Pour this mixture over the scampi, stir and leave to marinate for about one hour.

Finish the fritter batter by folding in the beaten egg white. Heat the oil to 190°C/375°F. At this temperature a 2.5 cm (1 in) cube of day-old bread will fry to golden brown in about 60 seconds.

Drain and dry the scampi, dip them in the batter to cover on all sides and deep fry them (see page 229), a few at a time, until golden brown, turning once. Drain the scampi on absorbent paper and serve at once with wedges of lemon to squeeze over them.

Home-made puff pastry with its 730 paper thin buttery layers is the foundation of all sorts of elegant and often inexpensive dishes. Try filling golden puff cases with lightly cooked shreds of leek, carrot and celery, and a little butter sauce, and see if this is not as delicious a first course as you will meet anywhere.

Use the same treatment for steamed asparagus tips. Or experiment with seafood, meat, and poultry fillings, varying the sauces appropriately.

Squares, rectangles and diamond shapes waste less pastry than the usual round vol-au-vent cases, though there will still be some offcuts of raw pastry. Stack the trimmings neatly – never screw them up in a ball – so they can be re-rolled to make cheese straws or palmiers.

The detailed instructions for cutting and baking the puff pastry which follow in the recipe can be adapted to make larger or smaller cases of any shape.

Feuilletées de Légumes d'Hiver

SERVES 4

puff pastry, one third of recipe (see page 84), or 400 g (14 oz)
1 egg, beaten

For the filling:
110 g (4 oz) carrot
110 g (4 oz) celery
225 g (8 oz) leek
30 g (1 oz) butter
salt and freshly ground white pepper

For the sauce:
2 egg yolks
1 teaspoon lemon juice
110 g (4 oz) butter
salt and freshly ground white pepper

Roll out the pastry on a cold, lightly floured surface to a rectangle about 20 × 40 cm (8 × 16 in). Using a ruler, and a metal pastry cutting wheel in preference to a knife which may drag the edges of the dough, trim the rectangle neatly. Divide the sheet of dough into eight 10 cm (4 in) squares. Dampen a heavy baking sheet by sprinkling it with water and arrange four squares of dough on it, spacing them well apart. Touch the edges of the pastry as little as possible. Brush the top of each piece of positioned dough with water and place a second square on top. Avoiding the edges, press them lightly together with your fingertips. Chill the prepared pastry well.

Again avoiding the edges of the pastry, brush the top of each square liberally with the beaten egg to glaze. Prop a wire drying rack about 5 cm (2 in) above the baking sheet with suitable ovenproof objects – at last a use for those stainless steel egg cups. Bake the pastry above the centre of a preheated hot oven (200°C/400°F, gas mark 6) for 25 minutes, or until well risen and golden. Puff pastry is temperamental stuff and the restraining rack prevents the odd maverick piece from rising too high and toppling over.

Cool the pastry on a wire rack until it is cold enough to handle, then carefully pull the tops off the feuilletées. Using a sharp pointed knife, cut away any uncooked layers in the centre, taking care not to break the fragile side walls. Return the cases to a very cool oven (110°C/225°F, gas mark ¼) for 5–10 minutes to finish drying.

To prepare the filling, cut the carrot, celery and leek into very fine julienne strips about 5 cm (2 in) long. Melt the butter in a heavy-based pan and add the vegetables. Cook them on a low heat, shaking or stirring the pan from time to time, until they are just soft, but not mushy or brown. Season to taste with salt and pepper.

To make the sauce, beat the egg yolks in a saucepan with the lemon juice and six tablespoons of water on a very low heat until the mixture is thick and light. Melt the butter in another pan, then whisk it, a little at a time, into the egg mixture. Continue whisking until all the butter has been added and the sauce has thickened a little. Season to taste with salt and pepper.

To assemble the dish, put a hot puff pastry base on each warmed plate and divide the vegetable mixture between them, letting a few strands of vegetable spill over the sides. Pour a little sauce into the centre of each case, and a little on the plates beside them. Top with the pastry lids and serve immediately.

The pastry cases for this dish may, of course, be baked in advance and reheated. The vegetables must be cooked at the last moment, but can be prepared in advance and kept in an airtight container in the refrigerator. The sauce needs last-minute attention, but with the help of a food processor, which allows you to pour boiling butter into the egg and water base, it takes only moments to make.

Blini, the hot pancakes traditionally served with caviare, are the best possible accompaniment to it. These yeast-raised pancakes are best when very freshly made and it is well worth searching out buckwheat flour to give them an authentic nutty taste. Salmon roe caviare or lumpfish roe take a step up in the world when given the full caviare treatment.

SERVES 6–8

Blini

225 g (8 oz) plain flour
225 g (8 oz) buckwheat flour
2 teaspoons dried yeast
600 ml (1 pint) milk
1/2 teaspoon sugar
2 large eggs, separated
30 g (1 oz) butter, melted
1 teaspoon salt

Sift the plain flour into a large mixing bowl and the buckwheat flour into a smaller one. Dissolve the yeast in a little of the milk heated to lukewarm (about 43°C/110°F) and sweetened with the sugar.

Make a well in the plain flour, pour the dissolved yeast into the dip and draw in the flour. Beat the mixture with a wooden spoon, adding enough warm milk to make a thick, smooth batter. Cover the bowl with a cloth and leave the batter to rise in a warm place until it is light and bubbly and has doubled in volume – this will take about one to two hours.

Beat in the buckwheat flour and enough of the remaining milk to produce a smooth batter with the thickness of double cream. Now beat in the egg yolks, melted butter and salt. Whisk the egg whites until they are stiff, but not dry, and fold them into the batter. Cover the bowl with a cloth and leave the batter to rise again in a warm place until it has doubled its bulk (one to two hours).

At this stage the batter may be left for several hours at kitchen temperature. If it is to be kept overnight, put it in the refrigerator and remember to allow it plenty of time to come back to room temperature before cooking.

To cook the blini, heat a crêpe pan or small heavy frying pan and grease it lightly with butter. Pour batter to a depth of about 7 mm (1/4 in) into the pan, swirl it to cover the base, and cook on a medium heat until the underside of the pancake is golden and small bubbles are bursting through on top. Flip it over and cook until the second side is golden too. Grease the pan before each addition of batter and continue in the same way until all the batter is used.

To keep blini hot, stack them on a plate over a pan of simmering water and cover them loosely with a clean tea towel or napkin.

Preparing the traditional accompaniments for caviare and blini – the separate bowls of soured cream, finely chopped hard boiled eggs, and finely chopped onion – can be done when the batter is rising. Only a small jug of melted butter needs last-minute attention.

Serve the caviare or lumpfish roe in a bowl set on a bed of crushed ice. Hand it round with the blini and let everyone help themselves to their own combination of cream, egg, onion and butter.

All kinds of vegetables can be stuffed to serve as hot or cold first courses, or as a light main dish. The recipe for stuffed artichoke hearts makes no use of the flesh on the leaves. Scrape this off with a teaspoon to use in soup, or serve the leaves cold on another occasion with a thick, mustardy vinaigrette dressing to dip them in.

Stuffed Artichoke Hearts

SERVES 6

3 tablespoons lemon juice
6 large globe artichokes
salt and freshly ground black
  pepper
110 g (4 oz) butter
55 g (2 oz) plain flour
450 ml (¾ pint) milk
170 g (6 oz) strong Cheddar
  cheese, grated
grated nutmeg to taste
225 g (8 oz) small mushrooms,
  sliced
6 rashers smoked bacon, grilled
  until crisp
4 tablespoons chopped parsley

Half-fill a large pan with water, add a tablespoon of salt and two tablespoons of the lemon juice and bring to the boil. Wash the artichokes, pull off the stalks and drop them into the boiling water. Boil them briskly, uncovered, for about 40 minutes, or until the outer leaves can be pulled off easily.

Drain the artichokes, heads down, until they are cool enough to handle, then pull off the leaves and carefully scrape away the chokes. Trim the hearts, season with salt and pepper and arrange them on a lightly buttered ovenproof dish.

Melt 55 g (2 oz) of the butter in a saucepan and stir in the flour. Cook the *roux* for a minute or two without allowing it to colour, then gradually stir in the milk. Cook on a gentle heat until the sauce thickens, then stir in 110 g (4 oz) of the cheese, the nutmeg, and salt and pepper to taste.

In another saucepan, melt half the remaining butter. Add the mushrooms with the remaining lemon juice and a little salt and pepper. Cook the mushrooms on a low heat until they have absorbed the butter and are beginning to brown. Add the finely chopped bacon and the parsley. Stir in just enough of the cheese sauce to bind the mixture.

34

Heap the mushroom mixture onto the prepared artichoke bottoms, sprinkle with the remaining cheese and dot with the remaining butter. Bake, uncovered, in a preheated moderate oven (180°C/350°F, gas mark 4) for about 15 minutes, or until lightly browned.

Reheat the remaining cheese sauce and serve it with the stuffed artichokes.

Open mushrooms, large and flat with dark brown gills, have much more flavour than infantile buttons. Grill them with garlic and parsley packed butter, or stuff and bake them as follows. Any open mushrooms large enough to take a spoonful of stuffing are suitable for this recipe.

Stuffed Mushrooms

SERVES 6

6–24 mushrooms, depending on
   size
1 clove garlic, crushed
salt
150 ml (¼ pint) natural yogurt
170 g (6 oz) fresh breadcrumbs
6 rashers streaky bacon, grilled
   until crisp
2 tablespoons melted bacon fat or
   butter
1 tablespoon finely chopped parsley
freshly ground black pepper

Peel the mushrooms and trim the stalks level with the caps. Mix together the garlic, salt and yogurt and stir in the breadcrumbs. Crumble the bacon into the stuffing and add the bacon fat or butter, parsley, and pepper to taste.

Divide the stuffing between the mushrooms and arrange them on a greased baking dish. Bake in a preheated moderately hot oven (200°C/400°F, gas mark 6) for 10–15 minutes, or until the mushrooms are tender. The exact time will depend on the size of the mushrooms.

Mushrooms with Snail Butter

SERVES 4

4 large open mushrooms, or 8
   smaller ones
110 g (4 oz) butter, softened
2 cloves garlic, peeled and chopped
at least 4 tablespoons chopped
   parsley
juice of ½ a lemon
salt and freshly ground black
   pepper

Peel the mushrooms and cut off the stalks level with the caps. Smear the peeled surface with a little of the butter, and arrange the mushrooms, butter side up, in a grill pan.

Mix together the remaining butter with the garlic, parsley, lemon juice, salt and pepper, and reduce the mixture to a smooth paste in a mortar or food processor.

Grill the mushrooms under a medium heat. When the tops are cooked turn them over and spread the garlic butter over the gilled surface. Grill until cooked through, raising the grill pan nearer the heat to finish them.

Serve the mushrooms just as they are, or with a sprig of parsley in the centre of each one, and fresh crusty bread.

Mushrooms cooked with cream or sour cream, flavoured sometimes with herbs (dill is a favourite), are lovely on toast or fried bread as a snack or savoury, or, on their own, as a vegetable. The full flavour of coriander seeds used in the next recipe is released only when the seeds are heated.

Mushrooms with Coriander

225 g (8 oz) button mushrooms
2 tablespoons fresh lemon juice
3 tablespoons olive oil
1 rounded teaspoon coriander
* seeds, crushed*
4 bay leaves
salt and freshly ground black
* pepper*

Wipe the mushrooms, trim the stalks, and quarter or slice them thickly. Sprinkle them with half the lemon juice.

Heat two tablespoons of the oil in a heavy frying pan and add the coriander. Almost immediately, add the mushrooms, bay leaves, salt and pepper. Shake the pan on a low heat, then cover the pan and cook the mushrooms until they are tender, but not browned.

Tip the mushrooms, bay leaves and all the juices into a shallow serving dish. Dribble over them the remaining oil and lemon juice. Serve hot or cold as a first course, or with plainly grilled poultry, lamb or pork.

Speaking personally, I draw the line at eating mussels raw. In the natural state their taste is uncomfortably reminiscent of oysters, now, alas, a memory. But cooked mussels are another and altogether safer matter.

In Corsica in summer there are *moules au four* sizzling irresistibly in garlic butter. And in Brittany, the best mussels I have tasted – the plainest too, just steamed open with a spoonful or two of white wine, shallot and parsley – are unfailingly good even in the most unprepossessing establishments.

Live mussels, invariably farmed and often Dutch, are my idea of a real bargain. A 2 kg (4½ lb) bag is enough for four or five people. Like all shellfish mussels should be cooked and eaten as soon as possible after they are taken from the sea. However, they will keep for at least 24 hours in the salad drawer of the refrigerator. Leave them wrapped in the perforated polythene sack in which they are sold, or tip them into a bowl and cover them loosely.

Farmed mussels seldom need a great deal of scrubbing to prepare them for the pot. Wash or scrub the shells to rid them of mud, seaweed and barnacles. Discard any mussels with broken shells and any that do not snap shut when tapped.

To freeze mussels, put them, cleaned, in a large saucepan with a couple of tablespoons of water. Cover the pan and cook them on a high heat, shaking the pan once or twice to redistribute the shells, until they open. This should take only a few minutes. Leave them to cool, then pack them for freezing, with or without their shells, and including the strained liquid released in cooking. The recommended freezer life of mussels is short: about one month. To use them, thaw them slowly in the refrigerator, and take up the recipe of your choice at the appropriate stage.

36

Moules au Four

2 litres (3½ pints) fresh mussels
2 large cloves garlic, crushed
4 tablespoons finely chopped
    parsley
110 g (4 oz) butter, softened
freshly ground black pepper to taste
4 tablespoons dry white
    breadcrumbs (optional)

Put the prepared mussels in a large, heavy saucepan with two tablespoons of water. Cover the pan and place it on a high heat. Shake it once or twice so that all the mussels come into contact with the heat, and cook until they open. Discard any that do not open of their own accord. Drain the mussels and remove one shell of each. Arrange them on the half shell in four shallow ovenproof dishes, in a single layer if possible.

Put the garlic, parsley, butter and pepper in a bowl and mix well together. Put a small teaspoonful of the mixture on each mussel. Sprinkle the top of each dish with the breadcrumbs, if you are using them.

Bake in a preheated very hot oven (240°C/475°F, gas mark 9) until the butter is bubbling briskly – this will take only 5–10 minutes. Be careful not to overcook the mussels or they will be tough. Serve this substantial first course with plenty of crusty French bread to dip in the buttery juices.

Prawns in sizzling garlic butter are another reliable winner. It is a first course that makes something memorable of those pathetically small cooked and shelled frozen prawns sold in packets everywhere. Serve them in individual ramekins with lots of hot French or granary bread to mop up the butter.

SERVES 6

Prawns in Garlic Butter

450 g (1 lb) frozen prawns, thawed
170 g (6 oz) butter
1–3 cloves garlic, very finely
    chopped
1 teaspoon Tabasco sauce
1 tablespoon fresh lemon juice
salt and freshly ground black
    pepper to taste
6 tablespoons, or more, finely
    chopped parsley

Last-minute assembly and brief cooking in a hot oven are essential for this dish. Overcooking the prawns makes them tough.

Drain the prawns well and divide them between six ovenproof ramekins. Set the ramekins on a baking tray.

Melt the butter in a small saucepan. Add all the remaining ingredients and bring to the boil. Pour the garlic butter over the prawns, dividing it equally between them. Transfer the prawns immediately to the top of a preheated hot oven (220°C/425°F, gas mark 7) and bake for 10 minutes, or until the butter is bubbling briskly again. Serve immediately.

Lobster thermidor is the classic dish and scampi thermidor a rather cheaper variation. Large prawns or scallops are equally flattered by a thermidor presentation.

Scampi Thermidor

SERVES 6–8

30 g (1 oz) butter
2 tablespoons finely chopped
    shallots
2 tablespoons finely chopped cooked
    ham
2 tablespoons plain flour
salt and freshly ground black
    pepper
1 bay leaf, crumbled
600 ml (1 pint) warm milk
2 tablespoons chopped parsley
2 egg yolks
2 tablespoons double cream
1 tablespoon fresh lemon juice
2 tablespoons dry sherry
1 teaspoon dry mustard
Worcestershire sauce to taste
680 g (1½ lb) raw shelled scampi,
    thawed if frozen
2 tablespoons finely grated
    Parmesan cheese
600 ml (1 pint) creamed potato
4 tablespoons finely grated
    Cheddar cheese
paprika

Melt the butter in a saucepan and add the shallots. Cook gently until they are transparent, but not coloured, then add the ham. Sprinkle the mixture with the flour and cook, stirring constantly, for a minute or two. Season with salt, pepper and the bay leaf, then gradually add the warm milk, stirring constantly. Add the parsley, then transfer the sauce to the top of a double boiler and cook it gently over hot water for about one hour, stirring from time to time.

Strain the sauce into a bowl in which you have whisked together the egg yolks, cream, lemon juice, sherry, mustard and Worcestershire sauce. Return the sauce to a gentle heat and cook, stirring constantly, until it has thickened a little more. Do not allow it to return to the boil or it may separate.

Poach the scampi, or steam them lightly, and drain well. Add the scampi to the sauce together with the Parmesan cheese. Keep warm.

Pipe an edging of the creamed potato round six or eight warmed ovenproof dishes and divide the shellfish and sauce between them. Sprinkle with the Cheddar cheese and a little paprika. Brown the dishes under a hot grill and serve immediately.

3

Starting Cold

A dinner party that begins with 'something cold' has become a culinary cliché only because cold first courses are so splendidly practical. The arguments in favour of dishes which can be prepared in advance need no rehearsal. Keen cooks, or the adventurous, grab the chance to spend a morning in the kitchen messing about with mousseline when the result is the kind of fish terrine that money cannot buy except in very good restaurants. Galantines, and pâtés encased in brioche or pastry are also for show-offs who enjoy creating dishes that are both spectacular and delicious. The cooking itself is at least half the fun of recipes like these and the reward that they taste as good as they look. The snag is, of course, that you do need time to put them together.

For those with neither the time nor patience for flashy cooking, the mousses, terrines, pâtés, dips and salads in this chapter include recipes for every season and most occasions. The speed with which food processors can chop or purée raw or cooked ingredients has made pâtés and terrines much easier and quicker to cook at home. The easiest can now be made in moments.

Without one of these machines only real enthusiasts are likely to turn their hands to delicate fish terrines, or to quenelles, both of which are based on the preparation of a perfect mousseline.

What with pounding and sieving the raw fish, cooling the purée on ice and beating in chilled cream a little at a time with pauses for further cooling between additions, mousseline without a food processor is a lengthy task. It is not exactly instant with one, but chilling the bowl and the ingredients thoroughly before beginning does cut out the need to work over ice.

The trickiest part of making mousseline remains the critical judgement of how much cream to add. Too much and the texture of the finished dish will be wet and coarse, too little and it will be rubbery. The texture to aim for is close, light and creamy. Test the mixture by poaching a teaspoonful in simmering water. Add more cream if it is too firm, more egg white if it is too loose.

SERVES 8

Terrine of Turbot with Scallops

255 g (9 oz) skinned and boned turbot
up to 450 ml (¾ pint) double cream, chilled
1 whole egg and 1 egg white
salt and cayenne pepper
8 large fresh spinach leaves
8 fresh scallops

To make the mousseline using a food processor, dice the fish and chill it well. Also chill thoroughly the processor bowl and blade and the cream. Purée the fish with the egg and egg white and gradually add two-thirds of the cream and season with salt and cayenne. Test the texture by poaching a teaspoonful of the mixture and add more cream if needed. Check the seasoning and keep chilled for up to two hours, until needed.

To make the mousseline by hand, mince the fish twice using the fine blade of the mincer. Using a pestle and mortar, purée the fish with the egg and egg white, then sieve the purée. Stand the bowl of purée in a larger bowl of crushed ice and chill it well. Gradually add two-thirds of the cream, a little at a time, working it thoroughly into the purée with a wooden spoon. Season the mousseline with salt and cayenne. Test the texture as described above.

Remove the tough stalks from the spinach, blanch the leaves in boiling water, then refresh them in cold water. Pat them dry.

Clean the scallops, but leave them whole. Poach them lightly in salted water and dry them well.

Generously butter a terrine of 900 ml (1½ pints) capacity and line it with spinach leaves. Half-fill the terrine with mousseline, then lay the whole scallops closely together down its length. Cover with the remaining mousseline and top with spinach. Tap the terrine sharply on a hard surface to settle the contents.

Cover the terrine with a lid or foil and stand it in a larger dish. Pour boiling water into the larger dish, ideally to come two-thirds of the way up the sides of the terrine. Transfer both to a preheated moderate oven (180°C/ 350°F, gas mark 4) and bake for 30 minutes, then test with a skewer. It will come out warm and clean when the terrine is cooked.

Rest the terrine for 10 minutes before turning it onto a warm plate to serve hot, or leave it to cool in the dish for serving cold.

Pâté of salmon en croûte is another recipe which uses fish mousseline: this time to bind pieces of whole fish which are cooked in a pastry case. The pastry used is a stronger than usual version of shortcrust which is reinforced with egg.

SERVES 8–10

Pâté of Salmon en Croûte

For the fish mousseline:
225 g (8 oz) skinned and boned
salmon or salmon trout
salt and cayenne pepper to taste
¼ teaspoon ground mace
1 egg white
250 ml (8 fl oz) double cream,
chilled

For the pastry:
340 g (12 oz) plain flour
½ teaspoon salt
170 g (6 oz) butter, chilled
1 egg
iced water to mix
1 egg yolk beaten with 1 tablespoon
water to glaze

For the filling:
340 g (12 oz) skinned and boned
salmon or salmon trout
½ teaspoon salt
freshly ground black pepper
30 g (1 oz) butter
2 tablespoons dry white wine
1 tablespoon cognac
2 tablespoons chopped fresh dill
2 tablespoons chopped fresh chives

For the aspic:
150 ml (¼ pint) fish or chicken
stock
salt
1 tablespoon gelatine crystals
1 tablespoon dry sherry

Make a salmon or salmon trout mousseline using the method explained in terrine of turbot with scallops (see facing page).

Make the shortcrust pastry in the usual way (see page 80), but using the whole egg, and chill it well before rolling out.

To prepare the filling, cut the fish into long strips about 1.25 cm (½ in) wide and thick. Season them with salt and pepper. Heat the butter in a frying pan until it froths, then add the fish. Fry it gently for only three or four minutes, just to firm the flesh. Transfer the fish to a plate to cool and sprinkle it with the wine and cognac.

To assemble the pâté, generously butter or oil a rectangular hinged metal mould about 25 × 7.5 cm (10 × 3 in) × 7.5 cm (3 in) deep. Alternatively, use a non-stick loaf tin of similar dimensions. Roll out three-quarters of the dough on a lightly floured surface to a long rectangle about 8 mm (⅓ in) thick. Lower the rolled dough carefully into the mould. Gently press the pastry against the base and sides of the mould so that it forms an even, crack-free crust which will be imprinted with the pattern of the tin. Trim the edges level with the top on the tin.

Drain the fish fillets and beat a little of the wine and brandy marinade into the mousseline. Spread a layer of mousseline over the base of the pastry and top it with a closely packed layer of fish, sprinkled with a layer of the herbs. Continue the layers to the top of the tin, finishing with a layer of mousseline.

Roll out the remaining pastry and trim it to make a lid. Dampen the edges of the walls of pastry with water and fit the lid in place.

Glaze the pastry by brushing it with the egg yolk and water. To allow steam to escape, cut a small hole in the centre of the lid and prop it open with a cylinder of several thicknesses of foil and crimp the edges of the pastry with the back of a fork. Brush the lid again with the egg glaze.

Set the mould on a baking sheet and bake in a pre-heated moderately hot oven (190°C/375°F, gas mark 5) for 15 minutes. Reduce the temperature to moderate (180°C/350°F, gas mark 4) and continue baking for another 1¼ hours. If the crust is browning too quickly, cover it loosely with foil.

When the pâté is almost cold, remove the foil chimney and tin. Chill it well.

To make the aspic, strain the stock through a fine sieve lined with a double layer of damp muslin or with kitchen paper, then season to taste with salt. Pour the stock into a small pan and sprinkle the gelatine on top. When it has swollen, heat gently until the crystals have dissolved completely. Cool the aspic and stir in the sherry. Chill a spoonful of aspic to check that it sets firmly enough, adding more gelatine if necessary.

Place a small funnel in the hole in the lid of the pâté and pour in a little of the aspic. If leaks in the pastry are revealed, chill the pâté again to set the jelly inserted, then continue filling with melted aspic until it will accept no more. Chill the pâté for several hours before serving it with a delicate cold sauce made by mixing good mayonnaise half and half with single cream and plenty of finely chopped fresh dill.

Fresh herbs are essential for a terrine of salmon and green peas, but the peas may be frozen. The texture of this terrine is fairly dense and its appearance, with two salmon pink layers separated by a vivid green one, is striking.

SERVES 8–10

Terrine of Salmon and Green Peas

400 g (14 oz) skinned and boned salmon
6 large eggs
150 ml (¼ pint) double cream
salt and cayenne pepper
450 g (1 lb) small green peas, fresh or frozen
6 tablespoons finely chopped parsley
3 tablespoons finely chopped chives

Purée the raw salmon in a food processor or by pounding it in a mortar. Gradually beat in three of the eggs and all but two tablespoons of the cream. Season the mixture with salt and cayenne and beat it until smooth.

Cook the peas by boiling them briefly in salted water, then drain them well. Purée them in a food processor or by pushing them through a *mouli légumes* or sieve. Add the remaining eggs and cream. Beat in the parsley and chives and season the mixture with salt and cayenne.

Generously butter a terrine of about 1.25 litres (2½ pints) capacity (a soufflé dish of comparable size will do instead) and spread half the salmon mousse evenly over the base. Now add all the pea purée and spread it evenly. Spoon the remaining salmon mousse over the top and spread it in an even layer.

Cover the terrine with a lid or foil and stand it in a larger dish. Transfer both to a preheated moderate oven (180°C/350°F, gas mark 4) and pour boiling water into the larger dish, ideally to come two-thirds of the way up the sides of the terrine. Bake the terrine for one hour, by which time the salmon should be beginning to shrink a little from the sides of the dish. Allow the terrine to cool, then refrigerate it until needed. Serve in thick slices.

This terrine does not freeze very successfully. The smooth texture of the pea mousse becomes grainy and wet.

Good smoked mackerel is rich and full of flavour. Whole fish are often, though not invariably, moister and better tasting than fillets, and are not difficult to bone at home. The flesh needs no further cooking and can be served, just as it comes, with a wedge of lemon. But it goes further and tastes even better made into a quickly prepared pâté. Adding softened butter to this oily fish may seem perverse, but it does give a smoother, firmer texture to the pâté than the cream specified in many recipes.

Smoked Mackerel Pâté

SERVES 6

285 g (10 oz) skinned and boned
  smoked mackerel
3 tablespoons freshly squeezed
  lemon juice
55 g (2 oz) butter, softened
1 teaspoon hot horseradish relish or
  English mustard
salt and freshly ground black
  pepper to taste

Reduce the mackerel to a smooth paste with a pestle and mortar, food processor, or by beating it in a bowl first with a fork and then with a wooden spoon. Beat in the lemon juice, butter, horseradish or mustard, salt and pepper. Spoon the mixture into one large or six small pots or ramekins and chill well before serving with toasted granary bread or crusty rolls.

Storecupboard ingredients make a quick tuna pâté.

Tuna Pâté

SERVES 4

200 g (7 oz) tin of tuna, drained
2 tablespoons mayonnaise
1 teaspoon curry powder
1 tablespoon dry sherry
salt and freshly ground black
  pepper to taste

Combine all the ingredients and pound or process them to a smooth paste. Transfer the pâté to a serving bowl, cover and chill well before serving with hot toast.

There are authentically Greek versions of taramasalata which include breadcrumbs, but the best and lightest taramasalata does not. It is made on the same principle as mayonnaise by beating oil into the fish roe base until the mixture is pale and fluffy. Smoked cod's roe is the usual basis of taramasalata. But if you come across real *tarama*, dried and salted grey mullet roe, you will be able to make the version which gave this recipe its name.

Taramasalata

SERVES 4–6

110 g (4 oz) smoked cod's roe
4 tablespoons fresh lemon juice
1 tablespoon onion juice (made in a
   garlic press)
150 ml (¼ pint) mild olive oil
1 tablespoon finely chopped parsley

If you are using cod's roe from the fishmonger choose a soft piece. Remove the skin then pound or process the roe until it is smooth. If you are using roe from a jar there is no need to soften it.

Using a food processor, or beating the mixture by hand, add the lemon juice, a little at a time, to the cod's roe, then beat in the onion juice and lastly the oil. As when making mayonnaise, the oil should be added very slowly at first, and the mixture beaten continuously until it has all been incorporated and the taramasalata is light in colour and texture. If it becomes too thick beat in a few tablespoons of boiling water to finish it.

Add more onion juice if you wish then serve the salad sprinkled with the parsley. It can be eaten with warm pitta bread or with thin, hot toast.

Smoked salmon mousse makes the most of offcuts which are much cheaper than perfect, wafer-thin slices. The trimmings are often sold in freezer packs. Although light textured, this mousse is rich and very satisfying, so serve small quantities. It can be offered in individual dishes with toast, or wrapped, parcel fashion, in slices of smoked salmon and accompanied by a few leaves of salad.

Smoked Salmon Mousse

SERVES 6–8

170 g (6 oz) smoked salmon
   trimmings
4 tablespoons water
1 teaspoon gelatine crystals
175 ml (6 fl oz) double cream,
   chilled
1 tablespoon cognac
1 tablespoon dry sherry
salt and cayenne pepper

Purée the salmon in a food processor, or using a pestle and mortar.

Put the water in a small pan and sprinkle the gelatine on top. When it has swollen, heat gently until the granules have dissolved completely. Stir the gelatine into the salmon purée.

Whip the cream until it holds soft peaks, then fold it into the purée. Stir in the cognac and sherry and season to taste with salt and cayenne.

Spoon the mixture into individual serving dishes, or one large dish, and chill to set.

Fish farming has greatly increased supplies of fresh trout though, for such a pretty fish, its flavour can be disappointingly dull. Make the most of its delicate taste in this light mousse. Serve it like a fish pâté in individual ramekins or in one larger dish, with fingers of hot toast or crusty bread. Dense, wholemeal bread, thinly sliced, makes good toast for this dish.

Fresh Trout Mousse

SERVES 6–8

340 g (12 oz) fresh trout, cleaned
900 ml (1½ pints) fish stock or
    lightly salted water
2 bay leaves
1 piece of lemon peel
a few parsley stalks
1 tablespoon gelatine crystals
2 tablespoons mayonnaise
1 tablespoon brandy
salt and freshly ground black
    pepper
150 ml (¼ pint) whipping cream
thin slices of lemon to garnish

Wash the fish in cold water. Bring the stock or water to the boil and add the bay leaves, lemon peel and parsley stalks. Poach the fish for five minutes in the stock and allow it to cool in the liquid.

Drain the fish and reserve 150 ml (¼ pint) of the strained poaching liquid. Remove the skin and bones from the fish and flake the flesh. Sprinkle the gelatine on the reserved stock. Leave it to swell and soften for a minute or two, then heat gently until it has dissolved completely.

Using a food processor or pestle and mortar, reduce the fish to a smooth paste. Stir in the reserved stock and mix well before adding the mayonnaise, brandy and salt and pepper to taste. Whip the cream until it forms soft peaks and blend it well with the fish mixture. Check the seasoning and pour the mousse into ramekins or one large bowl to set. Cover and refrigerate until about 30 minutes before serving with a garnish of lemon slices.

Forbidden brandy – 'But, darling, that was the *fine champagne* I was saving for the chairman/general/vicar/mother' – may be the very thing for the cook's morale, but it is too good for the *pâté de campagne*. Off-licence ordinary with a pretentious label and a price tag substantially less breathtaking than its flavour is the sort to make home-made pâtés taste luxurious. If the only bottle in the house is forbidden, use whisky.

Knowing exactly what has gone into a pâté or terrine (no gristle or grizzly bits) is one of the nice things about making it at home, and it is tempting to think that leaner meat will make a better one. It is a mistake I made many times until I learned that being too calorie conscious about the fat produces dry and crumbly results.

Too little seasoning is another common disappointment, and since it is *never* a good idea to eat raw pork, fry a spoonful of the uncooked mixture to check the taste before committing the rest to the oven.

Baking times will depend on the shape and thickness of the dish used as well as on the quantity and composition of the pâté mixture. To test whether it is fully cooked, pierce the mixture with a skewer. The emerging juices and surrounding fat should be clear and bloodless.

Dishes designed for cooking pâtés usually have a small hole in the lid to allow steam to escape. As with variable cooking times, the amount of moisture which will evaporate is not completely predictable. This, and the length of time the pâté is to be stored will govern the method of finishing it.

Most pâtés are much the better for a couple of days in the refrigerator to allow the flavours to develop and the texture to settle down. If the pâté is to be eaten within a few days of being made there is no need to do more than press it lightly under the weight of a few tins as it cools.

More elegantly, you can set it in aspic. Press the pâté for an hour and, before it is cold, pour off the liquid fat and juices. Skim off the fat and add a tablespoon of gelatine crystals to each 300 ml (½ pint) of stock before returning the stock to the dish. The jelly will then set firmly enough to slice with the pâté.

To keep pâté for more than a few days in the refrigerator it is best to discard the juices after pressing the meat for an hour, and to seal it completely with melted lard.

Neither gelatine nor lard are required if the dish is to be frozen. Just cool it under pressure and when it is quite cold turn out of the dish, wipe away any excess moisture and fat, wrap well and freeze.

Terrine of pork and green peppercorns is coarse pâté, robust and full of flavour.

Terrine of Pork and Green Peppercorns

MAKES ABOUT 1 kg (2¼ lb)

450 g (1 lb) pig's liver
450 g (1 lb) fat belly of pork
2 cloves garlic, finely chopped
55 g (2 oz) shallot or onion, finely chopped
½ teaspoon ground mace
1 teaspoon salt
1 tablespoon whole green peppercorns
225 g (8 oz) thinly sliced pork back fat or green streaky bacon
1 pig's trotter, split
1 medium onion, sliced
1 carrot, sliced
2 bay leaves
6 tablespoons brandy
6 tablespoons dry white wine

Chop the liver and pork very finely, or mince them coarsely. Mix together the meats, garlic, shallot or onion, mace, salt and whole peppercorns. Fry a small quantity of the mixture to test its seasoning, remembering that this will be less pronounced when the terrine is served cold.

If you are using pork back fat to line the terrine, chilling it well will make it easier to slice wafer thin. Alternatively, flatten thicker slices by beating them out. Use the back fat or bacon to line the base and sides of a terrine of about 1.25 litres (2½ pints) capacity.

Fill the terrine with the meat mixture. Place the trotter, onion, carrot and bay leaves on top. Pour in the brandy and wine and, if necessary, just enough cold water to bring the liquid up to the level of the meat.

Cover the terrine closely with a lid or foil and bake in the centre of a preheated cool oven (150°C/300°F, gas mark 2) for about four hours. Remove it from the oven and allow the terrine to cool a little. Discard the trotter and vegetables before the jelly sets. Cover the terrine and allow it to stand in the refrigerator for two or three days before serving it at room temperature.

The texture of this pâté is fairly coarse and free. It may be weighted as it cools to solidify the texture further.

Rough Country Terrine

SERVES 10–12

225 g (8 oz) chicken livers
170 g (6 oz) pig's or lamb's liver
55 g (2 oz) shallots
225 g (8 oz) lean pork (leg or shoulder)

Trim the chicken livers and cut out any yellow patches which would give the terrine a bitter taste. Likewise, trim any tubes and membranes from the pig's or lamb's liver. Peel the shallots and chop them roughly. Roughly chop the livers, pork and belly of pork (or lean and back fat).

450 g (1 lb) fat belly of pork, or
   half and half lean pork and pork
   back fat
salt and freshly ground black
   pepper
grated nutmeg
2 tablespoons brandy
2 tablespoons pine kernels
225 g (8 oz) unsmoked streaky
   bacon, thinly sliced

Put all these ingredients once through the coarse blade of a mincer. Add salt, pepper and nutmeg to taste. Stir in the brandy and pine kernels.

Cut the rinds off the streaky bacon and flatten and stretch each rasher by pressing it against a board with the back of a knife. Use the bacon to line a terrine, loaf tin or soufflé dish, leaving enough of the bacon draped over the sides of the dish to lap over the top of the pâté.

Fill the dish with the terrine mixture, then fold the bacon over the top. Cover with a lid, or loosely with foil, and stand the dish in a baking tin. Pour boiling water into the tin to a depth of 2.5 cm (1 in). Bake in a preheated moderate oven (180°C/350°F, gas mark 4) for about 20 minutes. Reduce the temperature to cool (140°C/275°F, gas mark 1) and continue baking for another three hours. Cool the terrine with a weight on it.

SERVES 6–8

Terrine of Duck

4 duck legs, or 1 whole duck
150 ml (¼ pint) red wine
4 tablespoons port or brandy
450 g (1 lb) fat belly of pork, or
   half and half lean pork and pork
   back fat
1 clove garlic, finely chopped
12 juniper berries
salt and freshly ground black
   pepper
170 g (6 oz) unsmoked streaky
   bacon, thinly sliced

Part roast the duck in a preheated hot oven (220°C/425°F, gas mark 7). Cook duck legs for about 10 minutes, or a whole duck for about 20. Set aside to cool.

Remove all the flesh from the duck, reserving some of the fat but not the skin. Cut the best pieces into long fillets and marinate them in the wine and port or brandy. Finely chop the rest of the duck meat. Put the pork once through the mincer using a coarse blade.

Mix together the finely chopped duck and minced pork with the garlic and juniper berries. Season generously with salt and pepper. Drain the fillets, add the marinade to the mixture and stir well.

Cut the rinds off the bacon and flatten and stretch each rasher by pressing it against a board with the back of a knife. Use the bacon to line a terrine, loaf tin or soufflé dish, leaving enough of the bacon draped over the sides to lap over the top of the pâté.

Put a third of the terrine mixture in the bottom of the dish and top with half the marinated fillets. Top with another third of the mixture and the remaining fillets. Finally add the remaining mixture and fold the bacon over the terrine. Cover with a lid, or loosely with foil, and stand the dish in a baking tin. Pour boiling water into the tin to a depth of 2.5 cm (1 in) and bake in a preheated moderate oven (180°C/350°F, gas mark 4) for about 20 minutes. Reduce the temperature to cool (140°C/275°F, gas mark 1) and continue baking for another two hours.

If the terrine is to be eaten within a few days of being made there is no need to do more than press it lightly under the weight of a few tins as it cools. Alternatively, the juices can be poured off when it has been pressed for an hour or so, skimmed, and firmed with gelatine before being poured back into the dish.

Galantines, which enjoyed their greatest popularity in Edwardian times, may be embellished with elaborate decorations and enriched with luxurious ingredients: *foie gras* and truffles. That said, the basic recipe is rich enough for most occasions. It makes an excellent dish for a cold buffet lunch or supper.

Galantine of Duck

SERVES 6–8

1 duck weighing 1.8–2.3 kg (4–5 lb)
2 tablespoons cognac

For the stock:
the duck carcass and giblets (not the liver)
2 large onions, chopped
1 carrot, chopped
1 stick of celery, chopped
2 bay leaves
salt
8 black peppercorns, crushed

For the stuffing:
3 duck or chicken livers
30 g (1 oz) pistachio nuts, blanched and skinned
2 shallots, or 1 small onion, finely chopped
225 g (8 oz) pork, lean and fat, minced
225 g (8 oz) veal, minced
1 egg, beaten
60 ml (2 fl oz) dry white wine
2 tablespoons cognac
1/2 teaspoon grated nutmeg
1/2 teaspoon saltpetre (optional)
salt and freshly ground black pepper to taste

To braise:
30 g (1 oz) butter
3 carrots, thinly sliced

Taking all the bones out of a raw duck without puncturing its skin in the wrong places is not as tricky as it sounds. But it does need a small pointed knife which is very sharp indeed, and a relaxed frame of mind. First cut off the wing tips and the next section of wing bone, leaving only the wing bone nearest the body.

Place the bird breast side down on a wooden board and cut the skin from neck to tail down the line of the spine. Cut and scrape the skin and flesh away from the bones, cutting through the ball and socket joints of the wings and legs to free the limbs from the body. Work down both sides towards the breast bone, taking particular care when cutting close to the ridge of the breast bone where the skin is stretched over the bone with almost no flesh.

Remove the bones from the wings and legs by scraping off the flesh from the inside of the bird and pulling the bones through.

Reserve the carcass and other bones for the stock. Sprinkle the cognac inside the duck and set it aside.

To make the stock, put the duck carcass, onions, carrot and celery in a saucepan and add 1·5 litres (2½ pints) of cold water. Bring to the boil, skim, then add the bay leaves, salt and pepper. Reduce the heat, cover the pan and simmer for about two hours.

To make the stuffing, cut some of the breast and leg meat from the boned duck and slice it in long slivers. Cut the livers into slivers and set both aside. Mix the pistachios, shallots or onion, pork, veal, egg, wine, cognac, nutmeg, saltpetre (if using to make the stuffing a rosy pink), and a generous quantity of salt and pepper. Fry a teaspoon of the stuffing in butter to test the seasoning. Adjust if necessary, remembering to season the mixture more highly for serving cold than if it were to be eaten hot.

3 sticks of celery, thinly sliced
3 onions, thinly sliced

2 egg whites
a few sprigs of fresh tarragon or
    chervil
watercress
1 orange, sliced

Place the duck on a flat surface, skin side down, and place half the stuffing mixture in a neat rectangular block in the centre. Arrange the slivers of breast meat and liver lengthways on top of the stuffing so that they will form an attractive pattern when the bird is cut in slices. Top with the remaining stuffing. Draw the skin up over the stuffing and sew the bird into a slack roll using a trussing needle and string (or a darning needle and button thread). Tuck the wings and legs under the duck, and secure them with string tied, not too tightly, round the roll.

To cook the duck, choose a heavy ovenproof casserole with a lid. Melt the butter and add the carrots, celery and onions. Soften the vegetables for about 10 minutes on a low heat, then place the duck, breast side up, on top of them and pour over the strained stock. Cover the casserole and cook in a moderate oven (180°C/350°F, gas mark 4) for 1½ hours. Remove the lid, pour off the stock leaving just enough to cover the vegetables, and brown the duck in the oven for another 30 minutes without the lid.

When the duck is cooked, return the stock to the casserole and leave the duck to cool in the liquid. When it is quite cold, lift it from the stock and wipe off the excess fat with kitchen paper. Remove the thread and string and chill the duck. Strain the stock and let it set to a jelly. Remove the fat carefully, then clarify the stock.

To clarify the stock, bring it to the boil and whisk in the two stiffly beaten egg whites. Let them rise up the pan, catching all the particles which would cloud the jelly, and whip the pan off the heat before it boils over. Without discarding the layer of egg white, return the pan to a low heat and simmer gently for 30 minutes. Strain the stock through kitchen paper, or a fine sieve lined with a double layer of muslin or cheesecloth. Leave the stock to cool, but do not let it set completely.

When the clarified stock is syrupy, but not too thick, arrange the duck on a serving dish and spoon a little of the stock over it. Decorate with the tarragon or chervil and glaze these too. (If the duck's skin has ripped or split at any stage of the preparation you can patch the damage at this stage with thin slices of orange.) Give the galantine one or two more coats of jelly, chilling it between applications.

To serve, garnish the plate with the watercress and orange slices and any remaining jelly, set firm and chopped into dice. As the middle slices are usually the best looking, cut the galantine in halves and slice it from the centre.

I confess that I would seldom go to the trouble and expense of baking brioches just for breakfast. What makes it worth the bother is the versatility of the basic dough and all the other guises in which it can be served. Small brioches can be hollowed out and filled, like vol-au-vent cases, with any number of hot or cold, sweet or savoury fillings. Fillet of beef can be served in a light casing of brioche, instead of the usual puff pastry which is the very devil to slice neatly. And best of all there is *foie gras en brioche*, the classic and unbeatable way to serve goose liver encased in a golden loaf of brioche. It is not only the best quality of tinned goose liver that looks and tastes magnificent this way. Dressed in brioche, humbler pâtés take on airs above their station, and a good garlic sausage is transformed.

Foie Gras en Brioche

SERVES 6

½ recipe brioche dough (see page 205)
1 egg yolk beaten with 2 tablespoons water to glaze
225 g (8 oz) tin of foie gras, bloc, terrine or mousse

Brush a small loaf tin about 18 × 10 cm × 7.5 cm deep (7 × 4 in × 3 in deep) with melted butter.

Roll out the brioche dough on a lightly floured surface to a rectangle approximately 30 × 15 cm (12 × 6 in). Brush it with the egg glaze. Brush the baton of foie gras with glaze and dust it with flour to help it to stick to the bread while baking. Place the foie gras lengthwise on the centre of the dough and roll it up. Fold the ends over the seam and place the roll, seam side down, in the prepared tin. Cover it loosely and leave it to rise until the dough has almost doubled in bulk.

Brush the top of the loaf with the remaining egg glaze and bake in a preheated moderately hot oven (200°C/400°F, gas mark 6) for 30–35 minutes, or until it is well risen and golden brown. Ease the loaf out of the tin and place on a wire rack to cool.

Filling the air gap between the filling and the loaf with aspic is an optional refinement. Tinned consommé, fortified with a little sherry and extra gelatine, does very well.

Chill the loaf very thoroughly before adding the aspic which should be cold and just on the point of setting. Make a hole in the top of the crust using an apple corer, and bore down until it reaches the filling. Feed in the aspic through a funnel or piping nozzle, then chill the loaf again to set it.

To serve *foie gras en brioche*, cut off the heels of the loaf, and divide the central portion containing the filling into even slices.

The livers of specially fattened geese and ducks have long been a delicacy prized by connoisseurs for their fine taste and texture. The rich but undiscriminating are keen on *foie gras* too, if only on the status-exalting attributes of anything that costs quite so much.

Oh to be rich, discriminating and slender as well. Or would that be too unbearably smooth? Perhaps it is just as well that trading regulations ensure that the chances of meeting fresh *foie gras* outside France are minimal, and that we are thus denied amazing dainties like slivers of hot fat goose liver with mushrooms on toast.

Preserved *foie gras* is sold in strictly controlled grades. If the tin or pot carries the words *au naturel* it should contain nothing more than cooked liver and seasoning. *Bloc* is the next grade and contains extra fat or a little stuffing. Then there are the preparations described as *purée*, *mousse* or *crème de foie gras*, all of which must contain at least 75 per cent fat liver.

Nothing the most skilled cook can do will turn the livers of conventionally reared geese or ducks into *foie gras*. They are simply too lean and too dense to be rendered as meltingly smooth as the real thing. But when it comes to mousses and purées, parfaits and the like, even a carton of frozen chicken livers can be groomed to take its place in high society.

Chicken liver parfait is better still made with duck or goose liver and can, of course, be based on a mixture of one or more types. It is very rich, very smooth, and so light in texture it is difficult to slice. It is best served in tiny ramekins or pots, or scooped from a larger dish.

Chicken Liver Parfait

SERVES 6

225 g (8 oz) chicken livers
salt and freshly ground black
 pepper
110 g (4 oz) butter
1½ tablespoons cognac
1½ tablespoons dry sherry
120 ml (4 fl oz) double cream,
 chilled

Thoroughly clean the chicken livers, removing every trace of green staining from the gall bladders which would make the dish bitter, and all stringy bits. Season the livers generously with salt and pepper.

Melt the butter in a heavy-based pot, add the livers and cook, uncovered, at the gentlest of simmers for 10–15 minutes, so that the livers are cooked through but not toughened. Remove the pan from the heat and set it aside until cool, then chop or process the livers with the butter and work the mixture through a fine sieve.

Beat in the cognac and sherry and set the bowl on crushed ice in a larger bowl. Whip the cream until it holds soft peaks then, working over the ice, beat it into the liver mixture, a spoonful at a time. Check the seasoning and divide the parfait between small individual serving dishes or spoon it into one larger dish. Cover and chill until needed. Serve with crusty bread or toast.

Chunks of ham set in a rich jelly crammed with chopped parsley and green peppercorns is delicious served as a first course with hot bread, or as a main dish with new or sauté potatoes and salad.

Ham and Herb Terrine

1 pig's trotter, split
900 g (2 lb) bacon joint
1 medium onion, chopped
1 carrot, chopped
1 clove garlic, crushed
1 stick of celery, chopped
150 ml (¼ pint) white wine
1 sprig of thyme
2 bay leaves
a handful of parsley stalks
6 tablespoons chopped parsley
2 tablespoons green peppercorns

Put the trotter and bacon in a large saucepan, cover with cold water, bring to the boil and drain immediately.

Return the bacon and trotter to the pan with the onion, carrot, garlic, celery, wine, thyme, bay leaves and parsley stalks. Pack them down and pour in cold water to cover. Bring to the boil, skim, cover the pan and simmer for three hours.

Strain the stock and set it aside to cool. When it is quite cold and has set to a jelly, scrape off the fat.

Cut the bacon into large dice and mix with the parsley and peppercorns. Pack the bacon into a terrine or another suitable mould. Heat the stock until it is just liquid and pour in sufficient to cover the bacon. Cool until set.

Perhaps because it is Italian, Parma ham tastes of summer even though we can buy it all year round. Maybe it seems summery because it is usually eaten with melon, though fresh figs or pears both make better combinations. It is such an easily prepared and universally enjoyed opening to any meal that it may seem to be gilding the lily to make it into something different.

I think my Parma ham mousse justifies taking the liberty. It can even be a storecupboard dish if you keep a tin of the sliced ham for gastronomic emergencies. Italian grocers cut the ham for you, and may sell offcuts and trimmings for less than the cost of perfect slices. They often stock the tins too.

Parma Ham Mousse

170 g (6 oz) Parma ham, very
  thinly sliced
4 tablespoons water
1 tablespoon gelatine crystals
150 g (¼ pint) double cream,
  chilled
1 tablespoon dry sherry
1 tablespoon cognac
salt and cayenne pepper
1 small ripe pear
juice of 1 lemon

For the garnish:
8 small lettuce or radicchio leaves
8 small basil leaves

Lightly oil four small ramekins. Line each with one or more slices of the ham, leaving enough draped over the sides of the dishes to cover them when they are filled. Chill until needed.

Purée the remaining ham using a food processor or pestle and mortar. Alternatively, chop it very finely indeed. Put the water in a small pan and sprinkle the gelatine on top. Leave it to soften for a few minutes, then heat gently until the crystals have dissolved completely. Mix the gelatine into the puréed ham.

Whip the cream until it holds firm peaks, then beat in the sherry and cognac. Fold the cream lightly into the ham mixture and season the mousse with salt (if it needs any) and cayenne.

Peel, core and cut the pear into small dice. Turn the pieces in the lemon juice. Drain and dry them and fold them into the mousse.

Spoon the mousse into the prepared ramekins and cover with the ham hanging over the sides of the dishes. Chill the mousse for an hour or more.

To serve, arrange two lettuce or radicchio leaves on each of four small plates. Turn out one mousse onto each plate and top with two fresh basil leaves. Almost any kind of freshly baked crusty bread goes well with this mousse.

Haricots verts, the dainty green beans beloved of restaurants, are available pretty well all year round, usually from Kenya. They are seldom inexpensive and, considering the cost, not always as fresh as they should be either. When they are fresh enough to snap crisply, very slender green beans can be shown off in this delicious salad first course dressed with cream and toasted hazelnuts.

Green Bean and Hazelnut Salad

SERVES 4

450 g (1 lb) small, fresh green beans
30 g (1 oz) shelled hazelnuts
150 ml (¹/4 pint) double cream, chilled
1 teaspoon hot English mustard
3 tablespoons fresh lemon juice
salt and freshly ground black pepper

Trim the beans and steam them, covered, until they are just tender, but still have a good bite of crispness. Plunge them immediately into cold water, then drain and dry them. Arrange the beans on a serving dish, cover and chill for an hour.

Cut the hazelnuts in slivers and toast them lightly under the grill. Leave them to cool.

Just before serving, mix the cream, mustard and lemon juice in a bowl and whisk lightly until the mixture is floppy, not stiff. Season the dressing to taste with salt and pepper and spoon it over the beans. Sprinkle the toasted nuts over the salad and serve.

Pears and prawns make a salad that is best rustled up at the last moment. The rate at which cut pears brown and avocados blacken can be slowed with lemon juice, but this does nothing to improve the taste or look of the salad.

Pears and Prawn Salad

SERVES 4

4 small lettuce leaves
4 sprigs of watercress
1 large, firm and ripe dessert pear
1 medium, firm and ripe avocado pear
225 g (8 oz) cooked, peeled prawns
120 ml (4 fl oz) single cream
1 tablespoon vinegar
salt and freshly ground black pepper
1–2 tablespoons chopped fresh coriander or parsley

Place a lettuce leaf and a sprig of watercress on each of four small plates. Quarter, peel and core the dessert pear, then cut each piece in thin slices. Keep the slices together while lifting them onto the plate, then press the pile gently to make a pretty fan of sliced fruit. Quarter, stone, peel and slice the avocado and arrange the fanned slices in the same way. Divide the prawns between the four plates.

Combine the cream, vinegar, salt and pepper and shake well together. Pour the dressing over the salads and sprinkle with the coriander or parsley. Serve immediately.

Gravad lax, the traditional Scandinavian dish of raw, marinated salmon, is most often served as a first course with an oil, vinegar and mustard dressing. In Sweden it appears as a main dish too, accompanied by poached eggs, buttered spinach and boiled potatoes. The fine, feathery leaves of fresh dill are an essential ingredient of the marinade and are usually used as a garnish too. If fresh dill is not available, use dried dill for the marinade and garnish the fish with fresh parsley or chives.

Marinated Salmon

SERVES 6–8

680 g (1½ lb) tailpiece of fresh salmon
2 tablespoons sea salt
1½ tablespoons granulated sugar
1 teaspoon crushed white or black peppercorns
1 tablespoon brandy (optional)
2 tablespoons chopped fresh dill, or 2 teaspoons dried dill

For the dressing:
4 tablespoons olive oil
1 tablespoon wine vinegar
1 tablespoon mild made mustard
½ teaspoon granulated sugar (optional)
salt and freshly ground white or black pepper
sprigs of fresh dill or parsley, or chopped chives to garnish

Bone the salmon, or ask the fishmonger to do it for you, to make two triangular fillets. Leave on the skin.

Mix together the salt, sugar, pepper, brandy (if you are including it) and dill. Spread a quarter of this mixture on the base of a dish and lay the first piece of salmon, skin side down, on top of it. Spread with half the remaining mixture and place the second piece of salmon, skin side up, on top. Rub the remaining salt mixture into the skin. Cover the fish with foil, weight it with a plate and a couple of tins from the storecupboard, and refrigerate it for up to five days, but not less than 36 hours.

To serve, slice the salmon either parallel to the skin or at an angle to it. It may be sliced thickly or thinly according to taste.

Mix or shake well together all the ingredients for the dressing. Arrange the sliced salmon on a serving dish and decorate it with the dill, parsley or chives. Serve the dressing separately.

Very fresh cod – the freshness is absolutely essential – served cold with good mayonnaise and a few capers to sharpen it up, is a more delicious summer dish than I, for one, would have believed before tasting it. Serve it as a first course on small plates. Put a lettuce leaf under each mound of fish and top with a slice of lemon.

Cod and Capers with Mayonnaise

SERVES 6

900 g (2 lb) middle cut of cod in one piece, on the bone and very fresh
2 tablespoons capers
150 ml (¼ pint) good mayonnaise

Steam the fish, covered, over simmering water for about 30 minutes, or until just cooked. Test it with the point of a knife inserted into the thickest part. It is cooked when the flesh loses its pinkish tinge and becomes a pearly, opaque white. A sure sign that the cod is really fresh is that a creamy curd forms between the flakes. Allow the fish to cool. When the fish is quite cold, remove all the skin and bones and flake the flesh into a bowl. Add the capers and mayonnaise and mix them gently together until the fish is well coated. Chill briefly before serving.

Thankfully it is only close friends and family who are likely to demand feeding at short notice. Not that *they* demand of course. But as protestations of going somewhere for a bite fade into mumblings about not going to too much trouble, who has not wondered how to stretch two chops between six?

Since not everyone has a freezer with anything suitable in it, or Parma ham slung from the rafters, or a side of smoked salmon somewhere handy, there is still a case for keeping a few well-chosen tins in the back of the storecupboard.

Fancy tins of things, particularly made up dishes like *coq au vin*, can be very disappointing and, for more than two people, costly with it. Basics like tomatoes, beans, tuna, anchovies, ham and mushrooms are much more versatile in an emergency.

Tonno e Fagioli

SERVES 6–8

2 × 400 g (14 oz) tins of white
  kidney beans, or other white
  beans
200 g (7 oz) tin of tuna packed in
  olive oil
5 tablespoons olive oil
1–2 tablespoons fresh lemon juice
  or wine vinegar
salt and freshly ground black
  pepper
1 small onion, sliced in thin rings
1 tablespoon chopped parsley
  (optional)

Rinse the beans under the cold tap, drain them well and put them in a bowl with the drained, flaked tuna.

Put the olive oil in a small screw-top jar with the lemon juice or vinegar, salt and pepper and shake well together.

Pour the dressing over the tuna and beans and mix them lightly together. Turn the mixture into one large serving dish or several small ones. Separate the onion rings and arrange them on top of the salad, then sprinkle with the parsley, if you have it.

All manner of dips and spreads make excellent first courses for informal summer eating. Serve any of them with chunks of crisp raw vegetables, with hot pitta bread, crusty rolls, toast or crackers.

Guacamole is eaten in a variety of ways on its home territory. Mexicans serve it as a sauce with meat, fish or beans, and as a dip or spread. They make it with fresh chillies, hot or very hot to taste, and with a variety of ingredients including green tomatoes, sweet peppers and onion or garlic.

Guacamole

SERVES 4

1 very ripe avocado
1 tablespoon fresh lime or lemon
juice
1 small tomato
1 tablespoon finely chopped onion
1 tablespoon finely chopped fresh
coriander leaves
salt and freshly ground black
pepper
Tabasco sauce or ground chilli

Peel, stone and mash the avocado. Stir in the lime or lemon juice. Peel the tomato after dipping it for 30 seconds in boiling water. Remove and discard the seeds and chop the flesh finely. Mix the avocado, tomato, onion and coriander and season to taste with salt, pepper and Tabasco or chilli. Chill before serving.

Creamed Aubergine with Walnuts

SERVES 6 OR MORE

450 g (1 lb) aubergines
1 clove garlic, crushed
55 g (2 oz) walnut pieces
4 tablespoons natural yogurt
salt and freshly ground black
pepper
walnut halves or chopped parsley to
garnish

Put the whole aubergines, stalks and all, in a shallow baking dish and bake in a preheated moderately hot oven (190°C/375°F, gas mark 5) for about 40 minutes, or until they are very tender. Leave them to cool.

Open the aubergines and scoop out the flesh. Discard the skins. Using a food processor, blender, or pestle and mortar, blend the aubergine, garlic, walnut pieces and yogurt to a paste. Season to taste with salt and pepper.

Serve creamed aubergine with walnuts at room temperature, garnished with the walnut halves or parsley.

Hummus

SERVES 6 OR MORE

400 g (14 oz) cooked chick peas
(tinned are fine)
4 tablespoons sesame paste (tahina)
4 tablespoons fresh lemon juice
2 cloves garlic, crushed
salt
4 tablespoons olive oil
1 tablespoon, or more, chopped
parsley

Using a food processor, blender, or pestle and mortar, blend the chick peas (well rinsed if they are tinned), sesame paste, lemon juice and garlic to a smooth paste. Season the mixture to taste with salt and add enough olive oil (or more lemon juice or water) to make a creamy dip. Serve at room temperature garnished with the parsley.

4

Egg Dishes

Idle speculation about the contents of other people's supermarket trollies whiles away the boredom of waiting to pay. At least it provides a distraction from the chocolate temptations on the run-up to the check-out.

What on earth is she going to do with six vegetable marrows, four bags of semolina and a box of bird seed? Dear me, that fish looks none too bright-eyed, madam. And ah yes; brown rice, orange juice, a jumbo bag of muesli and the biggest size of own-brand yogurt – that lot should sort out the poor fellow's complexion. I, meanwhile, was doing my best to look nonchalant about the five dozen eggs in my own basket. The embarrassment was self-inflicted of course. I had asked readers of *The Times* for advice on using up egg whites and, goodness, I got it.

You know the problem. One minute the fridge is cluttered with assorted vessels harbouring egg yolks of uncertain age. Then no sooner has much ingenuity been employed to disperse them, than it is the turn of the whites to collect and haunt you. And a couple of egg whites makes an awesome volume of meringue.

I had always found egg yolks easier to use up than their whites. Mixed with cream in an approximate proportion of two yolks to 150 ml (¼ pint) single cream, they make a handy liaison for thickening creamy soups and delicate sauces. Confectioners' custard and custard-based ice creams mop them up, as do the classic emulsion sauces, mayonnaise, hollandaise and béarnaise. But this was before I mentioned the superfluous whites problem in print. The most interesting of the readers' recipes made another article, but after using up all the eggs in that basket to test the recipes for publication it was a week or two before I felt like cracking another.

Eggs are certainly bigger now, if not better than they once were. Even if the beguilingly speckled brown ones are more likely to have been laid by new technology hens than by scratching farmyard fowl, they continue to seem the most pleasingly natural of foodstuffs. A new-laid egg is still one of the really good things in life, one that we city folk so seldom taste that it is the greatest treat.

The fresher the better is the rule for eggs, especially if they are to be simply cooked – boiled, poached or baked *en cocotte*. Meringue is the one exception. The best is made with elderly egg whites.

There are two ways to gauge the freshness of eggs. The first is to cover the raw egg with cold water and note how it lies. A new-laid egg has only a small pocket of air inside it. It is heavy and sinks until it sits square on the bottom with the round and pointed ends lying horizontally. After a week the porous shell of the egg will have allowed some of its moisture to evaporate. The air pocket will be bigger and the egg will sit tilted in the water. At two or three weeks the egg is still quite fit to eat but it has an even larger air pocket and almost floats. It stands, like a ballet dancer, balanced on the pointed end.

A raw egg broken onto a flat plate cannot disguise its age either. The rule here is that the older the egg the flatter it spreads. Both the yolk and particularly the white of a new-laid egg retain a rounded shape, and only a very small portion of the white is thin and watery.

Eggs are best stored in a cool place in preference to the refrigerator. However, if the fridge is the only cool spot you have, keep eggs with the salads and protect them from any strong smells they might absorb.

To store separated egg yolks or whites for a few days cover the container tightly and consign them to the fridge. I have never needed to freeze eggs, but the freezer guides say that it can be done successfully and give six months as the safe limit. Whites can be frozen just as they are, but yolks should be beaten with half a teaspoon of salt or sugar to every half dozen to prevent them thickening.

Oeufs en cocotte are simply eggs baked with cream. They are the easiest of hot first courses, and a little fresh tarragon or dill transforms the classic recipe.

Baked Eggs with Herbs

SERVES 6

30 g (1 oz) butter
6 large eggs, as fresh as possible
6 tablespoons double cream
2 tablespoons finely chopped fresh
   tarragon or dill
salt and freshly ground black
   pepper

Use half the butter to grease six small ovenproof cocotte dishes or individual ramekins. Break an egg into each dish.

Mix the cream with the tarragon or dill and season with salt and pepper. Top each egg with a tablespoon of the cream and dot with the remaining butter.

Stand the dishes in a large dish or roasting tin and pour in boiling water to come halfway up their sides. Bake the eggs in the centre of a preheated moderately hot oven (200°C/400°F, gas mark 6) for seven minutes, or a little longer. The whites should be set and the yolks still a little runny. Test them after seven minutes by tapping the sides of the dishes and give them a little longer if they are not quite done. Serve immediately.

Eggs Florentine, tender poached eggs served on a bed of creamed spinach and topped with a light cheese sauce, is a well-loved dish. Vary the classic recipe by substituting watercress and/or sorrel for a proportion of the spinach and add a few chopped spring onions too.

Eggs Florentine

SERVES 2

450 g (1 lb) fresh spinach
30 g (1 oz) butter
4 tablespoons double cream
salt and freshly ground black
*   pepper*
freshly grated nutmeg
4 large eggs

For the sauce:
15 g (1/2 oz) butter
15 g (1/2 oz) plain flour
250 ml (8 fl oz) milk
2 tablespoons freshly grated
*   Parmesan or sharp Cheddar*
*   cheese*
salt and cayenne pepper
paprika

Pull the stalks off the spinach and wash the leaves well. Blanch the leaves (and the watercress, sorrel and spring onions if you are adding them) for two minutes in boiling water, then plunge them immediately into cold water and drain well. Use your hands to squeeze out most of the moisture, then chop the spinach roughly.

Melt the butter in a saucepan and stir in the spinach. Cook it briefly on a medium heat, and when the mixture is becoming fairly dry, stir in the cream. Season to taste with salt, pepper and nutmeg and divide it between two shallow ovenproof dishes. Cover and keep warm.

Lightly poach the eggs. The whites should be just set and the yolks runny. Unless the eggs are newly laid, in which case they will retain their shape fairly well in an open pan, it may be better to use a poaching mould. Drain the eggs and arrange them on the spinach.

To make the sauce, melt the butter in a small pan and stir in the flour. Stir the *roux* on a low heat for a minute or two, then gradually add the milk, stirring constantly, to make a smooth, creamy sauce. Cook it for about five minutes before stirring in the cheese and seasoning to taste with salt and cayenne.

Pour the sauce over the eggs and spinach. Dust lightly with the paprika and brown under a hot grill. The paprika helps to make the sauce form those appetising dark brown blisters. Serve immediately.

Quails' Eggs en Brioche

SERVES 6

6 individual brioches (see page
*   205)*
2 tablespoons melted butter
12 fresh quails' eggs

For the sauce:
3 egg yolks
3 tablespoons water
salt and freshly ground black
*   pepper to taste*
170 g (6 oz) butter, softened
2 tablespoons lemon juice

Decapitate the brioches and scoop out the centres, leaving shells about 1 cm (1/3 in) thick. Brush the insides of the brioches with the melted butter and set the shells and lids on a baking sheet.

Drop the eggs into boiling salted water and boil them for just two minutes. Plunge them immediately into cold water. Shell the eggs and keep them warm in a bowl of warm – not hot – water until you are ready to assemble the brioches.

To make the hollandaise sauce, mix the egg yolks, water and a little salt and pepper in a small saucepan, or in the top of a double boiler if you prefer to make the sauce over indirect heat, in which case the water in the lower pan should be barely simmering. Whisk the mixture over a very low heat until it is thick and creamy. Whisk in the softened butter, a little at a time, until the sauce is thick and light. When all the butter has been added, remove the pan from the heat and whisk in the lemon juice. Adjust the seasoning.

Warm the brioche cases in a preheated moderate oven (160°C/325°F, gas mark 3) for about 10 minutes. Place a small spoonful of sauce in each case and top with two eggs. Add another spoonful of sauce and replace the lids on the brioches. Serve immediately, with the remaining sauce in a separate bowl.

It takes panache to make soufflés for guests, or at least a certain amount of confidence. The mystique which surrounds their construction continues to intimidate the most surprising people, and otherwise competent cooks are afraid to attempt soufflés even in the privacy of their own kitchens.

The great advantage to be won from all this mystification is the applause which greets a well-risen soufflé. Its perfection may be short-lived, but a soufflé always makes a good entrance. I like to bake them in individual dishes which allow everyone the pleasure of the first exploratory spoonful. So much hot air never looks quite the same spread on a flat plate.

Savoury soufflés flavoured with cheese, fish, game or vegetables, make first courses which can be fitted into almost any menu. Or they can be served as the main dish for lunch or supper. Most savoury soufflés are variations on a basic cheese soufflé mixture, the amount and strength of the cheese varying according to the additional flavouring ingredients.

There is nothing difficult about making good soufflés. They are, after all, nothing more than a thick, well-flavoured sauce lightened with meringue and baked so that the heat of the oven expands the air already beaten into the egg whites. As soon as they are out of the oven the air inside begins to cool and the expansion process goes into reverse. This is why soufflés are always served the minute they are ready and why it is not a good idea to open the oven door wide and slam it shut during their brief baking time.

But it is no reason to tiptoe round the kitchen talking in whispers and afraid to go near the oven. Take a look at the soufflé towards the end of the estimated cooking time; jog the dish gently to see whether it is firm enough to serve or needs another few minutes. Whether you like soufflés creamy in the centre or cooked right through is a matter of taste.

The basic points to watch when soufflé-making are these: the utensils used for beating the egg whites should be spotlessly clean and free of grease or water; the dishes should be straight-sided and well buttered, especially round the rims, before being dusted with breadcrumbs for savoury soufflés, granulated sugar for sweet ones; unless the dishes are very shallow, paper collars should not be needed for baked soufflés.

Cheese Soufflé

fine, dry breadcrumbs
45 g (1½ oz) butter
30 g (1 oz) plain flour
300 ml (½ pint) milk
4 large eggs, separated, plus an
   additional white
85 g (3 oz) Cheddar cheese, grated
30 g (1 oz) Parmesan cheese, finely
   grated
½ teaspoon dry English mustard
¼ teaspoon ground mace
salt and cayenne pepper to taste

Make one large soufflé in a dish of 1 litre (about 2 pints) capacity, or four smaller ones in 300 ml (½ pint) dishes. Butter the dish or dishes generously and sprinkle the insides with the breadcrumbs.

Melt the butter in a heavy saucepan and stir in the flour. Cook the *roux* on a gentle heat for a minute or two without allowing it to colour. Add the milk gradually, stirring constantly, to make a smooth, thick sauce. Cook the sauce gently for a minute or two, then remove it from the heat. Allow it to cool a little before beating in the egg yolks, one at a time, followed by the cheeses, mustard, mace, salt and cayenne.

Whisk the egg whites until they hold a stiff peak. Fold one large spoonful of the meringue into the cheese sauce to lighten it a little before gently folding in the remainder.

Turn the mixture into the prepared soufflé dish or dishes. Set the filled dish, or dishes, on a baking sheet and bake in the centre of a preheated hot oven (220°C/425°F, gas mark 7) for 12–15 minutes for the large soufflé, 8–10 minutes for the individual ones.

Stilton Soufflés

fine, dry breadcrumbs
55 g (2 oz) butter
45 g (1½ oz) plain flour
300 ml (½ pint) milk
4 eggs, separated, plus an
   additional white
110 g (4 oz) Stilton cheese,
   crumbled
salt and cayenne pepper to taste
1 teaspoon Dijon mustard

Butter four 300 ml (½ pint) soufflé dishes generously and sprinkle the insides with the breadcrumbs.

Melt the butter in a heavy saucepan and stir in the flour. Cook the *roux* on a gentle heat for a minute or two without allowing it to colour. Add the milk gradually, stirring constantly, to make a smooth, thick sauce. Cook the sauce gently for a minute or two, then remove it from the heat. Stir in the egg yolks, one at a time, then the cheese. Return the pan to the heat and stir until the cheese has just melted. Season it generously with salt, cayenne and mustard.

Whisk the egg whites until stiff and fold them gently into the cheese sauce. Divide the mixture between the prepared soufflé dishes. Set the filled dishes on a baking sheet and bake in the centre of a preheated cool oven (150°C/300°F, gas mark 2) for about 30 minutes, or until well risen and golden. Serve immediately.

Spinach Soufflé

fine, dry breadcrumbs
30 g (1 oz) butter
30 g (1 oz) plain flour
300 ml (½ pint) milk
55 g (2 oz) Gruyère or Cheddar
    cheese, grated
¼ teaspoon dry mustard
salt and freshly ground black
    pepper
freshly grated nutmeg
4 large eggs, separated
55 g (2 oz) streaky bacon, grilled
    crisp and crumbled, or cooked
    ham, finely diced
170 g (6 oz) cooked spinach,
    chopped, or frozen chopped
    spinach, thawed

Butter a dish of 1 litre (about 2 pints) capacity, or four to eight ramekins. Sprinkle the insides with the breadcrumbs.

Melt the butter in a saucepan and stir in the flour. Cook the *roux* for a minute or two on a moderate heat without allowing it to colour. Add the milk gradually, stirring constantly, to make a smooth, thick sauce. Add the cheese and cook gently until it has melted. Season generously with the mustard, salt, pepper and nutmeg.

Remove the sauce from the heat and allow it to cool a little before beating in the egg yolks, one at a time. Add the bacon or ham and spinach and stir them into the sauce.

Whisk the egg whites until they hold stiff peaks and fold them gently into the sauce using a metal spoon. Turn the mixture into the prepared dish or ramekins. Set the dish or dishes on a baking sheet and bake in the centre of a preheated moderately hot oven (190°C/375°F, gas mark 5) until well risen and golden. This will take 40–45 minutes for the big soufflé, 15–20 minutes for the little ones.

Asparagus is seldom cheap and a soufflé makes a little go a long way. The spindly home-grown asparagus sold loose during the season, and the rather bitter white French asparagus are both cheaper than the best English or Californian 'grass' and just as good for a soufflé.

Asparagus Soufflé

fine, dry breadcrumbs
225 g (8 oz) fresh asparagus
55 g (2 oz) butter
55 g (2 oz) plain flour
300 ml (½ pint) milk
4 tablespoons finely grated
    Parmesan cheese
4 large eggs, separated
pinch of ground mace
salt and freshly ground white or
    black pepper

Make one large soufflé in a dish of 2 litres (3 pints) capacity, or six smaller ones in 300 ml (½ pint) dishes. Butter the dish or dishes generously and sprinkle the insides with the breadcrumbs.

Trim the asparagus and steam it until just tender. Cut off the tips and reserve them to fill the soufflé. Purée the stems by pressing them through a sieve, or processing and then straining.

Melt the butter in a saucepan and stir in the flour. Cook the *roux* for a minute or two without allowing it to colour. Add the milk gradually, stirring constantly, to make a smooth, thick sauce. Cook the sauce for a minute more, stirring to ensure that it does not stick. Stir in the cheese and continue cooking until it has melted. Remove the pan from the heat and beat in the asparagus purée, then the egg yolks. Season well with the mace, salt and pepper.

Whisk the egg whites until they hold a stiff peak and fold them thoroughly into the asparagus mixture. Turn half the mixture into the prepared dish or dishes, top with the asparagus tips and cover with the remaining mixture. Stand the dish or dishes on a heavy baking sheet and bake in a preheated hot oven (200°C/400°F, gas mark 6) until well risen but still moist in the centre. This will take about 35 minutes for the large soufflé, 15–20 minutes for the small ones. Serve immediately.

'Take parsley, mint, savory, sage, tansy, vervain, clary [a variety of sage], rue, ditayn [a variety of oregano], fennel, southernwood; hew them, and grind them small; medle them up with eggs. Put butter in a dish, and put the mixture thereto, and bake, and mess it forth.' That is a fourteenth century recipe for *erbolates* or *herbolace*, a recognisable ancestor of today's herb omelette.

By the early eighteenth century *amletts* or *amulets* were commonplace enough for Richard Bradley to write in *The Country Housewife and Lady's Director* that 'Some like amletts, or frazes of eggs, with bacon, or with clary, or other high-tasted herbs, which every good housewife knows how to direct.'

An humungus omelette – humungus is not a real word but it describes the catch-all versatility of the dish perfectly – is an invaluable recipe for one-pan cooking when camping or bedsitting. The essential ingredients are onions, potatoes and eggs. It would be quicker to write a list of what cannot be added to the basic formula than to itemise all the successful variations. Ham, bacon, cheese, garlic, herbs, and other cooked vegetables are the most obvious additions. When courgettes and aubergines are cheap the opportunity to include them should not be missed.

Humungus Omelette

SERVES 4

at least 2 tablespoons oil or butter
1 large onion, finely chopped
1 small tin of new potatoes, or leftovers
110 g (4 oz) bacon or cooked ham, chopped
225 g (8 oz) courgettes or aubergines, sliced
6 large eggs
55 g (2 oz) hard cheese, grated or finely chopped
chopped herbs to taste
salt and freshly ground black pepper

The order of play for this recipe depends on whether the additional ingredients are raw or cooked. Heat the butter or oil in a large frying pan and cook the onion gently until it is soft, but not coloured. Add any other uncooked vegetables or chopped bacon and continue to cook gently until the vegetables are soft, the bacon is cooked, and the onion is golden. If all the ingredients in the pan are turning brown now the finished taste will be even better.

Add any cooked vegetables and the chopped ham. Beat the eggs and add the cheese, herbs, salt and pepper. Increase the heat a little and add the egg mixture to the pan. As the base of the omelette sets, scrape the cooked parts to the centre of the pan and allow the uncooked mixture to run to the edges. When the omelette is firm enough to turn, put a plate over the pan and invert the combination, sliding the omelette back into the pan to brown the uncooked side. If you have a grill, finish the omelette under a high heat instead of turning it over.

Serve the omelette hot, warm or cold and cut in wedges. Crusty bread and a simple salad are ideal accompaniments.

Many more people have heard of Scotch woodcock than could describe the dish or have ever tasted it. There are numerous versions to choose from. Escoffier, who seems never to have been certain whether he really approved of savouries, put capers in his sauce, sprinkled the finished dish with Parmesan and browned it. Chopped parsley is a more orthodox garnish.

Serve it in its traditional place at the end of a formal meal, or as a first course, or as a supper dish.

Scotch Woodcock

SERVES 2–8

12 anchovy fillets
85 g (3 oz) butter
4 thick slices crustless white bread

For the sauce:
4 yolks of large eggs
250 ml (8 fl oz) double cream
cayenne pepper
1 tablespoon chopped parsley

Mash together or blend the anchovy fillets with half the butter. Toast the bread lightly on both sides. Cut the slices in fingers, or small shapes if they are to be served as a savoury course at dinner. Spread the toast with the remaining butter, then with the anchovy butter. Arrange in one layer in a heated serving dish and keep warm. Mix the egg yolks in a small saucepan with the cream and a generous seasoning of cayenne. Heat the mixture, stirring constantly, to just below boiling point to make a thick, creamy sauce. Do not allow to boil or the sauce will curdle. Pour the sauce over the anchovy toast and serve at once, sprinkled with the parsley.

5

Cheese Themes

Presenting leftovers in such a way that those who receive them are not only truly grateful but quite unsuspecting is an art in itself. Success depends on an element of surprise which in turn rests on offering the dreaded remains in a form as different as possible from their earlier appearance at table. Cheese is the most amenable of ingredients for this kind of deception and the reason I never grudge buying really big pieces when I am entertaining is that there are so many good ways of using it up. Its character is invariably so radically altered by cooking that there is no evident association between last night's cheeseboard and tomorrow's soufflé or gratin.

The hard cheeses like Cheddar and Gruyère, and firm cheeses like Stilton are obvious choices for cooking as well as eating. Very hard cheese like Parmesan and pecorino romano are seldom eaten as they come, and soft cheeses like brie are hardly ever cooked. There are exceptions to every rule of course. A freshly cut piece of top quality mature Parmesan bought from a supplier whose turnover is so large that these huge cheeses have no chance to dry up, is an interesting choice to offer on a cheeseboard. Its sharpness and strength, the virtues that make it an invaluable cheese for cooking, are most enjoyable in small quantities.

At the opposite end of the cheese scale are the soft, white, fresh cheeses often sold loose or in cartons. Cream cheese and cottage cheese are the best known and most widely available of these but the selection seems to have multiplied bewilderingly in recent years and imported varieties have swollen the choice. The range of low-fat varieties alone is wide. Home-produced curd or cottage cheese, quark from Germany, Liptauer originally from Hungary, ricotta and mascapone from Italy, fromage blanc and petit Suisse from France are all commonly available.

The popularity of cottage cheese rests heavily on its low calorie count. A smoother, sharper low-fat cheese is easily made at home from fresh, natural yogurt. It is excellent in any recipe which calls for cottage cheese and in many that specify cream cheese. Make yogurt curd cheese with low-fat or whole milk yogurt. The fresher and blander tasting the yogurt the blander the resulting cheese will be.

Yogurt Curd Cheese

MAKES ABOUT 340 g (12 oz)

1 litre (1¾ pints) fresh natural yogurt

Line a large sieve with a square of damp muslin or cheesecloth and stand it over a bowl. Lightly beat the yogurt and pour it into the lined sieve. Gather up the corners of the muslin and knot them together. Hang the bag of whipped yogurt over a bowl in a cool place for at least four hours or, better still, overnight, by which time the whey will have dripped out.

Refrigerate the yogurt curd cheese and use it within three or four days. It is delicious seasoned with salt, pepper, garlic and fresh herbs.

Smooth mixtures of cream cheese and herbs make splendid sandwich fillings, or can be used instead of butter. Try basil and cream cheese with sliced tomato and fresh wholemeal bread, or a tarragon flavoured spread with thin slices of apple or chicken breast in granary rolls. Use a dill flavoured spread with salmon or tuna and cucumber fillings, chives for a mild onion flavour with egg. And for salad sandwiches try mixing larger quantities of mixed herbs into the cheese. Fresh full cream cheese or the low-fat varieties, including yogurt curd cheese, can be used for herb spreads.

Herb Cheese Spread

MAKES 225 g (8 oz)

225 g (8 oz) cream cheese, full cream or low-fat
4 tablespoons finely chopped basil, tarragon, dill or chives
salt and freshly ground black pepper to taste
single cream to thin if needed

Mix the cream cheese with the herbs and season it to taste with salt and pepper. If the cheese is too thick to spread, mix in just enough cream to give the consistency you need.

Dessert pears are at their best in late autumn and early winter. Serve them stuffed with a creamed Stilton mixture as a first course before game, or as a cheese course or pudding.

Creamed Cheese with Pears

110 g (4 oz) Stilton cheese, crumbled
1 small, ripe pear, peeled and roughly chopped
2 tablespoons finely chopped walnuts
2 tablespoons finely chopped celery
2 large or 4 small ripe pears, peeled
4 lettuce or radicchio leaves (optional)

Mix the cheese with the chopped pear and beat or blend to a smooth paste. Fold in the walnuts and celery. Chill the creamed cheese mixture.

Use the creamed cheese to fill halves of peeled pear, piling the mixture into the hollow left when the core has been removed. Alternatively, spoon or pipe the creamed cheese onto a leaf of lettuce or radicchio and arrange a fan of pear slices on one side of the leaf. (The pear halves or slices may be prepared a short while in advance and prevented from browning by keeping in iced water which has been acidulated with a little lemon juice or vinegar.) Serve well chilled.

Slices of grilled goats' cheese served with a small but carefully composed salad make an equally versatile opening or finish to a meal.

Petit Chèvre aux Endives

about 225 g (8 oz) log of semi-soft goats' cheese
6 radicchio (red endive) leaves
1 small Cox's Orange Pippin apple, peeled, cored and sliced
2 tablespoons chopped hazelnuts
1 tablespoon double or single cream
cayenne pepper

For the dressing:
1 tablespoon sherry vinegar
1 tablespoon dry sherry
3 tablespoons walnut oil
salt and freshly ground black pepper
1 teaspoon very finely chopped shallot

Try to find one of the small drum or log shaped semi-soft goats' cheeses sold whole. Ideally the diameter of the cheese should be about 4–5 cm (1½–2 in). Cut off the end rinds but not the rind on the side, and cut the cheese in 1.25 cm (½ in) slices. Allow one slice per serving as a cheese course, but perhaps two for a first course.

Arrange the washed radicchio leaves on six small plates and top with the apple slices. Toast the hazelnuts lightly and sprinkle them on the leaves.

Arrange the cheese slices on a sheet of foil in a grill pan and brush them with the cream, then sprinkle very lightly with cayenne. Turn the grill to high and make the dressing while it heats up.

Mix all the dressing ingredients and warm the dressing just a little before spooning some on each salad.

Lastly, grill the cheese lightly on one side only, until the top begins to bubble. Transfer the cheese to the prepared plates and serve immediately.

Really big soufflés, enough for say six to eight, are not really a practical proposition. On this scale the outside is inevitably overdone before the middle is warm, let alone cooked. And the alternative, individual soufflés, can only be tackled by those who have enough small soufflé dishes and an oven with unusually even heat distribution.

A hot cheese roulade is not quite as puffy and unstable as a full blown soufflé, but it is just as festive looking. Fillings can be varied to suit the occasion – cottage cheese and herbs for a light lunch, cream cheese and shellfish to begin a richer or posher meal.

SERVES 6–8

Cheese and Seafood Roulade

30 g (1 oz) butter
30 g (1 oz) plain flour
300 ml (½ pint) milk
55 g (2 oz) Parmesan cheese, freshly grated
5 eggs, separated
salt and cayenne pepper

For the filling:
225–340 g (8–12 oz) cooked fish or shellfish
225 g (8 oz) cream cheese
2 tablespoons finely chopped parsley
1 tablespoon finely chopped dill
salt and cayenne pepper
2 tablespoons melted butter
2 tablespoons freshly grated Parmesan cheese

Generously oil or butter a Swiss roll tray about 30 × 35 cm (12 × 14 in). Line it neatly with greaseproof paper or baking parchment and oil or butter that well too.

Melt the butter in a saucepan and stir in the flour. Cook the *roux* for a minute or two without allowing it to colour, then gradually add the milk, stirring constantly on a low heat to make a smooth sauce. Stir in the cheese and cook until it has melted completely, then remove the sauce from the heat. Beat in the egg yolks one at a time and season the sauce generously with salt and cayenne.

Whisk the egg whites until they hold stiff peaks and fold the meringue into the cheese sauce. Turn the mixture into the prepared tin and spread it evenly. Bake in a preheated moderate oven (180°C/350°F, gas mark 4) for about 15 minutes, or until the roulade is just firm.

As soon as it is out of the oven, cover the roulade with a clean tea cloth, then turn over the tin and cloth together, depositing the roulade on the cloth. Peel off the paper.

To prepare the filling, flake the fish, or break the shellfish into small pieces. Beat the cream cheese until it is smooth, adding a spoonful or two of cream or milk if it is too thick to spread on the delicate soufflé mixture. Spread the cream cheese on the roulade to within 1 cm (⅓ in) of each edge, sprinkle it with the herbs and season it with salt and cayenne. Scatter the fish or shellfish evenly over the cream cheese.

Now using the cloth to help fold the roulade, roll it, Swiss roll fashion, from one long side to the other.

Place the roulade on an ovenproof serving dish and brush it with the melted butter. Sprinkle with the Parmesan and bake for another 10–15 minutes at 180°C/350°F, gas mark 4. Serve the roulade in thick slices on warmed plates.

For a smoked salmon and avocado stuffing, mash the flesh of three ripe avocados and season it generously with lemon juice, cayenne and a little salt. Spread this mixture on the roulade and cover it with 225 g (8 oz) smoked salmon cut in slivers. Finish as above.

Beaufort is a hard French alpine cheese of the Gruyère family. Swiss Gruyère or Comté from France have similarly rich fruity flavours and can be substituted for Beaufort in this tart.

Beaufort and Walnut Tart

SERVES 6

340 g (12 oz) shortcrust pastry (see page 80)

For the filling:
170 g (6 oz) shelled walnuts, coarsely chopped
170 g (6 oz) Beaufort or Gruyère cheese, finely grated
1 tablespoon cornflour
300 ml (½ pint) milk
3 large eggs
150 ml (¼ pint) double cream
salt and freshly ground black pepper

Roll out the pastry thinly on a lightly floured surface and use it to line a loose-bottomed 25 cm (10 in) tart tin. If there is time, chill the pastry shell again before baking it blind. Just before baking, line the shell with greaseproof paper or foil and weight it down with dried beans. Set on a baking sheet and bake in a preheated moderately hot oven (200°C/400°F, gas mark 6) for 10 minutes. Remove from the oven and take out the beans and lining paper. Prick the base with a fork, reduce the temperature to moderate (180°C/350°F, gas mark 4) and bake the shell for another 10 minutes.

Spread the nuts then the cheese over the pastry. Mix the cornflour with a little of the milk in a bowl, then beat in the eggs, the remaining milk and cream. Season the custard to taste with salt and pepper and pour it into the tart. Return it to the oven and bake for about 40 minutes, or until the filling has set. Serve hot or warm.

Macaroni cheese is not usually anything to write home about. In fact school macaroni, when it was not an unspeakable pudding, was so high on macaroni and low on cheese that they served it in slabs. Lukewarm.

This one is very different. The creamy sauce is rich in cheese, parsley and spring onions, and the result is delicious. Serve it with a crunchy salad of Webb or Iceberg lettuce, or with home-made coleslaw (see page 164).

Green Macaroni Cheese

SERVES 3–4

170 g (6 oz) wholewheat or ordinary macaroni
55 g (2 oz) butter
6 level tablespoons plain flour
600 ml (1 pint) milk
225 g (8 oz) strong Cheddar cheese
6 tablespoons chopped parsley
6 tablespoons finely chopped spring onions
salt and freshly ground black pepper
paprika (optional)

Heat about 2 litres (3½ pints) of water in a fairly large saucepan until it boils, then throw in the macaroni. Boil the pasta, uncovered, until it is just tender, but not soggy. Drain the macaroni and rinse out the pan.

Melt the butter in the pan until it bubbles, then stir in the flour all at once. Cook the *roux* on a low heat for a minute or two without allowing it to brown, then gradually add the milk, stirring constantly.

Now add the cheese and stir until it melts. Add the parsley, spring onions and drained macaroni. Season the sauce to taste with salt and pepper.

Turn the macaroni into a buttered ovenproof dish and sprinkle a very little paprika over the top to help it brown. Bake it in a preheated moderate oven (180°C/350°F, gas mark 4) for about 45 minutes. Serve very hot.

Cheese pudding is the simplest of old fashioned dishes. It is comforting food – light and tasty and just the thing for lunch or supper when a soufflé would be too much trouble. It is that handy kind of recipe which can as easily be made for one or two as for six. Just double or triple the quantities and increase the baking time. Any well-flavoured cheese will do for this pudding which can be served on its own or with a crisp salad and crusty bread.

Cheese Pudding

SERVES 2–3

110 g (4 oz) sharp Cheddar cheese, grated
55 g (2 oz) fresh brown or white breadcrumbs
2 large eggs
450 ml (³/4 pint) milk
salt and freshly ground black pepper
freshly grated nutmeg to taste

Put all the ingredients in a large bowl, mix well and pour into a buttered ovenproof dish of about 900 ml (1½ pints) capacity. A small soufflé or pie dish is ideal. Bake the pudding in a preheated moderate oven (180°C/350°F, gas mark 4) for about 30 minutes, or until it is firm, golden and slightly puffed. Serve hot.

An alpine cheese fondue is the simplest of festive meals. A proper earthenware fondue dish, called a *caquelon*, is the best vessel for making it in, but a heavy casserole set on a heat-dispersing mat will do very well.

Cheese Fondue

SERVES 4

500 g (1 lb 2 oz) Gruyère, Emmenthal or Comté cheese, or a mixture of these
1 loaf crusty bread
1 clove garlic
300 ml (½ pint) dry white wine
salt and freshly ground black pepper to taste
1 tablespoon cornflour
3 tablespoons kirsch

Cut the cheese into small dice which will melt evenly. Cut the bread into bite-sized pieces, each with a portion of crust. If you are using a French loaf, cut the bread in thick slices then half or quarter each slice. Leave the bread uncovered to dry a little.

Cut the garlic clove and rub it round the fondue dish several times to give the fondue a delicate aroma of garlic. Pour in the wine and set the dish on a medium heat. When the wine is hot, but before it comes to the boil, add the cheese all at once.

Stir the mixture constantly with a wooden spoon as the cheese melts. The heat should be just sufficient to keep the fondue bubbling very gently, and the stirring continuous to prevent it catching. Add salt and pepper and the cornflour mixed to a smooth paste with a little wine or water. Lastly stir in the kirsch and cook the fondue for a moment or two longer before serving it.

Set the dish over a lighted spirit burner adjusted to keep the mixture gently bubbling as before. Give each diner a long fork and plenty of bread. Each then spears a piece of bread with a fork and twirls it in the cheese mixture. Turning the fork as the cheese-coated bread is lifted out discourages drips.

As the level of the melted cheese drops, a crust gradually forms on the bottom of the pot. When this crust is the only nourishment left, pour a little kirsch onto it and set it alight. The 'croûton' is the final alpine delicacy.

Strong ale with cheese is a dish that could be seen as an English cheese fondue, and this version is made with Double Gloucester cheese. This cheese is traditionally made from the milk of a breed of cows called Old Gloucesters. But it was the temperament of the breed rather than the quality of their milk which recommended them to an eighteenth century Duke of Beaufort. The cows hardly looked up from their fields as his foxhounds swept past, an attribute which struck him so forcibly that he ordered his tenants to stock only this phlegmatic breed.

Strong Ale and Cheese

SERVES 2

*110 g (4 oz) Double Gloucester
   cheese*
*1 tablespoon Tewkesbury or other
   made mustard*
150 ml (¹/4 pint) strong ale
2 thick slices crustless toast

Cut the cheese into thin slices and lay them in a thick layer in a shallow ovenproof dish. Spread the mustard on the cheese and pour over the ale. Bake in a preheated hot oven (230°C/450°F, gas mark 8) for about 10 minutes, or until the cheese has melted. Stir to blend the cheese with the ale and spoon the mixture onto the slices of hot fresh toast. Serve immediately.

Welsh Rarebit

SERVES 2

30 g (1 oz) butter
120 ml (4 fl oz) brown ale
*salt and freshly ground black
   pepper*
*110 g (4 oz) mature Cheddar
   cheese, grated*
2 thick slices hot buttered toast

Melt the butter in a small saucepan and add the ale, salt and pepper. Just before the liquid comes to the boil, stir in the cheese. Stir until the cheese melts, then pour the mixture over the toast. Brown under a preheated grill and serve immediately.

Endless variations on the next recipe are possible. Potted cheese spread thickly on hot crumpets and popped under a hot grill until golden and bubbling is a delight I recommend. Serve it cold too, with toast or crudités. Good, strong cheese is the essential ingredient of this recipe.

Potted Cheese

MAKES ABOUT 680 g (1½ lb)

450 g (1 lb) cheese, grated or crumbled
110 g (4 oz) butter
1 small glass of sherry, port or brandy
½ teaspoon grated nutmeg or mace
cayenne, mustard or curry powder to taste

Remove any hard rinds from the cheese, then pound it with the butter, sherry and seasonings in a mortar, or blend in a mixer. When smooth pack down into little jars or pots. To keep for more than a week seal the top with melted clarified butter (see page 227) or lard and cover with waxed paper and string. Store in a cool place.

Bulgarians make particularly mouthwatering spirals of phyllo pastry filled with cheese. The cheese they use for these savoury confections is called *brynza* and the pastries themselves, *banista*. If you can find no *brynza, feta* will do very well. Feta cheese and phyllo or strudel pastry are most usually sold in shops specialising in Greek or Cypriot foods.

Banista

MAKES 12

340 g (12 oz) brynza or feta cheese
4 tablespoons natural yogurt
1 large egg
freshly ground black pepper to taste
110 g (4 oz) butter, melted
12 sheets phyllo or strudel pastry

Crumble the cheese and rub it through a sieve. Add the yogurt and egg and beat the mixture to a smooth paste. Season with the pepper and transfer the mixture to a piping bag fitted with a plain nozzle of about 1 cm (⅓ in) diameter.

Brush two heavy baking sheets with a little of the melted butter.

Place a sheet of pastry on a clean cloth and brush it lightly with melted butter. Fold the pastry double by joining the long edges and brush the top surface with melted butter. Pipe a line of the cheese filling along one long edge of the pastry rectangle, leaving a space at each end. Using the cloth to lift the edge, roll up the pastry into a cylinder. Brush it with butter and curl the ends in opposite directions to make a curly S-shaped spiral. Transfer the pastry carefully to the baking sheet. Shape the remaining pastries in the same way.

Bake the banista in a preheated moderately hot oven (200°C/400°F, gas mark 6) for about 20 minutes, or until they are golden brown.

Serve the pastries hot or warm. Newly baked banista freeze well and can be reheated from frozen.

6

Pies, Pizza and Pasta

Soggy underside of quiche or less than crisp pork pie crust are encountered so often that it is silly to feel either surprise or disappointment. But one does. Pastry is one of the few foods I admit to being fussy about, not just because it took me rather a long time to learn to make it well, but because it seems only fair that any food which costs so many calories should justify its price with pleasure. And a pleasure good pastry certainly is. It is the foundation of England's many pies and France's famous tarts, and no nations put it to better use.

Our raised crust pies and savoury suet pastry puddings are uniquely English and the kind of dishes I try to make a point of serving whenever I have overseas guests. These doughs are a part of our culinary heritage that cannot be bought in packets; they have to be made at home. Hot water crust pastry for raised pies is a recipe that gives me particular pleasure, even when it seems, as it often does, that the greasy lump of dough will not submit to being moulded into an elegantly shaped and glazed 'coffyn', as the old recipes call it, to enclose tasty morsels of meat. Pie recipes like these have changed so little in essentials down the centuries that they send my mind wandering irresistibly into imaginary kitchens of very long ago.

The easy availability of packets of frozen puff and shortcrust pastry have taken away some, but happily not all incentive for making them. The taste of puff pastry made only with good butter is without question superior to the usual frozen brands, and this applies to shortcrust too. Variations in the richness of shortcrust and in the possible additional flavourings are further reasons for making your own pastry at least occasionally.

A similar argument – that top quality ingredients produce the best results – is equally true for home-made pizza. Cheap, colourful and tasty, pizza is a winner for inexpensive entertaining and great fun to make in large as well as small quantities.

Pasta is another dough-based treat. Fresh pasta bears so little resemblance to dried pasta that the difference in taste and tenderness is hard to credit until it is experienced. Filled pasta shapes – ravioli and cappelletti for example – are obvious candidates for making at home because the interest and quality of the stuffings can be varied so pleasingly. The case for making noodles is less obvious until fresh tagliatelli with a pungent home-made pesto sauce has been tasted.

So first to England's mighty pies.

Making raised pies takes time, but the results are so delicious that the effort is more than repaid. Once baked, they keep fresh in the refrigerator for about a week, but the pastry loses its special crunch quite quickly, so ideally they should be baked no more than a day before they are to be eaten. Freezing pies as soon as they are finished allows them to be made well in advance. Thaw them at room temperature for about 12 hours. Making several pies at one time is more practical than trying to construct one enormous pie.

Each of the three raised pies which follow has its own hot water crust pastry recipe, but they are interchangeable and any one formula may be used for all the pies. You will see that I have not included directions for raising a 'coffyn' of pastry by hand without a mould. This is because I have enough trouble making beautiful pies with the moulds. I keep meaning to try it the old way sometime.

Raised Game Pie

SERVES 6–8

For the filling:
450 g (1 lb) pheasant, grouse,
 partridge or hare, meat only
120 ml (4 fl oz) port
freshly ground black pepper
340 g (12 oz) lean pork
225 g (8 oz) smoked bacon, lean
 and fat
1 medium onion, peeled
1/2 teaspoon chopped sage
1 tablespoon chopped parsley
salt
zest of 1/2 a lemon, finely grated
225 g (8 oz) fresh pork sausage
 meat

For the jellied stock:
900 g (2 lb) veal bones and
 chopped game carcasses
1 medium onion, roughly chopped
1 carrot, roughly chopped
2 bay leaves
6 black peppercorns, crushed
salt

First prepare the filling ingredients. Cut the meat off the game and reserve the carcasses for the stock. Slice the meat into slivers about 5 cm (2 in) long × 7 mm (1/4 in) wide × 7 mm (1/4 in) thick. Reserve any trimmings. Marinate the strips in the port with a little pepper.

Put the game meat trimmings, pork, bacon and onion through the coarse blade of a mincer and mix the ground meats in a bowl with the sage and parsley. Season generously with salt, plenty of freshly ground pepper and the lemon zest. Mix well and set aside.

Roll teaspoonfuls of the sausage meat into balls and set them aside.

To make the stock, put the veal bones and game carcasses in a large pot with the onion and carrot. Cover with cold water and bring to the boil. Skim the stock, add the bay leaves, pepper and a little salt. Cover the pot and simmer for 2½ hours. Strain the stock through a fine sieve lined with muslin and discard the bones. Reduce it by fast boiling to about 300 ml (½ pint), then check the seasoning. Set it aside to cool.

To make the pastry, sift the flour and salt into a warmed mixing bowl. Make a well in the flour, drop in the egg yolk and cover it with flour. Heat the lard or lard and butter with the water in a small saucepan until the fat has melted, then bring to the boil. Pour it immediately over

74

For the pastry:
450 g (1 lb) plain flour
1 teaspoon salt
1 egg yolk
225 g (8 oz) lard, or half and half
    lard and butter
175 ml (6 fl oz) water
1 egg, beaten

the flour and stir vigorously with a wooden spoon until the dough is cool enough to handle.

Turn the dough onto a lightly floured surface and knead it until it is smooth and pliable. Cover the dough and rest it in a warm place for about 20 minutes.

To assemble the pie, lightly grease an oval or rectangular pie mould of about 1.5 litres (2½ pints) capacity, or line an 18 cm (7 in) round loose-bottomed cake tin with foil. Pat dry the strips of marinating game.

Roll out two-thirds of the pastry into a piece to line the mould. Fold the pastry in half and lower it carefully into the mould. Unfold it and ease it smoothly and evenly into the base and up the sides of the mould. Press the dough well into the join between the base and sides of the tin and into any indentations on a fancy mould. Ideally the lining should be not quite 1 cm (⅓ in) thick. If it is too thick there will be a layer of cooked but soggy dough between the meat and the crust.

Put half the minced pork and bacon mixture in the bottom of the lined tin. Cover with slivers of game, arranged lengthwise and interspersed with the sausage meat balls. Top with the remaining pork and bacon. Press the mixture in lightly and mould the top into a dome shape.

Roll the remaining dough to a thickness of 7 mm (¼ in). Lift it on a rolling pin and lay it over the filling. Press the lid on firmly and trim the pastry with a sharp knife. Decorate the edge and ensure a good seal by pressing firmly. Cut a 2.5 cm (1 in) cross through the pastry in the centre of the lid, and fold back the four points to make a good opening for escaping steam. Set a chimney of rolled foil in the hole to keep it open. Re-roll the pastry trimmings and cut decorative flowers and leaves. Stick them onto the pie lid with the beaten egg, then paint all the exposed pastry with beaten egg to glaze.

Set the pie on a baking sheet and bake in a preheated hot oven (230°C/450°F, gas mark 8) for 20 minutes. Reduce the temperature to moderate (160°C/325°F, gas mark 3), cover the pie loosely with foil and bake for another three hours. Remove the foil for the last 30 minutes of cooking time. Leave the pie in its mould until almost cold.

Remove the mould and slowly pour into the pie as much of the cool liquid stock as it will hold, using a small funnel or icing nozzle.

Leave the pie in a cool place for several hours before serving. The stock will set to a jelly and fill the gaps between the pastry and the meat which will have shrunk during cooking. Serve the pie cold, cut into slices or wedges.

Chicken and bacon pie has no lid, just a golden edging of plaited pastry which frames the filling.

Chicken and Bacon Pie

SERVES 6–8

For the pastry:
340 g (12 oz) plain flour
1 teaspoon salt
1 egg yolk
110 g (4 oz) lard
150 ml (1/4 pint) milk and water,
  half and half
1 egg, beaten

For the filling:
450 g (1 lb) boned chicken meat
225 g (8 oz) gammon in one piece
2 tablespoons chopped parsley
freshly ground black pepper
30 g (1 oz) butter
2 tablespoons dry white wine

For the jellied stock:
300 ml (1/2 pint) good chicken stock
  (not a cube)
2 tablespoons gelatine crystals

lemon slices to garnish

To make the pastry, sift the flour and salt into a warmed bowl. Make a well in the flour, drop in the egg yolk and cover it with flour. Heat the lard with the milk and water in a small saucepan until the fat has melted, then bring to the boil. Pour immediately over the flour and stir vigorously with a wooden spoon until the dough is cool enough to handle.

Turn the dough onto a floured surface and knead it until it is soft and pliable. Cover the dough and rest it in a warm place while you make the filling.

Chop the chicken and gammon into small dice, including any fat but discarding skin and tendons. Stir in the parsley and a generous seasoning of the coarsely ground pepper.

To assemble the pie, generously butter a rectangular hinged metal mould about 25 cm (10 in) long × 7.5 cm (3 in) wide × 7.5 cm (3 in) deep. Roll out the dough on a floured surface to a long rectangle about 1 cm (1/3 in) thick. Lower the rolled dough carefully into the mould. Gently press the pastry against the base and sides of the tin so that it will form an even, crack-free crust. Trim the edges flush with the top of the tin. Knead the offcuts and form them into a ball.

Fill the shell with the meat and dot the top with the remaining butter. Sprinkle the wine over the filling.

Roll out the pastry offcuts to a long strip about half the thickness of the pie crust. Cut the strip into narrow ribbons, like tagliatelli, and plait groups of three strands into a decorative edge for the pie. Paint the top edge of the pie crust with the beaten egg, and cover this with the plaited edging. Glaze it with beaten egg.

Set the pie on a baking sheet and bake it in a preheated hot oven (230°C/450°F, gas mark 8) for 20 minutes to set the pastry. Reduce the temperature to moderate (160°C/325°F, gas mark 3) and continue baking for another two hours. Check from time to time that the pastry is not becoming too brown; if it darkens too quickly cover it loosely with foil, removing it for the last 10 minutes of baking time.

Cool the pie in its tin, removing it only when the pie is quite cold. Pour the stock into a small pan and sprinkle the gelatine on top. Leave it to soften for a few minutes, then heat the gelatine gently until it dissolves completely. When it is on the point of setting, pour it into the pie to fill the gaps where the meat has shrunk away from the pastry crust. Arrange the lemon slices on top of the filling and glaze them with jellied stock. Chill the pie until needed.

Use leg or shoulder, including some fat, for pork pie, and be generous with the pepper.

Raised Pork Pie

SERVES 6–8

pork or veal bones
2 onions, quartered
2 bay leaves
2 sage leaves
1 sprig of thyme
1 sprig of parsley
salt and freshly ground black
   pepper
900 g (2 lb) pork, lean and fat

For the pastry:
450 g (1 lb) plain flour
1 teaspoon salt
1 egg yolk
225 g (8 oz) lard
150 ml (¼ pint) milk and water,
   half and half
30 g (1 oz) butter
1 egg, beaten

Put the bones in a pot with the onions, bay leaves, one sage leaf, thyme and parsley. Add 900 ml (1½ pints) of cold water and bring to the boil. Skim, and add salt and pepper. Simmer, partially covered, for about two hours, or until the liquid has reduced to about 600 ml (1 pint). Strain the stock, cool it and skim off the fat.

Cut the meat into small dice, discarding all skin and gristle, and mix it with 1½ teaspoons of salt, the second sage leaf, very finely chopped, and plenty of freshly ground pepper.

To make the pastry, sift the flour and salt into a warmed mixing bowl. Make a well in the flour, drop in the egg yolk and cover it with flour. Heat the lard with the milk and water in a small saucepan until the fat has melted, then bring to the boil. Pour immediately over the flour and stir vigorously with a wooden spoon until the dough is cool enough to handle.

Turn the dough onto a floured surface and knead it until it is soft and pliable. Cover the dough and rest it in a warm place for about 20 minutes.

Form a third of the pastry into a ball and keep it warm. Roll out the rest on a floured surface to about 1 cm (⅓ in) thickness. Use the pastry to line a buttered raised pie mould or loose-bottomed cake tin of about 1.25 litres (2½ pints) capacity.

Fill the pie to within 1.25 cm (½ in) of the top, packing the meat in well. Sprinkle two tablespoons of cold water over the filling and dot with the butter. Roll out the reserved pastry for the lid, dampen the top edges of the pie and press on the lid, sealing it well. Crimp the edges, cut a slit in the top for the steam to escape and use the pastry trimmings to make decorative leaves and flowers. Stick them onto the lid with the beaten egg, and finally brush the whole of the lid with egg to glaze.

Stand the pie on a baking sheet and bake in a preheated hot oven (230°C/450°F, gas mark 8) for about 20 minutes to set the pastry. Reduce the temperature to moderate (160°C/325°F, gas mark 3) and continue baking for another two hours. Check from time to time that the pastry is not becoming too brown; if it darkens too quickly cover it loosely with foil, removing it for the last 10 minutes of baking time.

Cool the pie in its tin. When it is almost cold, slowly pour in as much of the liquid stock as it will hold, using a small funnel or an icing nozzle to direct the stock through the hole in the top of the pie. When it is completely cold, remove the pie from its tin.

Variations on steak and kidney pudding are too numerous to evaluate. Some recipes call for stewing steak and many for rump. Some have the meat in cubes, some in strips beaten flat. Some call for onion, some for none. Many add just water to make a gravy, a few prescribe stock. Mrs Beeton's recipe has a suet crust made with milk instead of the usual water. And then there is the school of thought that favours cooking the steak and kidney before enclosing it in the crust. To add my own fourpennyworth of preference, I like the mild flavour of calf's kidneys better than pungent ox kidney.

A Steak and Kidney Pudding

SERVES 4

570 g (1¼ lb) rump steak
225 g (8 oz) calf's kidney
4 tablespoons seasoned flour
340 g (12 oz) self-raising flour
170 g (6 oz) shredded beef suet
1 teaspoon salt
water to mix
300 ml (½ pint) good beef stock

Remove all the skin and fat from the steak and cut it into strips about 2.5 cm (1 in) wide × 7.5 cm (3 in) long. Core, skin and cut the kidneys into small pieces. Beat the strips of steak with a rolling pin to flatten them, then dip each strip into the seasoned flour and roll it up round a piece of kidney.

Sift the flour into a mixing bowl, add the suet and salt and mix lightly together. Sprinkle the mixture with water, mix lightly with a fork, and continue adding water and mixing until it makes a dough which will just hold together. Sift a little flour over it and lightly roll out the dough on a floured board to a thickness of about 1 cm (⅓ in).

Line a well-buttered pudding basin of 1.5 litres (2½ pints) capacity with the dough, trimming the surplus from the edge and rolling it into a circle for the top. Or use the method described in the recipe for grouse pudding (see facing page). Arrange the meat in the basin and pour in enough stock to come about two-thirds of the way up the meat. Fold the dough lining which is proud of the meat towards the centre of the basin and dampen the edge. Top with the circle of dough and press down well to seal.

Cover the basin with buttered greaseproof paper and foil which have been folded together to make a 2.5 cm (1 in) pleat across the diameter of the basin and tie down firmly with string.

Stand the pudding in a large saucepan and pour in boiling water to come about halfway up the sides of the basin. Bring back to the boil, cover the pan and simmer for about three hours, taking care that the water does not go off the boil or the saucepan boil dry. Add boiling water as necessary to bring up the level.

Serve the pudding in its basin with a clean cloth pinned round it. Just before serving, cut a small round hole in the top of the pudding and pour in a little of the remaining stock.

For the grouse pudding which follows the crust is made not with suet, but with butter, an old variation which complements luxurious ingredients. These traditional puddings are a splendid method of cooking game of uncertain age which might be tough or dry. Any other game birds, or mixtures of birds and beef make excellent puddings.

Grouse Pudding

SERVES 4

2 grouse of uncertain age
1 onion, quartered
4 juniper berries, crushed
bouquet garni of parsley, thyme,
* celery and bay leaf*
salt and freshly ground black
* pepper*
225 g (8 oz) self-raising flour
85 g (3 oz) butter, chilled
1 teaspoon finely grated lemon zest
2 egg yolks
2 tablespoons iced water
2 tablespoons seasoned flour
170 g (6 oz) field or cultivated
* mushrooms, thickly sliced*
1 eating apple, peeled and sliced
* (optional)*

Cut the breast meat off the grouse and divide each breast into three portions. Cut off as much of the meat remaining on the birds as can be removed easily, and set all the flesh aside.

Break up the carcasses and put them in a pan with the onion, juniper berries and bouquet garni. Add 900 ml (1½ pints) of water and a little salt and pepper and bring to the boil. Reduce the heat, cover the pan and simmer for about 1½ hours. Strain the stock, which should measure about 300 ml (½ pint).

To make the crust, sift the flour and one teaspoon of salt and the same of freshly ground black pepper into a bowl. Cut the butter into small dice and toss them in the flour. Rub in the fat, using your fingertips or a pastry blender, until the mixture resembles fine breadcrumbs. Stir in the lemon zest. Mix the egg yolks with the iced water and stir well. Sprinkle the liquid over the flour mixture and toss together with a fork until the dough holds together. Using your hands, gather it into a ball and knead lightly.

On a floured surface, roll out the dough to a circle which will cover an upturned pudding basin of 1.5 litres (2½ pints) capacity. Cut a wedge from the circle, about a quarter of the total area, and re-roll this piece for the lid. Use the remaining dough to line the basin, dampening the edge to be joined.

Toss the grouse flesh in the seasoned flour. Mix the grouse, mushrooms and apple (if using) and pack them into the basin. Pour in enough stock to come about two-thirds of the way up the filling. Fold the dough lining which is proud of the edge of the basin over the filling and dampen the edge. Top with the lid and press lightly to seal.

Cover the basin with buttered greaseproof paper and foil which have been folded together to make a 2.5 cm (1 in) pleat across the diameter of the basin and tie down firmly with string.

Stand the pudding in a large saucepan and pour in boiling water to come halfway up the sides of the basin. Bring back to the boil, cover the pan and simmer for about 2½ hours, taking care that the water does not go off the boil or the saucepan boil dry. Add boiling water as necessary to bring up the level.

Serve the pudding in its basin with a clean cloth pinned round it. Just before serving, cut a small round hole in the top of the pudding and pour in a little more warm stock.

Quiche is a victim of its own popularity. Poor, even nasty, imitations of the genuine article have devalued it so drastically that it is dismissed as dull. Or worse, a quick quiche will do for the family but is not special enough to offer to friends.

Finding a good one is a treat. Its shortcrust pastry is crisp underneath as well as at the edges. The filling is light, creamy and well flavoured. And if you are really lucky, it is freshly baked, golden and still a little puffy.

Quiche has a reputation for freezing well, but reheating seldom completely erases the wrinkles which set in as it cools.

To make a quiche worth boasting about requires good ingredients – cream, not milk alone. Quiche Lorraine is the best-known and most-often economised on version of the dish. Variations on the theme include fish or vegetables in the filling. Some rely simply on herbs for flavour.

Pastry for the classic quiche is rich, short and plain. Making it with wholewheat flour is an increasingly popular and possibly more healthy alternative, and either plain or wholewheat pastry may be flavoured with cheese or turmeric. Delicately spiced turmeric pastry is particularly good with smoked fish fillings. Cheese pastry goes well with an onion and cheese flavoured custard.

Cooking the pastry shell right through before filling it is the most reliable method to ensure that the base of the quiche will be crisp too. By using a loose-bottomed flan tin with fluted sides it is sometimes, but not invariably possible to achieve a crisp base on pastry that is filled raw.

Quiche Lorraine

SERVES 6

225 g (8 oz) plain flour
½ teaspoon salt
110 g (4 oz) butter, chilled
1 egg yolk
4–6 tablespoons iced water

For the filling:
55 g (2 oz) lean bacon, diced
1 small onion (optional)
300 ml (½ pint) milk
4 large eggs
300 ml (½ pint) double cream
55 g (2 oz) Gruyère cheese, finely grated (optional)
salt and freshly ground black pepper

Sift the flour and salt into a large bowl. Cut the butter into small dice and toss them lightly in the flour. Rub in the fat, using a pastry blender or your fingertips, until the mixture looks like fine breadcrumbs.

Beat the egg yolk with four tablespoons of the water and sprinkle it over the flour mixture. Mix lightly together, adding a little more water if it is needed to make a firm dough. Press the dough lightly into a ball, wrap it in greaseproof paper and refrigerate for at least 30 minutes.

Lightly butter a 25 cm (10 in) quiche tin or dish. Roll out the pastry thinly on a lightly floured surface. Rest it for five minutes before lifting it carefully on the rolling pin and laying it gently over the tin. Ease the pastry into shape without stretching it, trim the edges and chill for another 10 minutes, or more if you have time.

Just before baking the pastry shell, line it with greaseproof paper or foil and weight it with dried beans. Set on a baking sheet and bake in a preheated moderately hot oven (200°C/400°F, gas mark 6) for 10 minutes, or 15 if using a china dish. Remove from the oven and take out the beans and lining paper. Prick the base with a fork, reduce the temperature to moderate (180°C/350°F, gas mark 4) and bake the shell for another 10 minutes, or 15 if using a china dish.

While the shell is baking, prepare the filling. Fry the bacon lightly to brown it a little. If you are using the onion, infuse it in the milk, then strain the milk into a bowl. Add the eggs and cream and beat lightly together. Now add the cheese if you are including it, and salt and pepper to taste.

Scatter the bacon over the pastry shell and pour in the custard. Return the quiche to the oven and bake it for about 40 minutes, or until the filling has set. Serve hot or warm.

The following are variations on the basic recipe.

Prawn Quiche with Cheese Crust
Add 45 g (1½ oz) finely grated Parmesan cheese to the pastry mix at the breadcrumb stage. Omit the bacon and add 225 g (8 oz) cooked, peeled prawns to the filling mixture. Cut down the milk to 150 ml (¼ pint). As with quiche Lorraine, the cheese and onion are optional. Two tablespoons of chopped fresh basil, or a smaller amount of chopped fresh dill, are good additional flavourings.

Smoked Haddock Quiche with Turmeric Crust
Add 1 tablespoon of ground turmeric to the sifted flour for the pastry. Omit the bacon, chéese and onion and add 225 g (8 oz) cooked, flaked smoked haddock to the filling mixture. Use only 150 ml (¼ pint) milk.

Mushroom Quiche with Wholewheat Crust
Substitute 255 g (9 oz) wholewheat flour (preferably wholewheat pastry flour) for the plain flour, and omit the egg yolk. As with quiche Lorraine the cheese and onion are optional and, in this case, so is the bacon. Add 340 g (12 oz) sliced and lightly sautéed mushrooms and cut down the milk to 150 ml (¼ pint).

Herb Quiche
A simple herb quiche shows off the flavours of parsley, chervil, tarragon, dill, chives and many other herbs to perfection. The custard should be lightly set and the pastry short and crisp. The choice of herbs will depend on which varieties are available as well as personal taste. Parsley and chives are a good basis for almost any mixture. For a particularly pretty finish float single leaves of chervil or flat-leafed parsley on the surface of the custard before baking it. Omit the bacon from the quiche Lorraine recipe and add at least four tablespoons of chopped fresh herbs. The onion is optional.

The pastry for asparagus tart is shorter and even crisper than basic shortcrust. It is made with more butter than usual, a delicious indulgence to complement the luxurious asparagus filling.

Fresh Asparagus Tart

SERVES 6

For the pastry:
170 g (6 oz) plain flour
¼ teaspoon salt
110 g (4 oz) butter, chilled
iced water to mix

For the filling:
680 g (1½ lb) fresh asparagus
milk (see method)
4 large eggs
300 ml (½ pint) double cream
salt and cayenne pepper

Sift the flour and salt into a bowl. Cut the butter into small dice and toss them lightly in the flour. Rub in the fat, using a processor, your fingertips, or a pastry blender, until the mixture looks like fine breadcrumbs. Sprinkle sufficient iced water onto the mixture to make a firm dough. Press the dough lightly into a ball, wrap it in greaseproof paper and chill for at least 30 minutes.

Lightly butter a 23 cm (9 in) round fluted tart tin which is about 5 cm (2 in) deep. Roll out the pastry on a lightly floured surface. It should be no more than 7 mm (¼ in) thick. Rest it for five minutes before lifting it carefully on the rolling pin and laying it gently on the tin. Ease the pastry into shape without stretching it, trim the edges and chill for another 10 minutes, or more if you have time.

Just before baking the pastry shell, line it with grease-proof paper or foil and weight it with dried beans. Set it on a baking sheet and bake in a preheated moderately hot oven (200°C/400°F, gas mark 6) for 10 minutes. Remove from the oven and take out the beans and lining paper. Prick the base with a fork, reduce the temperature to moderate (180°C/350°F, gas mark 4) and bake the shell for another 10 minutes.

While the shell is baking, prepare the filling. Trim and steam the asparagus until it is tender. As soon as it is cool enough to handle, cut off the tips and set them aside. Chop the remainder of the stalks into short lengths and purée them either by pressing them through a sieve, or using a processor or liquidiser. Sieve the purée and make it up to 300 ml (½ pint) with the milk.

Mix the diluted purée with the eggs and cream and season to taste with salt and cayenne: lightly if the tart is to be served hot or warm, a little more if you plan to eat it cold.

Arrange the reserved asparagus tips in the pastry shell and pour in the custard. Return the tart to the oven, still on moderate, and bake for about 40 minutes, or until the filling has set and risen a little. Serve hot or warm.

'Cornish pasties were tailor-made to survive life in an open fishing boat, and old recipes show clearly how drastically the formula varied depending on whether times were fat or lean. When catches were good pasty fillings would include beef, lamb or bacon. When the fishing was poor, seasoned potato was the fisherman's lot', or so I believed until that paragraph was published as the introduction to a recipe for the pasties.

The following letter from Mrs John de Gaynesford published on the leader page of *The Times* began a lively pasty correspondence.

'Sir, As a Cornishwoman living in exile (and of necessity resigned to seeing the humble, delicious Cornish pasty travestied in almost every cook-shop in the Kingdom) may I express my delight at the authentic recipe given by Miss Shona Crawford Poole in *The Times* on September 11 [1980].

While in no way detracting from the excellence of her recipe, may I however, offer one dissident comment on her assumption that the pasty derives from the fishing population of Cornwall? Cornish tradition has always held that the pasty originated among the copper and tin miners of the Duchy. Easily carried in a pouch suspended from his shoulder with his day's supply of candles, the pasty was the miner's food-supply for the day, sustaining him throughout the murderous 12 hour shift he worked at his pitch "below grass".

Sometimes the pasty contained meat and potato at one end, and apple at the other, thus constituting a complete meal in microcosm. A pointer to the pasty's mining origin lies in the distinctive ridge of thick, folded pastry, sealing it at the edge: this ridge was not intended to be eaten, but to serve as the handle by which the pasty was held – working at a tin or copper lode, the miner's hands would inevitably become contaminated with arsenic and other noxious substances, and the thick ridge of pastry was thus highly practical, and disposable.'

Here then is the approved recipe.

Cornish Pasties

MAKES 6

450 g (1 lb) plain flour
1 heaped teaspoon salt
225 g (8 oz) butter, or half and
　half butter and lard, chilled
iced water to mix
1 egg, beaten

For the filling:
340 g (12 oz) frying or braising
　steak, finely diced
225 g (8 oz) potatoes, diced
225 g (8 oz) onions, finely chopped
salt and freshly ground black
　pepper
1 tablespoon finely chopped parsley
stock or milk to moisten

Sift the flour and salt into a large bowl. Cut the fat into small dice and toss them lightly in the flour. Rub in the fat, using your fingertips or a pastry blender, until the mixture resembles fine breadcrumbs. Sprinkle sufficient iced water onto the mixture to make a stiff dough.

Roll out the dough on a lightly floured surface and cut six circles of about 15 cm (6 in) diameter using a saucer or tea plate as a pattern.

Mix together all the filling ingredients and divide the mixture into six portions, placing them in the centre of the six pastry circles. Brush the edges of the pastry with the beaten egg and draw them together over the filling to make the traditional boat-shaped pasty. Crimp the edges firmly to ensure a good seal. Cut a small slit on each side of the crimped seam on top of the pasties.

Arrange the pasties on a floured baking sheet and bake

in a preheated hot oven (220°C/425°F, gas mark 7) for 10 minutes. Reduce the temperature to moderate (180°C/350°F, gas mark 4) and continue baking for about 30 minutes, covering the pasties lightly with foil if they become too brown.

There are, if my arithmetic is right, 730 layers in proper puff pastry. And putting them there is a tricky business.

For many purposes a packet of frozen puff from the supermarket does very well, and the real stuff is a delicious but time-consuming luxury. That said, though, there are other recipes in which the buttery flavour and extra lightness of home-made puff pastry make all the difference.

'Cool it' is the answer to many of the problems puff pastry making poses. Quite apart from all the elegant and inexpensive dishes this one accomplishment makes possible, it is very pleasing to work such a miraculous transformation on an unpromising lump of dough.

Puff Pastry

MAKES 1.25 kg (2¾ lb)

500 g (1 lb 2 oz) plain flour
2 teaspoons salt
1 tablespoon lemon juice
250–275 ml (8–9 fl oz) iced water
500 g (1 lb 2 oz) unsalted butter

Sift the flour and salt onto a clean surface (preferably a marble slab and as cold as possible) and make a well in the centre of the heap. Mix together the lemon juice and iced water and pour about one-third of this liquid into the well. Using one hand to beat the mixture, and the other to support the walls of flour, draw in the flour until the centre has the consistency of a cream sauce. Add more water and continue mixing until you have a dough which can be formed into a ball.

Overworking the dough develops the gluten in the flour and makes the dough too elastic and difficult to roll later, so work it as little as possible, and form it into a ball. Wrap the dough in greaseproof paper and a damp cloth or foil to prevent it drying out and chill for at least 30 minutes.

Prepare the butter by working it with a knife or spatula into a block which measures about 15 × 10 cm (6 × 4 in). Place it between two sheets of greaseproof paper for easier handling, then chill it.

Ideally, the butter and dough should have roughly the same consistency when you begin to roll them together. As this makes the following stages easier, it is worth a little patience at this stage to achieve it.

Lightly flour the work surface and roll out the dough, working from the centre outwards, to a rectangle large enough to wrap the butter block with just a little overlap. Place the butter in the middle of the dough with the short sides facing you and the longer sides to right and left.

84

Fold the long sides to the centre and press the join lightly with the rolling pin, then fold in the top and bottom sections and press lightly again just to stick the envelope.

Starting with the rolling pin in the middle of the envelope, roll out the dough, working towards and away from your body only, to make a rectangle about 20 × 40 cm (8 × 16 in). The short sides should still face you. Use a ruler or long knife to nudge the edges straight and square up the corners.

Mentally divide the rectangle into thirds. Take the third nearest to you and fold it over the middle third, then bring the top third down over the other two. Square up the package and lightly tap the edges with the rolling pin. Press one shallow dent in the top with your knuckle to remind you that it has had one fold or turn, wrap as before with greaseproof paper and a cloth or foil and chill for at least 30 minutes.

Unwrap the pastry and have a good look at it. Three sides, two short and one long, have folds in them (think of the pages of a book). Place the pastry on a lightly floured surface with the spine of the 'book' on your left and the turn-marking dent uppermost. Roll it out again using the same method and to the same size as before. Fold it in three again, keeping the edges and corners square, and make two turn marks. Wrap it as before and chill for another 30 minutes.

You will see that, if after every rolling and folding you reposition the pastry with the spine of the 'book' on your left, you have automatically turned the pastry through 90°. And by counting the turn mark dents you have kept a check on the number of turns made.

Six turns in all are required, making 730 leaves in the pastry – not quite a *mille-feuille* in one hit. The third and fourth turns should be possible without chilling the dough between them, likewise the fifth and last. But if the dough becomes too warm and soft, pop it back in the fridge to stiffen up. If the worst happens and the butter starts to leak through the dough, dust the afflicted area with a little flour and chill well before carrying on. Take heart: you probably have 700 or more layers left.

After the sixth and last turn, mark and wrap the pastry as before and chill well before using it. It will keep in the fridge for several days, or it can be frozen with no ill effects.

Thaw frozen pastry in the refrigerator before rolling it out.

Rabbit Pie

SERVES 4

30 g (1 oz) butter or dripping
450 g (1 lb) onions, sliced in thin rings
1 plump rabbit, jointed
750 ml (1¼ pints) good stock
salt and freshly ground black pepper
bouquet garni of bay leaf and small piece of lemon zest
12 plump prunes, or 12 button mushrooms, or 4 artichoke bottoms, cooked and quartered
225 g (8 oz) puff pastry (see page 84)
1 egg yolk mixed with 1 teaspoon water

Melt the butter or dripping in a large saucepan and add the onions and rabbit pieces. Cook them together on a medium heat, turning frequently until they are well browned. Add the stock, salt, pepper and bouquet garni. Cover the pan and simmer for an hour, or until the rabbit is almost tender. Set aside to cool.

At this stage you may, if you wish, take the rabbit flesh off the bones.

Put the rabbit pieces in a pie dish with the onions and prunes or mushrooms or artichoke bottoms. Check the seasoning of the stock before pouring about 450 ml (¾ pint) into the pie dish. It should not quite cover the meat or fill the dish.

Roll out the pastry and use it to cover the pie dish, inserting a pie funnel to allow steam to escape. Glaze the crust with the egg yolk mixture and bake in a preheated moderately hot oven (200°C/400°F, gas mark 6) for 15 minutes. Reduce the temperature to moderate (180°C/350°F, gas mark 4) and bake for another 30 minutes. If the pastry starts to brown too much, cover it loosely with foil for the remainder of the cooking time.

Serve the pie piping hot with braised carrots or parsnips.

A glossy puff pastry lid signals that celebration fish pie is no ordinary pie, but a delicious mixture of shellfish and white fish in a creamy sauce sharpened with yogurt. (Yogurt haters will not know it is there, only that the fish tastes uncommonly good.) If prawns, crab or scallops are too expensive or not available, improvise with another mixture of fish and shellfish that adds up to 680 g (1½ lb).

Celebration Fish Pie

SERVES 4

55 g (2 oz) butter
55 g (2 oz) plain flour
150 ml (¼ pint) milk
150 ml (¼ pint) natural yogurt
150 ml (¼ pint) fish stock
340 g (12 oz) cooked cod or haddock, flaked
110 g (4 oz) cooked prawns or mussels, shelled
110 g (4 oz) cooked crab or lobster meat
110 g (4 oz) cooked scallops, diced

Melt the butter in a fairly large pan and stir in the flour. Cook the *roux* for a minute or two without allowing it to colour. Gradually add the milk, yogurt and stock, stirring constantly, to make a smooth sauce. Cook the sauce on a low heat for a minute or two.

Fold in all the fish, shellfish and spring onions, and season to taste with salt and pepper. Pour the mixture into a pie dish and set it aside to cool.

Roll out the pastry on a lightly floured surface and cut off a narrow strip long enough to edge the pie dish. Paint the lip of the dish with the beaten egg and stick down the strip of pastry. Paint the strip with egg and cover the pie

2 tablespoons finely chopped spring
  onions
salt and freshly ground black
  pepper
400 g (14 oz) puff pastry (see page
  84)
1 egg, beaten

with pastry. Trim and knock up the edge. Make a small
hole in the lid to let out the steam and hold it open with a
tube of foil if you have not used a pie funnel. Decorate the
crust with pastry trimmings or leave it plain. Brush the top
of the lid (not the edges) with beaten egg to glaze, and
bake in a preheated hot oven (220°C/425°F, gas mark 7)
for 20 minutes. Reduce the temperature to moderate
(160°C/325°F, gas mark 3) and bake for a further 25–30
minutes.

Christmas sweet pie from the north of England is a really traditional mince pie because it
contains meat and not just the suet which is all that is usually seen now of the old ways. In
Cumberland whole chops often appear in the pie, but in most places the meat, invariably lamb
or mutton, is diced.

SERVES 8

225 g (8 oz) lean and fat lamb, or
  mutton chops
225 g (8 oz) currants
225 g (8 oz) seedless raisins
225 g (8 oz) sultanas
170 g (6 oz) soft brown sugar
55 g (2 oz) chopped candied peel
  (optional)
juice and finely grated zest of
  1 lemon
1/4 teaspoon salt
1/4 teaspoon ground cinnamon
1/2 teaspoon grated nutmeg
freshly ground black pepper to taste
120 ml (4 fl oz) dark rum
225 g (8 oz) puff pastry (see page
  84)
1 egg, beaten

Christmas Sweet Pie

Dice the meat after discarding the skin and bones.
In a bowl mix all the remaining ingredients (except
the meat, pastry and beaten egg), and stir them well
together. Spread half the fruit mixture in the bottom of a
pie dish of 1.2 litres (2 pints) capacity and top with half the
diced meat. Repeat the layers, ending with a layer of
meat. Cover the dish with foil and bake it in a preheated
moderate oven (180°C/350°F, gas mark 4) for 1¼ hours.
Allow the dish to cool until quite cold. At this point in the
preparation it may be refrigerated for one or two days.

Roll out the pastry to a thickness of about 7 mm (¼ in)
and leave it to rest for 10 minutes. Cut a ribbon of pastry
the width of the rim of the pie dish. Paint the rim of the
dish with the beaten egg and arrange the ribbon of dough
neatly round it. Paint this edging with egg, then place the
pastry lid on the pie. Press it down lightly to seal, then
crimp the edge with a knife, using an upward movement.
Paint the top, but not the edges, of the pastry with the
beaten egg.

Bake the pie in a preheated moderately hot oven
(200°C/400°F, gas mark 6) for about 30 minutes, covering the pastry loosely with foil if it browns too quickly.
Serve hot or warm.

Butter tarts are good in their own right and make an interesting change from mince pies. They can be made in advance and frozen, and should always be served warm or hot.

Butter Tarts

MAKES 15–18

170 g (6 oz) plain flour
85 g (3 oz) butter, chilled
1 egg yolk
2 tablespoons iced water

For the filling:
55 g (2 oz) butter, softened
55 g (2 oz) soft brown sugar
110 g (4 oz) currants
*55 g (2 oz) shelled walnuts,
    roughly chopped*
1 egg white

Sift the flour into a bowl. Cut the chilled butter into small dice and toss them lightly in the flour. Rub in the fat, using your fingertips or a pastry blender, until the mixture resembles fine breadcrumbs. Mix the egg yolk with the iced water and sprinkle it onto the flour mixture. Mix lightly to form a dough, adding a little more water if needed, and gather it into a ball. Chill the dough for 30 minutes before rolling it out thinly on a floured surface. Use a round pastry cutter or tumbler to cut circles of the dough and use them to line a bun sheet or patty tin.

To make the filling, beat together the softened butter and sugar until the mixture is fluffy. Mix in the currants and nuts. In another bowl whisk the egg white until it is stiff, then fold the meringue into the butter mixture.

Drop a teaspoonful of the filling into each pastry case. Bake the tarts in a preheated moderately hot oven (190°C/375°F, gas mark 5) for about 15–20 minutes.

No one should be put off making pizza because it calls for yeast-raised dough. Once made and allowed to rise, the punched-down dough will keep for three or four days in the refrigerator ready to be used at a moment's notice. The tomato sauce base for all pizza toppings keeps even longer, and of course it can be made in large quantities and frozen in appropriately sized portions. Other topping ingredients – ham, cheese, anchovies, olives, shrimps and almost anything else that takes your fancy – are all sold tinned, frozen or in long-life packets. And once baked, whole pizzas freeze well, as do leftover portions.

In fact, home-made pizza is the best sort of storecupboard recipe, and for economy the classic kind is closest ordinary mortals can come to recreating the miracle of the loaves and the fishes.

Serve pizza with a lavish green or mixed salad, lots of inexpensive Italian wine (decanting improves it immeasurably), and add a very definite extra 'something' to the meal by passing round a bottle of wickedly hot, chilli-flavoured olive oil.

Wickedly Hot Oil

MAKES 600 ml (1 pint)

600 ml (1 pint) olive oil
30 g (1 oz) small dried red chillies

Pour the oil into a well rinsed and dried wine bottle. Add the chillies and cork the bottle. Shake it once a day for a week, after which the oil should be hot enough to sprinkle sparingly on cooked pizza.

Keep the bottle corked and in a cool, dark place, adding more oil whenever the level drops below 300 ml

(½ pint). The longer it is kept, the hotter it becomes, so treat a well-matured bottle with caution.

Hot oil can also be used to sprinkle on pizzas before they are baked.

Basic pizza dough can be made with fresh yeast, dried granular yeast or, simpler still, with 'easy blend' dried yeast which does not need to be activated in warm milk before it is incorporated into the dough.

Basic Pizza Dough

MAKES 2 LARGE PIZZAS

250 ml (8 fl oz) milk
½ teaspoon sugar (if using fresh or granular dried yeast)
15 g (½ oz) fresh yeast, or 1 teaspoon granular dried yeast, or 1 teaspoon easy blend dried yeast
450 g (1 lb) strong plain white flour
1 teaspoon salt
1 large egg
6 tablespoons olive oil

Using fresh yeast or granular dried yeast: heat the milk to lukewarm (about 43°C/110°F) and mix about one-third of it with the sugar and yeast in a small bowl. Leave it to stand until it can be stirred easily into a cream.

Sift the flour and salt into a large bowl. Mix the remaining warm milk with the egg and oil and stir lightly together. Make a well in the centre of the flour and pour in the yeast and egg mixtures all at once. Use a fork to mix the ingredients to a dough.

Using easy blend dried yeast: sift together into a large bowl the flour, yeast and salt. Mix the egg with the oil and milk and stir lightly together. Add the egg mixture to the flour all at once and mix well to form a dough.

Turn the dough, which will be very sticky at this stage, onto a well floured surface and knead it for about five minutes, or until the dough is springy and elastic. Now form it into a ball and put it in a plastic bag or cover with plastic food wrap and leave it in a warm place for one to three hours. Too high a temperature will kill the yeast so do not be tempted to hurry the rising process. The dough will rise perfectly well in its own time in a cool temperature which means that it can be left overnight to rise.

Punch the risen dough down to knock the air out of it and knead it briefly on a floured surface before rolling it out with a floured rolling pin. Pizza dough should generally be rolled fairly thinly – 7 mm (¼ in) is generally quite thick enough.

To store risen dough in the refrigerator, punch it down and re-form it into a ball. Return it to the bowl, cover and refrigerate for up to four days. The warmth of the dough may cause it to rise a little before it cools down, and when needed it can be used straight from the refrigerator.

Basic Tomato Sauce

6 tablespoons olive oil
900 g (2 lb) onions, sliced in thin
  rings
2 cloves garlic, finely chopped
900 g (2 lb) tin of plum tomatoes
  with their juice
1 teaspoon dried marjoram or
  oregano
salt and freshly ground black
  pepper

Heat the oil in a large pan and add the onions. Cook them slowly, uncovered, on a gentle heat for about 20 minutes or until they are soft but not coloured. Add the garlic and cook for a few minutes more before adding the tomatoes and their juice, the marjoram or oregano, and salt and pepper to taste. Cook slowly, uncovered, on a low heat for about 40 minutes, or until the sauce is becoming thick and much of the juice has evaporated. Stir the sauce from time to time to prevent it sticking, and break up the tomatoes against the side of the pan with a wooden spoon. Cool and use as directed.

The following recipe makes two large rectangular pizzas about 23 × 30 cm (9 × 12 in), the size of a standard baking sheet. Each will cut into six small portions, or three or four large ones.

Anchovy and Olive Pizza

1 recipe basic pizza dough (see page
  89)
1 recipe basic tomato sauce (see
  above)
2 × 55 g (2 oz) tins of flat anchovy
  fillets
110 g (4 oz) small black olives
225 g (8 oz) cheese, grated –
  mozarella, Cheddar, Gruyère,
  Parmesan, or a mixture of these
2 tablespoons olive oil or wickedly
  hot oil (see page 88)

Divide the dough into two equal pieces. Roll the first out thinly on a floured surface. Place it on a floured 23 × 30 cm (9 × 12 in) baking sheet and trim the shape to fit the sheet. Spoon half the tomato sauce over the dough and spread it close to the edge.

Drain the anchovy fillets and cut them in halves lengthwise. Arrange half of them on top of the tomato in lines or a trellis pattern. Scatter half the olives over the anchovies, then sprinkle the whole surface of the pizza with half the cheese. Dribble a tablespoon of the oil over the now oven-ready pizza.

Use the remaining ingredients to make the second pizza in the same way. Bake the pizzas in a preheated very hot oven (250°C/500°F, gas mark 9) for 20–25 minutes. To make sure they cook evenly, move the lower pizza to the upper shelf, and vice versa, halfway through the cooking time.

Variations: top with fresh or frozen shrimps instead of anchovies (there is no need to thaw frozen shrimps). Omit the anchovies and top with diced, cooked ham and sliced mushrooms sweated in butter or oil. Add one or more sliced green or red peppers to the tomato sauce halfway through its cooking time and top with capers.

Filled Crescent Pizzas

SERVES 6

110 g (4 oz) cooked chicken
110 g (4 oz) cooked ham
110 g (4 oz) Gruyère or Cheddar cheese, grated
1 clove garlic, very finely chopped
2 tablespoons chopped parsley
1 teaspoon dried thyme, or 1 sprig of fresh thyme
4 tinned tomatoes
salt and freshly ground black pepper
1 recipe basic pizza dough (see page 89)
1/2 recipe basic tomato sauce (see facing page)
4 tablespoons grated Parmesan or Cheddar cheese
2 tablespoons olive oil or wickedly hot oil (see page 88)

Chop the chicken and ham very, very finely and mix them in a bowl with the Gruyère or Cheddar cheese, garlic, parsley, thyme and tomatoes. Stir vigorously to blend the ingredients into a reasonably coherent stuffing and season it to taste with salt and pepper. A food processor speeds this task, but beware of over-processing the mixture, which should have a rough texture.

Divide the dough into two equal pieces and roll the first out thinly on a floured surface. The shape to aim for is a large oval about 30 cm (12 in) long × 23 cm (9 in) wide.

Place half the stuffing mixture in a sausage shape along the length of the oval about 2.5 cm (1 in) in from one long edge. Roll the dough very loosely round the stuffing, sealing the ends of the roll by dampening the dough and pressing the edges together. Carefully lift this creation onto a well floured baking sheet, curling the ends a little as you lay it down to form a crescent shape.

Top the pizza with half the tomato sauce (a quarter of the whole recipe) and sprinkle it with half the Parmesan or Cheddar cheese and half the oil.

Use the remaining ingredients to make the second pizza in the same way. Bake the filled pizzas in a preheated very hot oven (250°C/500°F, gas mark 9) for 35–40 minutes.

A number of pasta recipes include water and/or oil. This one has eggs, flour and salt only, and behaves better for it.

Egg Pasta

SERVES 4–6

3 large eggs
310 g (11 oz) unbleached strong white flour or plain flour
1 teaspoon salt

To make pasta by hand: beat the eggs lightly in a small bowl. Sift the flour and salt onto a clean work surface. Make a well in the centre and add the eggs. Using one hand to beat the mixture, and the other to support the walls of flour until the eggs have been incorporated, work the eggs gradually into the flour to form a stiff dough. Knead the dough until it is smooth and elastic (about five minutes).

To make pasta in a food processor: fix the metal blade in the bowl. Drop in the eggs and process them briefly. With the machine running add the flour and salt through the feed tube. Continue processing until the dough forms a ball, and then for another 60 seconds to knead it.

To roll the dough by hand: divide it into two or three pieces. Cover the dough waiting to be rolled to prevent it drying out. Roll the dough on a lightly floured surface, working quickly and lightly until it is as thin as required – not much more than 2 mm (1/10 in) thick for fettucine (narrow noodles) and thinner for tagliatelli which are broader noodles about 7 mm (¼ in) wide, or for stuffed pastas like ravioli.

To roll the dough in a pasta cutting machine: take an egg-sized piece of dough (covering the remainder to keep it moist), dust it with flour and work it through the rollers, dusting again with flour as often as necessary. Put each piece of dough twice through the thickest setting of the rollers, then work down through the finer settings until the pasta is as thin as required.

To cut noodles by hand: fold a sheet of dough into a loose roll and use a sharp knife to cut it into strips. Open out the noodles and leave them to dry for at least five minutes before cooking them.

To cut noodles in a machine: simply pass the rolled dough through the appropriate cutting rollers and allow the pasta to dry for at least five minutes before cooking it.

Cook the noodles in plenty of boiling salted water, adding a handful at a time so that the water does not go off the boil. Freshly made noodles may need as little as one minute's cooking when the water returns to the boil. The longer the noodles have dried, the longer they will take to cook. Take care not to overcook them though. They should still have a little bite.

A good deal of mystique surrounds pesto, the finely pounded mixture of fresh basil leaves, pine nuts, and garlic, with Parmesan and pecorino cheese, that brings an instant whiff of Mediterranean summer to a bowl of steaming pasta. Perfection is an admirable goal, but fussiness spoils the fun. Pounding the ingredients by hand in a marble mortar is said to produce a finer result than whizzing them all together in a blender or food processor. Genoese basil, which has smaller leaves than the kind usually grown and sold here, may have the better flavour, but one should not forgo pesto on that account either.

Then there is the matter of the correct cheeses. Decent Parmesan is easy enough to come by, but Sardinian pecorino made from ewes' milk is another thing. Roman pecorino is easier to find outside Italy, but failure to locate a source of Sardinian or Roman is an insufficient excuse for pesto deprivation.

Serve pesto sauce with freshly made, or at least freshly cooked pasta, tagliatelli, fettucine, or spaghetti. Tip the pasta into a large bowl and add a spoonful or two of the pungent pesto. Toss with two forks to mix.

Pesto

85 g (3 oz) fresh basil leaves
2 cloves garlic, peeled and crushed
30 g (1 oz) pine kernels
1 teaspoon salt
55 g (2 oz) Parmesan cheese,
  freshly grated
30 g (1 oz) pecorino cheese, freshly
  grated
8 tablespoons olive oil
30 g (1 oz) butter, softened

To make pesto traditionally in a mortar, put the basil leaves, garlic, pine kernels and salt in the mortar and grind them to a smooth paste. Add the cheeses and incorporate them into the basil mixture, then transfer the paste to a larger bowl and beat in the oil and butter.

To make pesto in a blender or food processor, put all the ingredients except the cheeses into the machine and process them until smooth. Add the cheeses and process again briefly, or beat in the cheeses by hand for a coarser texture.

Herb and Cheese Ravioli

1 recipe egg pasta (see page 91)
110 g (4 oz) fresh ricotta, or sieved
  cottage cheese
55 g (2 oz) Parmesan cheese,
  freshly grated
2 tablespoons finely chopped fresh
  parsley or basil, or a mixture of
  the two
1 egg yolk
salt and freshly ground black
  pepper
freshly grated nutmeg

Make the pasta, but do not roll it until you are ready to assemble the ravioli. Keep the dough covered.

Mix the ricotta or sieved cottage cheese with the Parmesan and herbs. Bind the mixture with the egg yolk and season it to taste with salt, pepper and nutmeg.

If you are rolling the dough by hand, divide it into two equal pieces and roll each until it is very thin.

Place quarter-teaspoonfuls of the filling at regular 3.5 cm (1¼ in) intervals on one sheet of dough. Lay the second sheet of dough over the first. Using floured fingers, or a small lump of dough, press the two sheets of pasta together between the blobs of filling. Work out from the centre, trapping as little air as possible.

Use a pastry wheel to cut the pasta into neat squares – each a pillow of dough enclosing a morsel of filling. Place the ravioli in a single layer on a lightly floured tea cloth or greaseproof paper. Allow it to dry for two hours before cooking, turning it over halfway through the drying time.

To cook the ravioli, bring at least 2.5 litres (4½ pints) of lightly salted water or light chicken stock to the boil. Add the ravioli and cook until the liquid returns to the boil, then reduce it immediately to a simmer. Poach the ravioli for about five minutes, or until the pasta is cooked but still has a little bite. Drain it immediately.

Toss the ravioli in a little butter or cream and serve it very hot with freshly grated Parmesan. Alternatively, serve it with a cream and tomato sauce, or with a sauce of your own devising.

Ham and Cheese Ravioli

SERVES 4–6

1 recipe egg pasta (see page 91)
170 g (6 oz) cooked, lean ham
45 g (1¹/₂ oz) Parmesan cheese,
* freshly grated*
45 g (1¹/₂ oz) crumbly cheese
* (Lancashire or Cheshire),*
* freshly grated*
4 or 5 tablespoons double cream or
* white sauce to bind the mixture*
salt and freshly ground black
* pepper*
freshly grated nutmeg

Make the pasta, but do not roll it until you are ready to assemble the ravioli.

Chop or mince the ham very finely. Add the cheeses and bind the mixture with the cream or white sauce. Season it to taste with salt, pepper and nutmeg.

Continue as for herb and cheese ravioli (see page 93).

Chicken and Pork Ravioli

SERVES 4–6

1 recipe egg pasta (see page 91)
30 g (1 oz) butter
1 small onion, finely chopped
1 clove garlic, crushed
110 g (4 oz) chicken breast,
* roughly chopped*
110 g (4 oz) fillet of pork, roughly
* chopped*
2 tablespoons finely chopped
* parsley*
¹/₂ teaspoon finely chopped thyme,
* tarragon or rosemary*
2 tablespoons double cream
salt and freshly ground black
* pepper*

Make the pasta, but do not roll it until you are ready to assemble the ravioli.

Melt the butter in a frying pan and add the onion. Cook on a low heat until the onion is soft, but not browned. Add the garlic, stir for a moment, then add the chicken and pork. Fry the mixture gently until both meats are well cooked, without allowing them to take too much colour.

Mince or very finely chop the mixture. Add the herbs and stir in the cream. Season it to taste with salt and pepper.

Continue as for herb and cheese ravioli (see page 93).

Because it is freshly cooked, spaghetti with mussels is not a dish that looks or tastes as if it comes from tins and packets. Mussels can be bought in tins. Make sure that they are packed in their own juices or in brine. Precise quantities are not vital to the success of this recipe which serves three as a main course, and up to six as an appetiser.

Spaghetti and Mussels

SERVES 3–6

2 tablespoons olive oil
1 clove garlic, finely chopped
400 g (14 oz) tin of tomatoes and
* their juice*
salt and freshly ground black
* pepper to taste*

Heat the oil in a saucepan and add the garlic. Fry it for a moment or two before adding the tomatoes, salt, pepper and bay leaves. Break up the tomatoes with a wooden spoon and bring the sauce to the boil. Reduce the heat and simmer the sauce, uncovered, while the spaghetti cooks.

3 bay leaves
340 g (12 oz) spaghetti
285 g (10 oz) tin of mussels,
* drained*

Bring a large pan of salted water to the boil and add a few drops of oil. Slide the spaghetti into the water without allowing it to come off the boil. Boil the spaghetti briskly, uncovered, until it is almost tender but still has a little bite in the centre of each strand. Drain the pasta and tip it into a large, heated serving bowl.

Add the mussels to the tomato sauce and simmer for a moment or two until the shellfish is hot. Remove the bay leaves and pour the sauce over the spaghetti. Serve immediately.

Spaghetti alla carbonara is one of the ways bacon and eggs are eaten in Italy and the recipe does not include cream as it sometimes does in Anglo-Italian restaurants. The bacon should ideally be *pancetta*, a sweet tasting unsmoked variety which looks rather like a giant salami. It is often found in Italian grocers. British bacon, smoked or unsmoked to taste, is an acceptable substitute.

SERVES 4–6

Spaghetti alla Carbonara

225 g (8 oz) pancetta or streaky
* bacon, in one thick slice*
4 cloves garlic, peeled
2 tablespoons olive oil
30 g (1 oz) butter
4 tablespoons dry white wine
salt and freshly ground black
* pepper*
450 g (1 lb) spaghetti
3 large eggs
85 g (3 oz) Parmesan cheese,
* freshly grated*
3 tablespoons finely chopped
* parsley*

Chop the *pancetta* or bacon into sticks or dice, and bruise the garlic with the flat of a knife. Heat the oil and butter together in a small saucepan and add the *pancetta* or bacon and garlic. Cook them together until both are golden, then add the wine. Boil until the wine is well reduced, then discard the garlic. Keep warm.

Cook the spaghetti, uncovered, in plenty of boiling salted water and drain it as soon as it is tender but still has a little bite in the middle of each strand.

Meanwhile, break the eggs into a warmed serving bowl. Add the cheese and parsley and a generous sprinkling of freshly ground black pepper. Beat lightly together. Add the hot spaghetti and toss it in the egg mixture until it is well coated. The eggs form an instantly creamy sauce and need no further cooking. Add the *pancetta* or bacon with its fat and toss the spaghetti again to mix the ingredients. Serve immediately.

7

Fish and Shellfish

No fish tastes better than the one you hooked yourself, nearly lost, landed triumphantly and cooked in the open air while its sparkling scales were still ten times brighter than anything you will see on a fishmonger's slab.

Freshness really matters with fish which is why fish from the freezer is such a boon. Because it is frozen so soon after it is caught it can be, and often is, a much better bet than fresh fish which is not as fresh as it might be. Pointers to freshness are clear, full, shiny eyes; bright red gills and a clean smell.

Good fishmongers, like rural bus services, are thin on the ground and becoming fewer and further between all the time. The pity of this is not that frozen fish is necessarily inferior, but that the variety of types available is so restricted and anything much bigger than a small trout has to be cut to fit a packet.

It does not seem at all likely that fish farming, which supplies more of our fish every year, will result in a greater variety of species being offered for sale. But one good thing it does mean is much more and much cheaper salmon.

Fishermen and fishmongers can spot the differences between wild and farmed salmon at several paces. In fact the spots are one of the telltale signs. But let me begin where this particular tale began.

I wanted a sea trout (alias salmon trout) for a variation on a seventeenth century salmon recipe. It was to be stuffed with butter, herbs and soft breadcrumbs, and baked in a flaky pastry waistcoat that leaves the head and tail poking out of a golden crust. The result is one of those handsome dishes that draws gasps of pleasure from those about to eat it. And it tastes every bit as good as it looks.

Yes madam, we have salmon trout, said the fishmonger, they are farmed. Madam backed off to wait for the wild fish which were due in a few days. But I missed them, then the local man ran clean out of both kinds, and the nearest alternative source had no salmon trout either. They did have small salmon though. Farmed, not cheap, but less costly than the larger wild fish which were too big for the recipe anyway. So I bought one.

But by this time I was becoming a little confused. What about the salmon's long journeyings to far-away oceans and the romance of its return to the river of its birth at spawning time? How could such wanderers be raised in captivity, and would they be worth eating?

Salmon farming is a major industry in Norway and an increasingly important one in Scotland where the fish thrive in vast sea water cages or netted enclosures. Greater knowledge of breeding, feeding and nurturing techniques has raised the state of the art to its present level. Now you are as likely to be offered a farmed fish as a wild one, but how can you tell which is which, and does it matter?

The spots are one indication. Farmed salmon tend to have a greater concentration of dark spots not just on the back of the fish, but below the lateral line and on the gills. They are often more humpty-backed too, rather like a picture of a salmon jumping. The tail may have a straighter cut to it than the V-shaped tail of a wild fish, and the fins and tail are more likely to be eroded. The damage is due to a harmless parasite and not, as one might have feared, by the fish beating their fins against the bars of captivity.

The cooked flesh of farmed salmon is generally agreed to be softer than that of its wild relations, but whether or not this is a bad thing is debatable. Opinions vary. Fishermen and connoisseurs, self-appointed and otherwise, generally favour wild fish, though not everyone claims that it actually tastes better.

Sea, or salmon trout, also farmed in salt water, are less widely available. Fresh water fish farms are also producing large rainbow trout specially fed to produce pink, salmon coloured flesh, but changing the colour of its flesh cannot make rainbow trout taste like sea trout.

Now back to the recipe which started all this. It requires a whole fish which, when cleaned, should weigh about three pounds or a little more. I have tried it with sea trout and with a small salmon, and can see no reason why it should not be an equally good way to cook a large rainbow trout or the tailpiece of a big salmon.

The only problem with the recipe is skinning the fish: I have an uncommonly obliging fishmonger who was willing to try, and from the look of dismay on his face obviously felt that the rather ragged looking result was an insult to his professional skills. It made no difference to the success of this lovely dish, so don't be afraid to tackle the job yourself with a sharp knife if the fishmonger balks at doing it for you.

Sea Trout in Pastry

SERVES 4–6

1.35 kg (3 lb) salmon trout, skinned but with the head and tail left on
55 g (2 oz) fresh white breadcrumbs
120 ml (4 fl oz) hot milk
85 g (3 oz) butter, softened
2 tablespoons chopped chervil or parsley
1 tablespoon chopped chives
1 teaspoon chopped tarragon or fennel leaves
salt and freshly ground black pepper
450 g (1 lb) puff pastry (see page 84), home made or bought
4 tablespoons double cream
1 egg, beaten
lemon slices and sprigs of watercress to garnish

Wash the fish in cold water and pat it dry inside and out. To make the stuffing, soak the breadcrumbs in the milk and squeeze out any excess moisture. Mix the damp breadcrumbs, butter, chervil or parsley, chives and tarragon or fennel, season to taste with salt and pepper and beat the mixture well. Spoon the stuffing into the cavity of the fish.

Roll out the pastry thinly to a rectangle which is not quite as wide as the length of the fish, and at least three times its width.

Brush both sides of the fish with the cream and place it on the pastry. Without stretching the pastry, draw it up over the sides of the fish, leaving the head and tail sticking out. Dampen the edges of the pastry and press them firmly together. Trim the pastry with a sharp knife or scissors to make a fin-like seam along the length of the fish. Leave the seam plain, or crimp it decoratively, and press the pastry close to the fish at each end to make a good seal. Place the fish on a heavy baking sheet which has been greased and floured, and chill for about an hour.

Just before baking, brush all the exposed pastry except the cut edge of the seam with beaten egg. Bake in a preheated moderately hot oven (200°C/400°F, gas mark 6) for 20 minutes. Reduce the temperature to moderate (180°C/350°F, gas mark 4) and continue baking for a further 30 minutes. If the pastry takes on too much colour cover it loosely with foil, removing it for the last few minutes of the baking time.

Serve the fish on a large, warmed plate, garnished with the lemon slices and watercress. It may be served in thick slices like traditional salmon steaks which are cut clean through the backbone of the fish, or the pastry may be lifted off and sections of the flesh lifted from the bones. Spoon a little of the buttery stuffing onto each serving. New potatoes and a simple green salad go perfectly with this dish.

Sea or salmon trout are preferred by many people to the king of fish himself. Their more delicately flavoured pinkish flesh is frequently moister than that of the salmon proper, but more attractive still is the size of the fish. Salmon trout usually weigh from 900 g to 1.8 kg (2 lb to 4 lb) and thus one fish makes a pleasingly dramatic and very easily prepared dish for a dinner party. Baking in foil is the simplest method of getting a salmon trout right.

Most recipes for baked salmon trout specify butter for serving hot, and oil if it is to be served cold. As no oil tastes quite as nice as butter, and anyway the fish will probably be skinned if it is to be served cold, this distinction seems superfluous. A 1.35 kg (3 lb) salmon trout will serve six, and a 1.8 kg (4 lb) fish, eight. Hollandaise sauce or mayonnaise, hot new potatoes, and a crisp salad complete the feast.

Baked Sea Trout

SERVES 6

55 g (2 oz) butter
1 salmon trout weighing 1.35 kg
  (3 lb), cleaned
2 or 3 sprigs of parsley
1 sprig of tarragon or dill
1 lemon, sliced
4 tablespoons seasoned flour

Generously butter a large piece of kitchen foil. Spread the rest of the butter in the cavity of the fish and tuck into this pocket the parsley, tarragon or dill and several lemon slices.

Dust the fish all over with the seasoned flour. Place it on the foil and bring the foil up over the fish, making a folded seam. Fold the ends up to make a loose parcel. Place the fish on a big baking sheet and bake it in a preheated moderate oven (180°C/350°F, gas mark 4) for 35 minutes. Open up the parcel so that the top side skin can colour a little and bake the fish for another 10 minutes.

To make sure the fish is cooked, insert the point of a sharp knife into the flesh at the thickest point. If the flesh moves easily from the bone it is ready. Rest the fish in a warm place for a minute or two before serving it on a warmed plate with the remaining slices of lemon arranged down its length.

Poached salmon steaks may be served hot or cold. A classic hollandaise sauce or melted butter accompany the hot version; home-made mayonnaise or a favourite bottled brand with cold salmon.

Poached Salmon Steaks

SERVES 4

4 middle cut salmon steaks
  weighing 170–225 g (6–8 oz)
  each
1.2 litres (2 pints) fish stock (see
  page 232)
4 tablespoons dry sherry, or
  150 ml (¼ pint) dry white wine
juice of ½ a lemon

Wash the salmon steaks quickly in cold water and pat them dry. Bring the fish stock to the boil in a fish kettle or casserole which is large enough to hold the fish in one layer. Add the sherry or wine and the lemon juice. Carefully lower the steaks into the bubbling stock and simmer them very gently for four to five minutes only. Remove from the heat immediately.

To serve hot, leave the steaks in the stock for five

99

minutes before lifting them out carefully. To serve cold, leave the fish in the stock until it is quite cold before lifting it out. Either way, hot new potatoes and a crisp green salad are unbeatable accompaniments to poached salmon.

Cooking fish for any longer than it takes to turn the flesh from semi-transparent to opaque only toughens and dries it. It is ready as soon as the flesh separates easily into flakes. The following recipe for halibut poached in dry cider is a luxurious, cream enriched dish which can be adapted as a cooking method for any firm-fleshed fish. Try more fish stock or dry white wine instead of the cider and experiment with smaller quantities of cream or crème fraîche (see page 227).

Poached Halibut in Dry Cider

SERVES 4

4 × 170 g (6 oz) halibut fillets
  (suprêmes, *see method*)
salt and freshly ground white
  pepper
30 g (1 oz) butter
55 g (2 oz) carrot, cut in fine strips
55 g (2 oz) celery, cut in fine strips
55 g (2 oz) leek, cut in fine strips
120 ml (4 fl oz) fish stock
300 ml (½ pint) dry cider
4 tomatoes, peeled, deseeded and
  very finely chopped
250 ml (8 fl oz) double cream
finely chopped parsley to garnish

Suprêmes are skinless fillets of large fish, each of which is big enough to make one portion. Halibut is usually sold in steaks. But if you buy one piece large enough for four servings, it can be skinned and a flat fillet cut from each side of the spine, top and bottom.

Dry the fish and season it lightly with salt and pepper. Melt the butter in a heavy sauté or frying pan and add the carrot, celery and leek. Sauté them gently for a minute or two without allowing them to brown, then add the fish. Add the stock and cook on a high heat. The stock should be bubbling briskly. Allow the stock to reduce to just a few tablespoons, then add the cider. Continue poaching until the fish is cooked.

Ideally, the fish will be cooked and the liquid reduced to about 150 ml (¼ pint) simultaneously. If the liquid is reducing too fast, cover the pan until the fish is ready. As soon as the fish is cooked, remove it from the pan and keep it warm.

If there is more than 150 ml (¼ pint) of liquid in the pan, reduce it to that quantity by fast boiling, then add the tomatoes and cream. Shake or stir the sauce over a medium heat to blend the cream and stock and continue cooking until the mixture has reduced by about half and thickened a little.

Arrange the halibut on warmed serving plates. Add any juices which have run out of the fish to the sauce, unless this will thin it down too much, then adjust the seasoning. Pour the sauce over the fish and sprinkle each portion with a little of the parsley.

Mediterranean Baked Fish

3 tablespoons light olive oil
1 medium onion, sliced in rings
1 clove garlic, finely chopped
1 small red pepper, deseeded and
  cut in thin strips
225 g (8 oz) tomatoes, peeled,
  deseeded and roughly chopped
1 tablespoon chopped parsley
150 ml (¼ pint) dry white wine
salt and freshly ground black
  pepper
2 steaks of firm-fleshed white fish
12 small black olives (optional)

Heat the oil in a heavy-based pan and add the onion rings. Cook them gently until they are almost tender, but not browned. Add the garlic and cook for a moment or two longer before adding the red pepper, tomatoes, parsley and wine. Season to taste with salt and pepper and simmer, uncovered, for about 10 minutes or until the vegetables are tender.

Arrange the fish steaks in one layer in an oiled oven-proof dish that holds them without too much room to spare. Pour the tomato sauce over the fish. Scatter the olives (if you like them) over the sauce and cover the dish closely with foil. Bake in a preheated moderately hot oven (200°C/400°F, gas mark 6) for 25–30 minutes, or until the fish is cooked. Test it by inserting a pointed knife or skewer into the thickest part of the flesh. Serve immediately with new potatoes or boiled rice.

The idea for the next recipe comes from Sweden where I once sampled a large firm-fleshed lake fish which fed 10 for lunch. The flavour and texture of that fish was not unlike salmon, but was creamy white rather than pink. It had been split open and baked flat on a huge salver and under a herb flavoured blanket of moist stuffing.

This version of the dish uses a large trout weighing 680–900 g (1½–2 lb). Alternatively, smaller fish, other types and fillets could be baked this way.

Trout in Hiding

1 trout weighing about 680–900 g
  (1½–2 lb)
55 g (2 oz) butter
85 g (3 oz) fresh white
  breadcrumbs
6 tablespoons finely chopped
  parsley
2 tablespoons finely chopped chives
  or spring onion tops
1 tablespoon finely chopped dill or
  fennel leaves
2 large eggs
175 ml (6 fl oz) single cream
2 tablespoons dry white vermouth
salt and freshly ground black
  pepper

Clean the fish, removing the head and tail. Open it along the whole length of the underside and prise out the backbone, taking with it as many smaller bones as possible. Pick out any remaining bones. Press the fish flat and arrange it, skin side down, on a well-buttered baking dish which holds it without too much room to spare.

Mix together all the remaining ingredients except the butter. Spoon the mixture over the fish, smooth it into an even layer and dot with the remaining butter.

Bake the dish, uncovered, in a preheated moderately hot oven (200°C/400°F, gas mark 6) for about 40 minutes, or until the fish is cooked. Test by inserting the point of a knife or skewer into the thickest part of the flesh. Serve immediately with new potatoes and a green salad.

In Wales and in the Pyrenees trout are cooked with bacon. In the French version of the recipe the pan is deglazed with a little vinegar after the fish have been fried to make an excellent, instant sauce.

Trout with Bacon

SERVES 4

4 plump trout
225 g (8 oz) smoked bacon, lean
  and fat
30 g (1 oz) butter
4 tablespoons seasoned flour
1 clove garlic, finely chopped
2 tablespoons white wine vinegar
2 tablespoons chopped chives or
  parsley

Gut the fish, cut off the fins and wash and dry them.

Cut the bacon into dice or narrow strips and put them in a cold frying pan. Heat slowly and steadily until the fat runs and the bacon is cooked and beginning to crisp, then add the butter.

Coat the fish with the seasoned flour and add them to the pan. Cook for about five minutes on each side, turning carefully only once. Lift the fish from the pan and arrange them on a warm serving dish. Drain the bacon and sprinkle it over the fish. Keep warm.

Fry the garlic briefly in the fat remaining in the pan. Remove the pan from the heat and stir in the vinegar. Pour the sauce immediately over the fish, sprinkle with the chives or parsley and serve with plainly boiled new or old potatoes.

Nuts and trout are another well-tried combination. Usually sliced almonds or hazelnuts are fried golden brown in butter after the fish has been sautéed, and the nuts then sprinkled over the fish. But the nuts can also be used to coat the fish before baking them.

Baked Trout with Almonds

SERVES 4

4 plump trout
55 g (2 oz) butter, melted
110 g (4 oz) almonds, very finely
  chopped or coarsely ground
salt and freshly ground black
  pepper
1 lemon

Gut the fish, cut off the fins and wash and dry them. Paint them with the melted butter, coat them with the almonds and season lightly with salt and pepper. Place the fish in one layer in a well-buttered baking dish and spoon any remaining melted butter over them.

Cook them in a preheated moderate oven (180°C/ 350°F, gas mark 4) for about 20 minutes. Serve immediately from the baking dish with a freshly cut wedge of lemon to squeeze over them.

Creamed coconut is the basis of delicious and unusual marinades for fish, or shellfish. It is sold by Indian grocers and many supermarkets in hard white blocks which keep for months in the refrigerator. It is diluted in hot water to make a thick coconut cream, or thinned further to a milk. If you cannot find ground cardamom, buy the pods, which may be white, green or brown, then extract the hard round seeds and grind them in a mortar.

Spiced Coconut Marinade

MAKES 300 ml (½ pint)

110 g (4 oz) creamed coconut
175 ml (6 fl oz) hot water
1 small onion, finely chopped
1 clove garlic, crushed
1 teaspoon ground cardamom
½ teaspoon ground chilli
4 tablespoons fresh lime or lemon
*   juice*

Break up the creamed coconut and pour the hot water over it. Leave it for a minute or two to soften, then beat it to a smooth cream.

Using a food processor, blender or pestle and mortar, reduce the onion and garlic to a paste. Add the coconut cream, then the cardamom, chilli and lime or lemon juice. Blend until smooth.

Marinate cubes of firm-fleshed fish like monkfish, Dover sole, haddock, cod or fresh tuna for an hour or two, then thread them on skewers, sprinkle with salt and grill, preferably over charcoal. Baste with the marinade once or twice while cooking. Mediterranean prawns, sold raw, scampi and the white cushions of fresh scallops are suitable shellfish for this marinade.

Creamed coconut also flavours and thickens the elusively spiced sauce of this delicate and delightful fish curry.

White Fish Curry

SERVES 4

1 small onion, finely chopped
1 clove garlic, finely chopped
2.5 cm (1 in) cube of fresh green
*   ginger, finely chopped*
2 tablespoons clarified butter (see
*   page 227) or peanut oil*
10 whole cardamom pods
680 g (1½ lb) haddock or cod,
*   filleted, skinned and cut in big*
*   cubes*
350 ml (12 fl oz) boiling fish stock
*   or water*
55 g (2 oz) creamed coconut, grated
1 tablespoon fresh lemon juice
salt and freshly ground black
*   pepper*
4 tablespoons, or more, finely
*   chopped coriander leaves or*
*   parsley*

Using a pestle and mortar or food processor, reduce the onion, garlic and ginger to a smooth paste. Heat the butter or oil in a heavy-based flameproof casserole and fry the paste gently for about five minutes. Add the cardamoms and fry for a moment or two longer. Add the fish and turn it in the hot fat to seal each piece on all sides. Remove the casserole from the heat.

Stir the boiling stock or water into the creamed coconut and stir until the liquid is smooth. Pour this mixture over the fish, add the lemon juice and season to taste with salt and pepper. Cover the casserole and cook in a preheated moderate oven (160°C/325°F, gas mark 3) for 15 minutes, or until the fish is just cooked, but not falling apart. Sprinkle with the coriander or parsley and serve with plainly boiled *basmatti* rice, or golden saffron rice (see page 159).

Kedgeree is the most accommodating of dishes. It is equally good for breakfast, lunch or supper and is obligingly tolerant of careful reheating. The essential ingredients are fine smoked haddock, preferably on the bone and smoked as opposed to dyed, *basmatti* rice and lots of butter.

Kedgeree

SERVES 4

450 g (1 lb) smoked haddock
225 g (8 oz) basmatti *rice*
110 g (4 oz) butter
1 teaspoon ground turmeric
3 whole cloves
3 whole cardamom pods
1/2 teaspoon caraway seeds
10 cm (4 in) cinnamon stick,
  broken in pieces
salt and freshly ground black
  pepper
4 eggs

Put the haddock in a shallow pan, cover with boiling water and poach lightly on a low heat for 10 minutes. Drain the fish, reserving the liquid. Remove and discard the skin and bones and break the flesh into large flakes.

Wash the rice in cold water and leave it to soak while you prepare the spices.

Melt half the butter in a heavy-based pan which has a tightly fitting lid, and add the turmeric, cloves, cardamoms, caraway seeds and cinnamon. Stir the spices for a moment or two on a medium heat. Drain the rice and add it to the spices. Stir well to coat each grain with butter, then add about 250 ml (8 fl oz) of the reserved fish stock and bring to the boil. Immediately the rice boils, turn the heat very low, clamp on the lid and cook the rice for about 10 minutes, or until all the stock has been absorbed and each grain is tender and separate. If all the stock is absorbed before the rice is tender, sprinkle a little cold water onto the rice, cover the pan and continue cooking until it is tender.

Fluff up the rice with a fork and season with a little salt, if needed, and a generous quantity of the pepper.

While the rice is cooking, hard boil the eggs. Shell and quarter them while they are still hot.

Cut the remaining butter into dice and add to the rice, together with the flaked fish. Mix lightly together and turn the kedgeree into a warm serving dish. Decorate with quarters of hard boiled egg and serve very hot.

Soft herring roes are usually sold frozen now, or thawed from a large block. Small packs weighing just under a pound are a useful freezer standby. Thaw the roes completely before cooking them.

Herring Roes on Toast

SERVES 4

450 g (1 lb) soft herring roes
4 tablespoons seasoned flour
4 tablespoons bacon fat, butter or
   oil
4 slices thick buttered toast
8 rashers bacon, crisply grilled
freshly ground black pepper

Separate the herring roes and dip them in the seasoned flour to coat all sides. Heat the fat in a heavy frying pan, add the roes and sauté for about two minutes on each side. The outside should be pale gold and just a little crisp, the inside creamy. Divide the roes between the slices of toast and top with the bacon. Sprinkle with the pepper and serve very hot.

Perhaps I have been unlucky, if a chance to eat lobster can be seen as any kind of hardship, but some I have eaten in restaurants have been a sorry disappointment – even a disgrace. Tough flesh, claws with more air in them than meat, and barely an inkling of the tenderness, the fresh sweet taste of lobsters remembered, of lobsters simply grilled or boiled, served hot with melted butter or cold with mayonnaise.

Seeing the creatures alive is not the guarantee of freshness and quality it is widely supposed to be. For if they have been too long out of the sea, they become lethargic, lose weight and live off their own flesh – for weeks if conditions are right. Angry, skittish lobsters that feel heavy for their size are the ones to choose. And don't expect too much of tired lobsters which have been 'tickled up' by wily restauranteurs. The doziest of them can be teased into shaking a leg to a hungry customer.

Now we come to the business of what to do with a live lobster. To store it for a short while before cooking, put it in an empty bath, or wrap it loosely in newspaper and pop it into the salad chiller of the refrigerator.

Opinions differ on the most humane way to kill a lobster. Drowning it in cold fresh water is a method favoured by some. Others prefer stabbing it in the back, between the head and body, but this may alarm the squeamish because its involuntary reflexes continue to operate for a while after it is dead. Putting it in cold water and bringing it to the boil has its advocates. But the system most widely subscribed to is to plunge the lobsters head first into boiling water. This is the method I use and, contrary to ghoulish myth, they do not utter piteous squeaks or rattle the lid of the fish kettle.

Boiling lobster is the simplest method of preparation for the home cook, and is unbeatable anyway. A small lobster weighing 570–680 g (1¼–1½ lb) will serve two as a first course, one as a main dish.

Boiled Lobster

SERVES 4

3 tablespoons salt
300 ml (½ pint) white wine
4 live lobsters weighing 570–680 g
   (1¼–1½ lb) each

Half-fill a large fish kettle, or two large pans, with water and add the salt and wine. Bring the liquid to a rolling boil and add the lobsters, head first. Cover with the lid and return the liquid to the boil as quickly as possible. Allow the lobsters to boil briskly for 8–10 minutes, according to size. They will turn from greeny-blue to red almost immediately, and be bright, brick red when cooked.

If the lobsters are to be eaten hot, take them from the liquid as soon as they are cooked. For serving cold, leave them to cool in the cooking water.

To open a cooked lobster for serving hot or cold place it, underside down, on a board. Take a knife which is strong, sharp and pointed and insert it into the joint between the head and tail. Cut decisively through the tail towards the fin. Repeat the cut in the opposite direction from the centre joint through the head. Crack the claws.

Only the gut, which runs in a dark line through the tail section, and the little pocket of grit in the head end need to be removed. The papery white gills at the top of the head are edible, but may be discarded. The red coral and the creamy green liver, known as tomalley, are delicious and not to be missed.

Melted butter, sharpened if you like with a little fresh lemon juice, is the simplest and best sauce for hot boiled lobster, and a few new potatoes are all that is required to make a dish for the gods.

Good, plain mayonnaise (see page 224), rather than one of those more highly flavoured mayonnaise based sauces, is the best possible accompaniment to cold lobster.

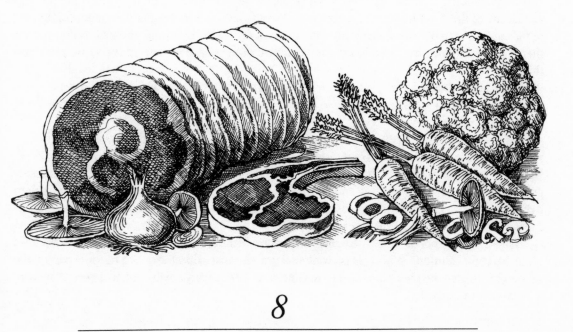

8

Meat

Early cookery books commonly contained repellently explicit instructions on how to choose good meat and ways to tell if it was less than fresh, diseased, or worse. We take it for granted now that meat is fresh and safe but how necessary that knowledge must once have been.

Old engravings of livestock being driven through London's streets, of the markets at Eastcheap, Newgate Shambles and Smithfield, and of the grazing fields at Islington where drovers rested their herds before bringing them into town emphasise vividly the merits of refrigeration. What can urban life have been like when a million cattle a year were driven through the city's streets as they were in the mid-nineteenth century? What price public health when beasts were slaughtered in the gutters?

Salt curing was one of the most successful ways of keeping meat wholesome for long periods without refrigeration and it was a technique exploited to the limit by British naval ships on months-long voyages.

In the winter of 1677 Samuel Pepys, Secretary of the Admiralty Commission, established new victualling allowances for the navy. For 6d a day in harbour, 7¾d at sea and 8d south of Lisbon, the contractors were to provide a daily ration to every seaman of a gallon of beer, a pound of biscuit and two pounds of English salted beef, or of bacon and pork, on four days a week. On the other three cod, haberdine (salt cod) or Poor John (salt hake), two ounces of butter and four of Suffolk cheese were the fare below decks.

Suffolk cheese, like its counterpart from Essex, was hard, strong tasting, and never enjoyed wide acclaim except for its cheapness.

In ships sailing south of latitude 49N an alternative diet was prescribed. Flour, rusks, raisins, currants, olive oil, pickled suet, stockfish (air-dried cod) and rice were washed down with a quart of wine or half a pint of brandy. Rum came later.

As Pepys noted at the time: 'Englishmen, and more especially seamen, love their bellies above everything else, and therefore it must always be remembered in the management of the victualling of the Navy that to make any abatement from them in the quantity or agreeableness of the victuals is to discourage and provoke them in the tenderest point, and will sooner render them disgusted with the King's service than any other one hardship that can be put upon them.'

That heavily salted beef, stored for months and sometimes years in wooden casks, can scarcely have been a treat any more than its successor in the sustenance of British fighting men, canned corned beef.

The version of salt beef consistently spoken well of nowadays is the Jewish one and the reasons for its good reputation are not difficult to work out. It is lightly salted and lightly spiced. But even more important is the cut of beef chosen, which should be brisket. This coarsely grained meat is layered with fat and is transformed by careful preparation into a succulent delicacy. The fat is absolutely necessary to the flavour and tenderness of the result, and any excess can be cut off when the beef is served.

The saltpetre specified for the brine, potassium nitrate, is increasingly difficult to get hold of, at least in London. Where it is available the chemist will stock it. The purpose of the saltpetre is to give the pickled meat a rosy glow, and without any it will cook to a greyish brown. The taste is unaltered.

Salt Beef

SERVES 8–10

170 g (6 oz) sea salt
2 teaspoons saltpetre
85 g (3 oz) Demerara sugar
2.3–2.7 kg (5–6 lb) boned brisket,
 not rolled
1 clove garlic, quartered
1 teaspoon mixed pickling spice
1 teaspoon black peppercorns,
 crushed
4 bay leaves
1 large onion, quartered

Mix together the salt, saltpetre and sugar and rub the mixture into the beef on all sides. Sprinkle the garlic, pickling spice and pepper over the meat. Put the brisket in a large earthenware bowl or casserole with two bay leaves and cover with cold water. Stand the container in a cool place, or in the refrigerator, and turn the meat daily for 7–10 days. By this time the liquid will appear offputtingly slimy, but as long as it is fresh smelling, all is well.

Take the meat from the brine and wash it well in cold water before rolling and tying it neatly.

Put the beef in a large pan or flameproof casserole and cover with cold water. Bring slowly to the boil and skim it carefully. Add the onion and the remaining bay leaves. Cover the pot and simmer the beef *very* gently for about four hours, or until tender.

Serve it hot in the English fashion with carrots, onions and parsnips added to the pot for the last 40 minutes of cooking time, and suet dumplings (see facing page) popped in for the last 20 minutes. Plain boiled or mashed potatoes, cooked separately, a jug of the hot stock and a little fiery mustard complete this traditional meal. Or serve the beef Jewish fashion with potato latkes (see page 157).

Suet Dumplings

225 g (8 oz) self-raising flour
salt and freshly ground black
pepper
110 g (4 oz) shredded suet
cold water to mix

Sift the flour, salt and pepper into a bowl, add the suet and toss together with a fork. Stirring the mixture with a round-bladed knife, gradually add enough cold water to form a soft dough. Shape the dough into small dumplings, flouring your hands to prevent sticking. Cover the pan to which the dumplings are added and cook them in simmering stock for 15–20 minutes. If the stock is boiling too fast the dumplings will disintegrate, and if it is off the boil they will be leaden.

While hot salt beef is generally sliced rather thickly, cold salt beef should be carved in thin slices. For serving cold the beef is best pressed. Remove any large pieces of fat before placing the meat in a suitable dish or tin and cooling it under weights.

Corned beef is the name given to salt beef in Ireland and in the United States. For a hash you can use tinned, corned or bully beef instead.

SERVES 4

Corned Beef Hash

55 g (2 oz) butter
1 large onion, finely chopped
1 clove garlic, finely chopped
680 g (1½ lb) cooked potatoes,
fresh or tinned
340 g (12 oz) cold salt beef or
tinned corned beef, diced
225 g (8 oz) tin of tomatoes,
drained
1 large egg
salt and freshly ground black
pepper
½ teaspoon dried rosemary
1 tablespoon chopped parsley

Melt half the butter in a heavy frying pan and add the onion. Fry slowly until it is tender and beginning to brown, adding the garlic just before the onion is ready.

Transfer the onion to a large bowl and add the potatoes, roughly chopped, and the corned beef. Break up the tomatoes and add them to the bowl with the egg, salt, pepper, rosemary and parsley. Mix the whole lot thoroughly together. At this stage it looks an unappetising lumpy mess.

Melt the remaining butter in the frying pan until it sizzles, then tip in the hash and fry gently until a golden brown crust forms on the underside.

If you have a well seasoned or non-stick pan it should be possible to turn the hash without breaking the crust. Place a large dinner plate over the pan and, holding plate and pan together, turn the hash onto the plate, then slide it back into the pan. If it has stuck, turn it over in sections and pat it back into shape. Fry the second side until it too is golden brown and the middle of the mixture is cooked.

Serve the hash immediately with green beans, a crisp green salad, or with a tomato salad.

For a whole piece of beef served *en croûte*, fillet steak is the best bet. It is sure to be tender, and its flavour, though less emphatically beefy than other cuts, can be bolstered by a layer of stuffing between the meat and pastry. Some recipes incorporate liver pâté in the stuffing, but I prefer the less elaborate onion and mushroom mixture given here.

Fillet of Beef en Croûte

SERVES 4

450 g (1 lb) fillet of beef, in one
 piece
freshly ground black pepper
55 g (2 oz) butter
110 g (4 oz) onions, finely chopped
170 g (6 oz) mushrooms, finely
 chopped
1 clove garlic, finely chopped
2 tablespoons finely chopped
 parsley
2 tablespoons cognac
salt
285 g (10 oz) puff pastry, home
 made (see page 84) or bought
1 egg, beaten

Trim the fillet and sprinkle it generously with the pepper. Heat the butter in a heavy frying pan until it foams. Add the meat and brown it evenly on all sides – this will take about 10 minutes. Take out the meat and set it aside to cool.

Add the onions to the pan and fry gently until they are soft, but not browned. Add the mushrooms and continue cooking until they too are soft. Add the garlic, parsley and cognac and cook gently until the liquid has disappeared. Season with salt and pepper and set the stuffing aside until it is quite cold.

Roll the pastry thinly on a lightly floured surface, then paint it lightly with the beaten egg. Spoon half the stuffing onto the pastry as a base for the meat. Place the beef on top of it and spoon the remaining stuffing over it.

Wrap the pastry over the meat to form a parcel. Join the long edges on top of the meat in a pinched-up frill, and the ends in the same fashion. Trim with scissors. Avoid overlapping the pastry in folds which would cook unevenly, and trim off the excess.

Cut one or two small slits in the pastry top to let out steam, and brush the top with beaten egg, avoiding the cut edges of the frill. Place the meat on a baking sheet which has been lightly sprinkled with water and bake in a preheated hot oven (230°C/450°F, gas mark 8) for 10 minutes. Reduce the temperature to moderate (180°C/350°F, gas mark 4) and bake for another 20–30 minutes. Rest in a warm place for five minutes before serving in thick slices.

On these cooking times the meat will be medium rare, that is, pink in the middle. If you prefer it browner or pinker, cook it for a longer or shorter time before wrapping it in the pastry.

Of the dozens of versions of steak au poivre, this is my favourite. Whether the steaks are small or thick, you should be able to fit all six into one large frying or sauté pan.

Steak au Poivre

SERVES 6

6 fillet steaks
4 tablespoons green peppercorns
1/2 teaspoon dried thyme
1/2 teaspoon dried rosemary
1/2 teaspoon dried tarragon
1/2 teaspoon salt
1 tablespoon moutarde de Meaux
2 tablespoons peanut oil
30 g (1 oz) butter
4 tablespoons cognac
1 tablespoon mild French mustard
300 ml (1/2 pint) single cream

Trim the steaks and pat them dry. Mix together the peppercorns, thyme, rosemary, tarragon, salt and *moutarde de Meaux*. Spread the mixture on both sides of the steaks.

Heat the oil in a heavy frying or sauté pan until it is hot, then add the butter which should melt and froth quickly. Before the butter starts to burn, add the steaks, and as soon as the first side is sealed, reduce the heat and cook them as quickly and evenly as you can, turning them over when they are half done. There is no substitute for judgement here as the time they take to cook will depend on the thickness of the meat and how well done you like it.

A chef will test meat by pressing it with his fingers – like choosing a Camembert. It is a skill that takes practice to develop. Failing such expertise, the only alternative is to jab one of the steaks with a pointed knife and see how it is doing.

When the steaks are very nearly as cooked as required, sprinkle them with the cognac and ignite it immediately. As soon as the flames have died down, transfer the steaks to a heated serving dish. Stir the mild mustard into the pan juices, followed immediately by the cream. Stir or shake the sauce and let it boil until reduced by about a quarter. Check the seasoning and pour it over the steaks. Serve the steaks immediately with new potatoes, or green salad.

When is a stew not a stew? When it is a casserole? Well, not really. The distinctions, in truth, are hopelessly blurred.

Both are made with meat and vegetables cooked in liquid and it is tempting to draw a line between recipes which are usually cooked on top of the stove and those traditionally consigned to the oven. Put plain-speaking stews on the back burner and casseroles in the oven. But Irish stew with its un-stirrable layers of meat and potato is an oven dish if ever there was one.

Or it might be claimed that stew is good solid British fare, and casseroles are fancy foreign mutton parading as lamb. Not so though. To stew comes from the Old French *estuier*, meaning to shut up or enclose; the very same word that gave us the fish ponds, or stews, of old England. And just to be difficult, casserole, based to be sure on the French *cassole*, has been English verbal currency for the best part of four centuries.

From the point of view of current English usage, a better distinction can be found in the presentation of these dishes than in their preparation. Which makes stews unpretentious family fare, and casseroles what they are called when anyone else is listening . . . except Irish stew of course.

This braised ox-tail recipe with its rich, shiny sauce, amply repays the pains taken in its preparation. Reducing the cooking liquid twice before the final braising encourages the gelatine to come out of the ox-tail and make a rich glossy gravy.

Braised Ox-tail

SERVES 4

1.5 kg (3¼ lb) ox-tail
salt and freshly ground black
　pepper
3 tablespoons oil, preferably peanut
55 g (2 oz) onion, finely chopped
55 g (2 oz) leek
55 g (2 oz) carrot
55 g (2 oz) celery
200 ml (⅓ pint) red wine
1 litre (1¾ pints) brown stock (see
　page 234)
3 tablespoons tomato purée
1 bay leaf
1 sprig of thyme

For the garnish:
225 g (8 oz) carrots
225 g (8 oz) turnips
110 g (4 oz) button onions, peeled
30 g (1 oz) butter (optional, see
　method)
30 g (1 oz) parsley, finely chopped

Cut the ox-tail into pieces 2.5–5 cm (1–2 in) thick and season with salt and pepper. Heat the oil in a heavy flameproof casserole, add the ox-tail and sauté until it is well browned. Add all the vegetables and brown them well.

Add the wine and cook on a high heat until it has reduced to just a few tablespoons, then add one-third of the stock and continue boiling until it too is well reduced.

Now add the remaining stock, the tomato purée, bay leaf and thyme. Cover the casserole and braise in a preheated moderately hot oven (190°C/375°F, gas mark 5) for about 2½ hours, or until the ox-tail is very tender.

While the ox-tail is cooking, prepare the vegetables for the garnish. To turn the carrots and turnips is an optional refinement. Use a sharp knife to shape the vegetables into elongated miniature rugby balls about the size of a large teaspoon. Uniformity is the aim and it takes practice, but the results do give a well-finished appearance to the completed dish. The offcuts can, of course, be used for soup or stock.

When the ox-tail is tender, take the pieces from the casserole, skim the fat from the sauce, then pass it through a fine sieve, pressing through as much of the *mirepoix* as possible. Return the sauce and ox-tail to the casserole and add the carrots, turnips and onions. Cook the braise for another 30 minutes. Adjust the seasoning to taste and serve sprinkled with the parsley.

The vegetable garnishes may be cooked separately in the butter and added to the braise when it is served.

The flavour of topside is splendidly rich and beefy, which is why cooks going back to the cauldron days have browned it in dripping and cooked it on a bed of vegetables with just enough liquid to make it succulent when cooked right through.

Eliza Acton's recipe for braising a rump of beef weighing seven or eight pounds demonstrates the larger joints common in the mid-nineteenth century. Rump was the name then for topside and is still among Scottish names for the cut. Other current regional names include corner cut, corner piece and corner case, best end, hinderbone, hind lift and buttock.

How reassuring Eliza Acton's plain speaking recipes must have been when all cooking appliances ran on solid fuel and thermostats were a thing of the future.

'TO STEW A RUMP OF BEEF   This joint is more easily carved, and is of better appearance when the bones are removed before it is dressed. Roll and bind it firmly with a fillet of tape, cover it with strong cold beef broth or gravy, and stew it very gently indeed from six hours to between seven and eight; add to it, after the scum has been well cleared off, one large or two moderate-sized onions stuck with thirty cloves, a head of celery, two carrots, two turnips, and a large faggot of savoury herbs. When the beef is perfectly tender quite through, which may be known by probing it with a sharp thin skewer, remove the fillets of tape, dish it neatly, and serve it with a rich *Espagnole*, and garnish with forced tomatas, or with a highly flavoured brown English gravy, and stewed carrots in the dish.

'This is the most simple and economical manner of stewing the beef; but should a richer one be desired, half roast the joint, and stew it afterwards in strong gravy to which a pint of mushrooms, and a pint of sherry or Madeira, should be added an hour before it is ready for table. Keep it hot while a portion of the gravy is thickened with a well-made brown roux, and seasoned with salt, cayenne, and any other spice it may require. Garnish it with large balls of forcemeat highly seasoned with minced eschalots, rolled in egg and bread-crumbs, and fried a fine golden brown.

'Plainly stewed 6 to 7 or 8 hours. Or: half roasted then stewed from 4 to 5 hours.'

Hot English mustard or fiery horseradish go well with the slightly sweet flavour of a traditional pot roast cooked with plenty of root vegetables.

Pot Roast of Beef

SERVES 4–6

55 g (2 oz) butter or dripping
1.8 kg (4 lb) rolled topside of beef,
  in one piece
450 g (1 lb) onions, peeled and
  quartered
225 g (8 oz) carrots, scraped and
  halved
225 g (8 oz) turnips or parsnips,
  peeled and cut in chunks
1 leek, cut in 2.5 cm (1 in) lengths
1 sprig of fresh thyme, or ½
  teaspoon dried thyme
150 ml (¼ pint) drinkable red
  wine or beef stock
salt and freshly ground black
  pepper

Melt the butter or dripping in a heavy flameproof casserole large enough to hold the meat and vegetables without too much room to spare. Add the meat and brown it well on all sides. Take out the meat, add all the vegetables and brown them lightly. Return the meat to the casserole, making sure that there is a good layer of the vegetables underneath it. Add the thyme and wine or stock and a generous seasoning of salt and pepper. Cover the casserole and cook in a preheated cool oven (150°C/300°F, gas mark 2) for about three hours, or until the meat is tender.

Transfer the meat to a heated serving dish and surround it with the vegetables. Serve the stock separately, as it is, or thickened to make a conventional gravy.

Carbonade of beef, a fairly liquid dish of beef cooked slowly in beer, is popular in the Low Countries. I have been making the simplest possible version for years and prefer this to more complicated variations which may well be more authentic. Some recipes call for Guinness which, of course, makes a beautifully dark gravy, but you can use any beer from lager to stout. Brown ale has my vote.

Carbonade of Beef

SERVES 6–8

1.35 kg (3 lb) braising steak
salt and freshly ground black
    pepper
2 tablespoons olive oil
30 g (1 oz) butter
680 g (1½ lb) onions, peeled and
    thinly sliced
1 tablespoon plain flour
600 ml (1 pint) brown ale

Cut the steak into large cubes and season it generously with salt and pepper. Heat the oil in a heavy flameproof casserole, add the meat and brown it quickly on all sides. Lift out the beef and add the butter to the casserole. Reduce the heat, add the onions and brown them evenly without allowing them to burn. Sprinkle them with the flour and mix well. Return the meat to the casserole and add the beer. Bring to the boil on top of the stove, then cover the casserole tightly and cook in a preheated slow oven (150°C/300°F, gas mark 2) for three hours, or until the meat is very tender.

Adjust the seasoning and serve the carbonade piping hot with plenty of fluffy mashed potato or with flat ribbons of pasta. The dish tastes even better if it is cooled and reheated, and cooling makes it easier to remove any surplus fat from the gravy. It freezes well too.

A well made osso bucco, or *ossi buchi alla milanese*, is one of the great dishes of the world. The thick slices of shin of veal simmered until meltingly tender with white wine and tomatoes, are lifted into a class all their own by a finishing flourish of *gremolata*. This unique and essential garnish is a mixture of chopped parsley and garlic with shreds of finely grated lemon zest. Because the bone marrow is a particular delicacy of osso bucco I like to serve it with creamed potatoes. A saffron-scented milanese risotto (see page 159) is its customary partner.

Most recipes specify 5 cm (2 in) thick slices of shin of veal. This is probably the right size for meat from calves that are barely weaned, but it is too thick when it comes from older and larger animals. A minimum thickness of 2.5 cm (1 in) is about right for slices from the broad end of the leg. From the thin end of the leg the choice is between serving one very thick slice or two or more of much the same thickness as the larger slices.

Osso Bucco

SERVES 6

45 g (1½ oz) butter or clarified
    butter (see page 227)
6 slices shin of veal
300 ml (½ pint) dry white wine
425 g (15 oz) tin of Italian plum
    tomatoes

Melt the butter in a heavy flameproof casserole which has a tightly fitting lid. Add the meat and brown it lightly on both sides. Arrange it in the casserole in one layer so that the marrow is not lost and pour in the wine. Cook on a high heat until the wine has reduced by about one-third, then add the tomatoes and their juice. Allow this too to

114

*300 ml (¹/₂ pint) light stock or
    water*
*salt and freshly ground black
    pepper*
*30 g (1 oz) parsley, very finely
    chopped*
1 clove garlic, very finely chopped
2 teaspoons finely grated lemon zest

reduce a little, then add the stock or water and season with salt and pepper. Cover closely and cook in a pre-heated very cool oven (110°C/225°F, gas mark ¹/₄) for two to three hours, or until the meat is very tender.

I like the very thin, well flavoured gravy that this recipe makes, especially when the dish is served with creamed potatoes to mop it up. It may of course be reduced by fast boiling or thickened to taste.

Mix the parsley, garlic and lemon zest. Sprinkle the mixture on the osso bucco just before serving or hand round the *gremolata* separately.

When speed is of the essence it takes no longer to rustle up an elegant sauté dish than to grill a frozen chop. Sautéing calls for lean, tender pieces of meat: the very cuts which shrivel and dry if cooked too long. This wonderfully fresh-tasting sauté of veal with lemon comes from Roger Vergé's *Cuisine of the Sun*, a book filled with lovely Mediterranean recipes from his restaurant, the three-star *Moulin de Mougins* near Cannes.

SERVES 2

Medallions of Veal
with Lemon

1 ripe juicy lemon
¹/₂ teaspoon sugar
60 g (2 oz) butter
*about 300 g (10 oz) veal fillet
    (tenderloin), cut into 4 pieces
    and trimmed of fat and sinews,
    or 2 first grade veal cutlets,
    trimmed of their fat*
*salt and freshly ground black
    pepper*
4 tablespoons dry white wine
1 tablespoon chopped parsley

Pare off the zest of half the lemon as thinly as possible with a potato peeler and cut into thin julienne strips. Put these in a small pan with cold water and bring to the boil. Drain and refresh under the cold tap. Return the blanched zest to the pan with the sugar and one table-spoon of water and cook until the water has evaporated and the zest is a beautiful bright yellow. Remove from the heat and set aside.

Heat one-third of the butter in a frying pan, and meanwhile season the pieces of veal on both sides with salt and pepper. When the butter begins to sizzle, add the veal and cook on a moderate heat, allowing about five minutes on each side. Remove the meat and keep hot. Pour away the cooking butter but do not wash the pan. Pour in the wine and deglaze the pan over a moderate heat, scraping up the caramelised juices from the bottom of the pan and allowing the wine to reduce until there is only a generous tablespoonful left. Add the remaining butter and mix very well to amalgamate the sauce. Add the parsley, taste and season with salt and pepper.

Arrange the veal on two hot plates. Add to the sauce the juices which have run out of the meat. Pour the sauce – there will be very little of it – over the meat and garnish each medallion with a slice of peeled lemon and a pinch of the cooked julienne of lemon zest.

Vergé suggests risotto or fresh young vegetables cooked in butter to accompany the veal.

115

Leg and shoulder joints of spring lamb are smaller than those from older animals later in the year. So for more than four servings a festive looking crown roast or guard of honour may be a better choice. Best end of neck, which comes from behind the shoulder and therefore a good deal further back than its name suggests, is the cut used for both these roasts.

Given a little warning, butchers are usually pleased to exercise their skill, making up crowns and guards of honour to order. It is a bit of a fiddle, but not difficult, to do at home. For either roast, ask for two matching best ends of neck or racks (six to eight rib bones each) taken from the same lamb and ask the butcher to chine them; that is, to saw through the spine, and in this case to remove it.

If the rack has a piece of shoulder blade between the first couple of ribs, cut it out. Now cut across the rack about 10 cm (4 in) in from the tips of the rib bones. Remove the fatty layer of meat to expose the ends of the bones and scrape them clean with a sharp knife.

To form a guard of honour roast stand the two racks upright facing each other with the bones arching inwards and press them together so that the bones interlock across the top. Tie the roast firmly in about three places along its length. To make sure the guard of honour maintains an aspect of military precision in the oven you can weave a long length of string in between the criss-crossed ribs, then bring the ends back along the outside of the bones to tie them at the end you started.

To form a crown roast stand the two racks back to back, bones on the outside, meat on the inside, and bend them into a circle. Stitch the ends together with a couple of loops of string and a trussing needle.

Unless you like lamb very well cooked, it is not a good idea to stuff either of these roasts. Season them with salt and pepper, and set them on a rack in a roasting tin. Roast in a preheated hot oven (230°C/450°F, gas mark 8) for 10 minutes to sear the meat, then reduce the temperature to moderate (180°C/350°F, gas mark 4) and cook for another 25–35 minutes, or until the meat is cooked as you like it. Test by piercing the meat with a skewer. The juice will run red when the meat is rare, pink when it is lightly cooked and clear when it is well done.

Rest the meat in a warm place for 5–10 minutes before serving. Both guard of honour and crown roasts are child's play to carve at table. Simply cut down between the rib bones and these joints fall into neat cutlets.

Good lamb is so juicy and tender that it can be served as rare as fillet steak. For a special occasion wrap it in puff pastry.

SERVES 4–6

Loin of Lamb in Puff Pastry

900 g (2 lb) boned loin of lamb
55 g (2 oz) butter
225 g (8 oz) onions, chopped
110 g (4 oz) lamb's liver, roughly chopped
30 g (1 oz) shelled hazelnuts, chopped
½ teaspoon dried tarragon, or 1 sprig of fresh tarragon when available

Ask the butcher to bone a loin of lamb. A piece weighing about 1.25 kg (2¾ lb) will weigh about 900 g (2 lb) when boned and trimmed. Trim away most of the fat on the outside of the joint, leaving a layer which is wafer thin. Roll the meat into a sausage shape and tie it in one or two places with string.

Spread half the butter on the lamb and part-roast it in a preheated hot oven (230°C/450°F, gas mark 8) for 30 minutes. This is long enough for meat which will be pink inside at the completion of cooking. Add another five

salt and freshly ground black
  pepper
450 g (1 lb) puff pastry, home
  made (see page 84) or bought
1 egg yolk

minutes or so for medium-done, and 15 minutes for
well-done. Transfer the lamb to a plate to cool.

Melt the remaining butter in a pan, add the onions and
fry until they are soft, but not coloured. Add the liver and
fry it very briefly just to firm it. Cool the mixture, then
mince or chop it very finely. Stir in the hazelnuts and
tarragon and season to taste with salt and pepper.

Roll the pastry very thinly on a floured surface. Spoon
half the onion mixture onto the pastry as a base for the
meat. Remove the string, place the lamb on it and top with
the remaining stuffing.

Dampen the edges of the pastry with water and wrap it
over the meat in a parcel, joining the long sides on top of
the meat in a pinched-up frill, and the ends in the same
way. Resist the temptation to overlap the pastry in folds
which would cook unevenly, and trim off the excess.

Cut one or two small slits in the pastry top to let out
steam, and brush it with the egg yolk. Place the meat on a
greased baking sheet and bake in a preheated moderately
hot oven (190°C/375°F, gas mark 5) for 30–35 minutes,
or until the pastry is golden and crisp. Serve in thick slices
with bitter orange (see page 242) or redcurrant jelly.

Lamb steaks cut from the leg make a substantial grill. The slices should be 1.25–2 cm
(½–¾ in) thick and will have a small piece of bone in the centre. Chump chops and lamb
cutlets are also suitable for this recipe.

SERVES 4

Grilled Lamb Steaks

4 leg of lamb steaks
1 clove garlic, crushed
salt and freshly ground black
  pepper
fresh or dried herbs to taste: thyme,
  marjoram, tarragon and
  rosemary
3 tablespoons olive oil
2 tablespoons fresh lemon juice

Pat the steaks dry and arrange them on a plate. Mix
together all the other ingredients for the marinade and
pour it over the meat. Marinate the steaks for an hour or
two at room temperature, turning them once.

Insert two skewers in an X-shape horizontally through
each steak to keep it flat during cooking, then grill them
under a preheated very hot grill for about six minutes on
each side. Baste the meat with the marinade during
cooking, and make sure the meat is heat-sealed on both
sides before reducing the heat if it is cooking too quickly.

Serve with baked potatoes and plenty of crisp green
salad.

Shoulder of lamb is cheaper than leg, and very good for roasting. The meat is all the sweeter for the fat layers in this cut which is best roasted slowly.

Roast Shoulder of Lamb

SERVES 4

1 shoulder of lamb weighing
    1.35–1.6 kg (3–3½ lb)
1 clove garlic, peeled
2 tablespoons plain flour
salt and freshly ground black
    pepper

For the gravy:
150 ml (¼ pint) light lamb or
    chicken stock
½ teaspoon dried tarragon, or
    fresh when available
salt and freshly ground black
    pepper
1 tablespoon redcurrant jelly
    (optional)
1 teaspoon cornflour (optional)

Pat the meat dry. Cut the garlic into thin slices and, using your fingers, insert the slivers into the meat. Dust the joint on both sides with the flour, salt and pepper, then place it, cut side down, on a rack in a roasting tin. Roast in a preheated moderate oven (180°C/350°F, gas mark 4) for 25 minutes per 450 g (1 lb) plus 25 minutes more. (Add another 15 minutes if the meat is cold from the refrigerator.)

Rest the meat in the oven with the heat turned off and the door half open for about 10 minutes before carving.

While the meat is resting, make the gravy. Skim all the fat from the juices in the roasting tin and add the stock. Stir to dissolve the crusty bits from the tin, then add the tarragon, salt, pepper and redcurrant jelly, if used. For thin gravy, simply bring to the boil, strain and serve. For thicker gravy blend the cornflour with a little water and stir into the liquid. Bring to the boil and keep at boiling point for a minute or two before straining and serving.

Baked potatoes cooked without fat are a better accompaniment with shoulder of lamb than the traditional roast potatoes.

A boned, spiced leg of lamb is not as highly seasoned as the ingredients suggest. As with some of the more interesting curries, the spices enhance rather than mask the flavour of the lamb.

Spiced Roast of Lamb

SERVES 6–8

1 boned leg of lamb weighing about
    1.35 kg (3 lb)
30 g (1 oz) green ginger, peeled and
    finely grated
1 teaspoon salt
30 g (1 oz) butter
2 medium onions, finely chopped
2 tablespoons ground coriander

To baste:
150 ml (¼ pint) natural yogurt
110 g (4 oz) butter, melted
2 tablespoons ground cumin
1 teaspoon ground cardamom
1 teaspoon ground cinnamon
2 teaspoons ground cloves

Trim the lamb of skin and lay it out flat, slashing the meat where necessary. Mix together the ginger and salt and rub this mixture into the meat on all sides. Set it aside.

Melt the butter in a pan, add the onions and fry gently until they are soft. Add the coriander and continue frying until the onions are well browned. Spread this mixture on the side of the meat from which the bone has been cut. Roll it up with the onion on the inside and tie it securely with string. Some of the onion will inevitably ooze out, and the roll is unlikely to be a neat one, but it will shape up more convincingly when cooked.

To make the basting mixture, mix the yogurt, melted butter, cumin, cardamom, cinnamon and cloves.

To spit roast the meat, cook it on maximum heat for about 15 minutes, or until well browned, basting it several times with the yogurt mixture. Continue cooking according to the appliance manufacturer's directions for roast lamb, basting frequently.

To roast in the oven, set the meat on a rack and place a tin to catch the drippings on the shelf below. Roast in a preheated very hot oven (230°C/450°F, gas mark 8) for 15 minutes, or until well browned, basting several times with the yogurt mixture. Reduce the temperature to moderate (180°C/350°F, gas mark 4) and continue roasting for about 1½ hours, basting the meat frequently.

When the meat is cooked, set it aside to rest while you make the spiced gravy. Skim the excess fat from the pan juices and add to them about 150 ml (¼ pint) of water and any remaining basting liquid. Bring the mixture to the boil, scraping up the pan juices to make a rich gravy. Reduce the mixture to a thick sauce by fast boiling and season to taste. Serve it with the meat which should be cut in fairly thick slices.

This rich and subtle curry is based closely on a recipe for *badami roghan josh* which appears in Madhur Jaffrey's *An Invitation To Indian Cooking*.

SERVES 4–6

Lamb in Dark Almond Sauce

6 tablespoons vegetable oil, preferably peanut
6 whole cloves
1 or 2 dried chillies (optional)
12 whole black peppercorns
6 whole cardamom pods
900 g (2 lb) shoulder or leg of lamb, cubed
1 tablespoon ground cumin
2 tablespoons ground coriander
4 tablespoons ground or finely chopped almonds
6 cloves garlic, peeled and chopped
15 g (½ oz) fresh green ginger, peeled and coarsely chopped
1 teaspoon ground turmeric
½ teaspoon ground nutmeg or mace
225 g (8 oz) onions, finely chopped
3 tablespoons natural yogurt
225 g (8 oz) fresh or tinned tomatoes, peeled and coarsely chopped
salt

Heat the oil in a heavy frying pan and add the cloves, chillies, peppercorns and cardamoms and fry them for a moment or two on a medium heat. Add about one-third of the meat and fry it in the spiced oil until it is browned on all sides. Transfer the meat to a heavy flameproof casserole, leaving the spices in the oil, and brown the remainder of the meat in the same way. Put the cumin, coriander and almonds in another small, heavy pan and cook them dry on a medium heat until the almonds turn a rich coffee colour.

Mix together these roasted spices with the whole spices from the oil and the garlic, ginger, turmeric and nutmeg or mace. Blend the mixture until smooth using an electric blender or pestle and mortar, and adding up to 120 ml (4 fl oz) of water to make a thick paste.

Cook the onions in the oil remaining in the frying pan until they are lightly browned. Add the spicy paste and cook on a medium heat for a few minutes, stirring constantly. Stir in the yogurt, a little at a time, then add the tomatoes and continue to cook the mixture for a few minutes more. Add salt to taste. Add the sauce to the meat in the casserole, stir well, cover the casserole and cook on a low heat until the meat is tender, which will take one to two hours depending on the cut used. Alterna-

119

tively, cook the casserole in a preheated cool oven (150°C/300°F, gas mark 2) for about two hours.

The method of making curry using a paste is simple and works equally well with meat, fish, poultry and vegetables. Stock may be used instead of water. So may natural yogurt, stabilised before cooking so that it does not curdle by mixing one tablespoon of cornflour to each 150 ml (¼ pint) of yogurt. Small quantities of fresh green ginger, very finely chopped and blended with yogurt, give a fine tang.

Lancashire hot pot is typical of the homely dishes that are simply delicious when well made and not at all nice when sloppily done. The natural sweetness of best end of neck of lamb cutlets will be spoiled if too much fat is left on them, or every scrap removed. So trim them to leave a narrow band of fat that will hold the chops in shape without making the dish too greasy. This is one of the few dishes in which lamb stock is an improvement.

Lancashire Hot Pot

SERVES 6–8

1.35 kg (3 lb) best end of neck of lamb cutlets
salt and freshly ground black pepper
450 g (1 lb) onions, peeled and sliced in rings
900 g (2 lb) potatoes, peeled and thickly sliced
600–900 ml (1–1½ pints) good stock
30 g (1 oz) butter

Trim the cutlets of excess fat and leave them on the bone. The shape of a traditional hot pot dish is round and straight sided so a large soufflé dish or casserole will do very well.

Season the cutlets with salt and pepper and arrange them standing round the edge of the dish with bones towards the outside and meatiest ends down. Tuck the onions and potatoes in layers between the cutlets, seasoning each layer, and ending with a good layer of potato on top. Pour in the stock to within 1.25 cm (½ in) of the top layer of potato and dot the top of the dish with the butter.

Cover the dish and bake it in a preheated cool oven (150°C/300°F, gas mark 2) for three hours. To brown the top, remove the cover, increase the temperature to moderately hot (190°C/375°F, gas mark 5) and bake for a further 30 minutes.

In the days when oysters were the food of the poor, a few, say six, would be included in a hot pot. Now they are a very optional refinement.

Highly spiced meat kebabs can be moulded, sausage-fashion round skewers, or shaped into flat patties. Serve them with Indian or Arab bread, lemon wedges, onion rings, and a dish of natural yogurt mixed with finely chopped cucumber and onion, salt and pepper.

Seekh Kebabs

SERVES 6

*900 g (2 lb) lean lamb, minced
   twice*
*55 g (2 oz) fresh white
   breadcrumbs*
4 cloves garlic, crushed
*2.5 cm (1 in) cube of fresh ginger,
   crushed*
*30 g (1 oz) fresh coriander leaves
   or mint, finely chopped*
1 tablespoon garam masala
2 teaspoons salt
1 teaspoon ground coriander
1 teaspoon ground cumin
1 teaspoon ground cinnamon
1 teaspoon freshly grated nutmeg
1 teaspoon cayenne pepper
1 egg

Combine all the ingredients and mix well. Then pass the mixture once more through the mincer, or process it briefly. Chill for at least two hours, or overnight, to give the flavours time to blend and develop. Form the meat into kebabs or patties and grill, preferably over charcoal, basting frequently with sunflower or peanut oil, or with a mixture of melted butter and lemon juice.

Meatballs can be differently dressed in so many ways that a good, basic recipe is useful and versatile. A Greek recipe coats them in a piquant yogurt sauce. Americans eat them with a fresh tomato sauce and Swedes serve them dry. Curried meatballs are very good too. Try adding finely chopped garlic to the basic mixture, or ring the changes on the herbs.

Meatballs

SERVES 4

1 large onion, very finely chopped
*450 g (1 lb) finely minced lean beef
   or lamb*
110 g (4 oz) fresh breadcrumbs
1 egg, beaten
2 tablespoons chopped fresh parsley
*1 tablespoon chopped fresh oregano,
   or 1 teaspoon dried oregano*
*salt and freshly ground black
   pepper to taste*
55 g (2 oz) plain flour
*4 tablespoons vegetable oil for
   frying*

Mix thoroughly together in a large bowl the onion, meat, breadcrumbs, egg, parsley, oregano, salt and pepper. Form the mixture into balls, taking a teaspoonful at a time and rolling it in the palms of your hands, then in the flour.

Heat the oil in a heavy sauté or frying pan, add the meatballs and fry them, a few at a time, for about four minutes, turning once. Transfer the meatballs to a warm dish and keep them warm in a low oven.

To make the piquant Greek sauce, whisk together 150 ml (¼ pint) natural yogurt with the same amount of water and a tablespoon of cornflour. Add this mixture to the pan juices left after frying the meatballs and heat together, stirring constantly, until the sauce thickens. Adjust the seasoning to taste and return the meatballs to the pan to coat them with the sauce. Serve with buttered noodles or spaghetti.

Fillet or tenderloin of pork is the basis of this speedily made sauté.

Pork Medallions with Mustard Cream Sauce

SERVES 4

680 g (1½ lb) pork tenderloin
2 tablespoons plain flour
salt and freshly ground black
    pepper
2 tablespoons clarified butter (see
    page 227) or peanut oil
1 small onion, finely chopped
250 ml (8 fl oz) dry white wine, or
    lightly seasoned chicken stock, or
    a mixture of both
1 tablespoon pale Dijon mustard
150 ml (¼ pint) crème fraîche (see
    page 227) or double cream

Choose thick pieces of tenderloin and cut them in 1.25 cm (½ in) thick slices across the grain to make round medallions or cushions of meat which look like miniature fillet steaks. Dust the pork with the flour and season it with salt and pepper.

Heat the butter or oil in a large sauté or frying pan until it foams, then add the pieces of pork in one layer. Cook them on a medium to high heat, turning once. As soon as the meat is lightly browned and cooked, transfer it to a warm plate and keep it warm while making the sauce. A very cool oven preheated to 110°C/225°F, gas mark ¼ is ideal.

Add the onion to the pan and cook, stirring, until it is transparent and lightly browned. Pour in the wine or stock and boil the liquid, scraping up the pan juices and bits to flavour the sauce. Cook briskly until half the liquid has boiled away, then stir in the mustard, followed by the cream. Stir the sauce until it is well blended, allowing it to reduce a little more. Check the seasoning, then strain the sauce.

Divide the sauce between four warm plates and arrange the medallions of pork on top of it. Add a small heap of lightly buttered noodles or rice generously sprinkled with finely chopped parsley. Serve immediately.

Buttered papers and a simple stuffing ensure that baked pork is moist and tender.

Papered Pork

SERVES 4

450 g (1 lb) fillet (tenderloin) of
    pork, or 4 boneless chops
30 g (1 oz) butter
1 small onion, finely chopped
110 g (4 oz) fresh brown or white
    breadcrumbs
2 tablespoons finely chopped
    parsley
pinch of finely chopped rosemary or
    tarragon

If using tenderloin divide it into four pieces of equal size and split them lengthwise without cutting right through. In the case of chops cut a slit pocket in each one.

Heat the butter in a small pan, add the onion and fry until it is tender, but not browned. Stir in the breadcrumbs and herbs and season to taste with salt and plenty of freshly ground black pepper. Divide the stuffing between the four pieces of meat and wrap the meat around the stuffing.

Cut out four large ovals of greaseproof paper or foil

salt and freshly ground black
    pepper
85 g (3 oz) butter, softened
pinch of ground mace

about 25 cm (10 in) long × about 15 cm (6 in) wide. Spread each paper generously with the softened butter, then sprinkle with salt, pepper and a very little mace.

Wrap each piece of meat loosely in a buttered paper and twist the ends tightly to seal. Arrange the parcels in a shallow baking dish and bake in a preheated moderate oven (180°C/350°F, gas mark 4) for 35 minutes if the pork is wrapped in greaseproof paper, 45 minutes if it is wrapped in foil. Serve the parcels as they come out of the oven, allowing each person to open one on the plate.

Made with fresh asparagus and best ham this is a dainty dish indeed. It is also good made with standby tins of ham and asparagus.

SERVES 6

Baked Ham and Asparagus Rolls

15 g (½ oz) butter
12 thin slices cooked ham
24 cooked asparagus spears
300 ml (½ pint) single cream
salt and freshly ground black
    pepper
45 g (1½ oz) Parmesan cheese,
    finely grated

Butter a shallow ovenproof dish just large enough to hold all the ham and asparagus rolls in one layer without too much room to spare.

Place two asparagus spears on each slice of ham. Top the asparagus with a teaspoon of the cream, a little salt and freshly ground black pepper and a teaspoon of the Parmesan. Roll up each slice of ham round its asparagus filling and arrange the rolls in the prepared dish. Pour the remaining cream over the dish and sprinkle the top with the remaining Parmesan.

Bake in a preheated cool oven (140°C/275°F, gas mark 1) for about 30 minutes, or until the cream is bubbling. Brown the cheese under a hot grill and serve immediately with crusty bread.

Tripe, as everyone knows, is the stomach lining of herbivorous ruminant mammals, usually cattle. The first stomach, the largest one, is the rumen, and this supplies tripe with a texture that looks like a face flannel. The appearance of honeycomb, the most widely prized variety of tripe, is self-explanatory. It comes from the second stomach, called the reticulum. The third stomach, called the ometum, is a continuation of the second and used to provide a flimsy tripe called 'bible tripe' which even Scottish tripe cleaners can no longer be persuaded to prepare. The fourth stomach, the abomasum, is said by *The Shorter Oxford Dictionary* to be the true digestive stomach of ruminants. This is the stomach that provides 'black' tripe, which, in serious tripe-fancying circles, is the most sought after of all.

What then is real tripe? It is all the kinds mentioned so far, but it has not been messed about. It has been cleaned by scraping, and it is raw. It is cheap and plentiful in parts of the north of England and Scotland. But in London and the south the only kind we can buy is precooked and bleached with hydrogen peroxide. As a result it looks and tastes harmless enough and can be used without further ado in recipes calling for cooked tripe.

Unbleached tripe looks even less attractive than the bleached kind but it has a great deal more taste, and a much nicer texture. To prepare it for recipes which call for cooked tripe simply wash it well and simmer it gently in water for five hours. Pressure cooking cuts the time dramatically.

Pigs' pettitoes and the feet of oxen crop up in many tripe recipes and in reality are less frightful than they sound. Pigs' trotters are sold scrubbed and raw and the recipe for *tripes à la mode de Shadwell* explains what to do with them.

To obtain feet of oxen ask the butcher for cow heel and he will produce a well boiled, scarcely recognisable clod of bone and gristle, and hew it into pieces on request. What these extremities add to the finished dish is a succulently gelatinous gravy so full of body that when cold a lump of it will almost bounce.

Tripes à la mode de Caen is a dish cooked, ideally, in quantities that are by today's standards gargantuan. Classic recipes begin with the tripes of one ox and go on to include all four of the brute's feet. The tripes alone would weigh between 15 and 25 pounds.

Old recipes also make much of the need to place substantial slabs of beef fat over the tripe and to seal the casserole with a layer of flour and water paste which will bake hard in the 10 hours required to transform the contents into a triumph of gastronomy. But scale the recipe for a large domestic casserole, use a couple of layers of kitchen foil to make sure the lid is really tight, and with a modern, thermostatically controlled oven, the fat and paste may safely be dispensed with.

A disadvantage of making a smaller quantity is that the amount of liquid needed is disproportionately large. Unless the cider is very dry, use no more than 1 litre (1¾ pints) and reduce the gravy by fast boiling at the end of the cooking time. Bleached tripe shrinks to about half its original size and weight when cooked in this way, so add double the amount specified in the recipe and cut it in larger than usual pieces.

Tripes à la Mode de Caen

SERVES 4

1 kg (2 lb 3 oz) raw, unbleached
   tripe
½ a cow heel
225 g (8 oz) onions, chopped
225 g (8 oz) carrots, sliced
salt and freshly ground black
   pepper
a handful of parsley, or parsley
   stalks
1 sprig of thyme
1 bay leaf
1 clove
1 litre (1¾ pints) good dry cider
4 tablespoons Calvados or brandy

Cut the tripe into 5 cm (2 in) squares and the cow heel into large pieces.

Line a heavy casserole with the onions and carrots and place the pieces of cow heel on top. Season with salt and pepper, then add the tripe. Tie the parsley, thyme, bay leaf and clove into a bouquet garni and bury it in the tripe. Add the cider and enough water to cover the tripe (the exact amount will depend on the shape of the casserole), and the Calvados or brandy.

Cover the casserole as tightly as possible using foil and the lid and cook in a preheated moderate oven (160°C/ 325°F, gas mark 3) for one hour. Reduce the temperature to very cool (120°C/250°F, gas mark ½) and continue cooking for another nine hours.

To serve the dish fish out the tripe and strain the stock, discarding the vegetables and any undissolved pieces of cow heel. Keep the tripe warm and reduce the stock by fast boiling to about 900 ml (1½ pints). Return the tripe to the gravy, bring it back to the boil and adjust the seasoning. Serve very hot, preferably in heated bowls.

Shadwell is the East End district of London where Louis Heren, ex-foreign correspondent and a former deputy editor of *The Times* grew up. This was his mother's recipe.

Tripes à la Mode de Shadwell

SERVES 4–5

2 pig's trotters
900 g (2 lb) cooked tripe
225 g (8 oz) tin of sauerkraut, drained
1 large onion, chopped
1 celery stalk, chopped
5 black peppercorns
2 cloves
1 clove garlic
1 sprig of thyme
1 bay leaf
salt and freshly ground black pepper
150 ml (¼ pint) dry white wine
4–8 tablespoons Calvados (optional)

Put the trotters in a saucepan with 2 litres (3½ pints) of water. Bring to the boil, skim, cover the pan and simmer gently for two hours. Bone the trotters, chop up the soft bits and reserve the stock.

Cut the tripe into 5 cm (2 in) squares.

Put the trotter pieces in the bottom of a heavy casserole and place the tripe on top. Add the sauerkraut, onion and celery. Tie the peppercorns, cloves, garlic, thyme and bay leaf into a bouquet garni and bury it in the casserole. Pour in sufficient reserved stock to cover the contents.

Bring the casserole to the boil on top of the stove, then seal it tightly with kitchen foil and the lid. Cook in a preheated cool oven (150°C/300°F, gas mark 2) for three hours. Just before serving, skim any fat from the gravy, adjust the seasoning to taste and stir in the wine and Calvados, if used. Reheat and serve very hot.

This is how my grandmother cooked tripe.

Tripe with Onions

SERVES 4–6

110 g (4 oz) smoked bacon, lean and fat, diced
900 g (2 lb) onions, sliced
55 g (2 oz) plain flour
1.2 litres (2 pints) milk
900 g (2 lb) cooked tripe
a handful of parsley, or parsley stalks
1 stick of celery, chopped
1 sprig of thyme
1 small piece of lemon zest
1 bay leaf
salt and freshly ground white or black pepper
grated nutmeg to taste
2 tablespoons chopped parsley

Put the bacon in a heavy pan and cook on a low heat until the fat begins to run. Add the onions, cover the pan and allow them to sweat until they are transparent. Stir in the flour and cook the mixture for a minute, stirring well. Gradually add the milk, bring slowly to the boil and stir until the sauce has thickened.

Cut the tripe in 5 cm (2 in) squares and add to the sauce. Tie the parsley, celery, thyme, lemon zest and bay leaf into a bouquet garni and add it to the tripe. Season to taste with salt, pepper and nutmeg. Cover the pan and simmer on a very low heat for about two hours.

Just before serving sprinkle the dish with the parsley and serve piping hot.

It was in *Le Gavroche*, the first British restaurant to win three rosettes in the *Guide Michelin*, that I tasted a dish of calf's kidney in a mustard sauce that was nothing short of exquisite. The pieces of kidney were rosy inside and perfectly tender. The sauce was smooth, shiny and plainly rich in wine, cream and softly flavoured French mustards. There was mystery too. Why did such lightly cooked kidney not bleed, even a little, into the sauce? This puzzle was solved on a subsequent visit when I was invited to watch the dish being prepared. This is how I now do it at home.

Calf's Kidney in Three-mustard Sauce

SERVES 2

1 calf's kidney
2 tablespoons rendered kidney suet
  or clarified butter (see page 227)
sea salt
55 g (2 oz) butter
2 tablespoons very finely chopped
  shallot
150 ml (¼ pint) dry white wine
150 ml (¼ pint) veal stock
150 ml (¼ pint) double cream
1 tablespoon Dijon mustard
2 teaspoons moutarde de Meaux
1 teaspoon tarragon mustard
freshly ground white pepper to taste
1 tablespoon finely chopped parsley
  and chives, mixed

Put the serving dish in a cool oven (140°C/275°F, gas mark 1).

Cut the kidney into bite-sized pieces and trim off any bits of suet and the white core. Heat the rendered suet or clarified butter in a sauté pan or heavy frying pan until it is smoking hot. Tip in the prepared kidney and a pinch of salt and fry quickly, stirring constantly, to cook the pieces on all sides. As soon as the kidney is sealed on the outside and still pink in the middle, tip the pieces and their cooking fat into a sieve and leave them to drain over a bowl while you make the sauce. A fair amount of blood will drain out too, but this does not mean the kidney is undercooked.

Still working on a high heat, add 15 g (½ oz) of the butter to the pan until it froths, then add the shallot. The heat should be fierce, but not so hot as to burn the butter which would give the sauce a toffee taste. Fry the shallot until it is transparent, but not coloured. Add the wine and boil the mixture vigorously until it has reduced to about four tablespoons. Add the stock and continue to boil until the liquid has again reduced to about four tablespoons. Now add the cream, allow the sauce to return to the boil and cook it, shaking or stirring, until it has reduced to about 150 ml (¼ pint).

Reduce the heat, and from now on do not allow the sauce to boil. Add the remaining butter and allow it to melt, stirring constantly to incorporate it smoothly and thicken the sauce. Stir in the mustards and season to taste with salt and the pepper.

Tip the drained kidney into the warmed serving dish and reheat in the oven for about one minute. Now add the kidney to the sauce and stir together for a minute or two, still making sure the sauce does not boil. Pour the mixture into the warmed dish and sprinkle with the herbs. Serve immediately with lightly buttered flat noodles or rice.

Brains, delicate in both taste and texture, are unjustly neglected. They are usually sold by the set rather than by weight, and a set of calf's brains will feed two as a first course, one as a substantial main dish. Smaller lambs' brains are similar in taste and texture. Treat either kind in the same simple manner.

Brains in Black Butter

SERVES 2–4

2 sets of calves' brains, or 4 lambs'
2 tablespoons wine vinegar
salt
110 g (4 oz) butter
freshly ground black pepper
1 tablespoon capers (optional)
1 tablespoon finely chopped parsley

Soak the brains in cold water for one hour, then drain them and pick off any chips of bone, blood vessels and loose membrane.

Put the brains in a pan and cover them with cold water. Add half the vinegar and a teaspoon of salt. Bring to the boil, cover the pan and poach the brains on a low heat for about 15 minutes, or until they are firm.

Drain the brains, and when they are cool enough to handle peel away the outer skin and any remaining visible blood vessels. Place the brains between two plates and allow them to cool under light pressure. Refrigerate them until needed.

Melt three-quarters of the butter in a frying pan and cook on a high heat until it is brown, not black despite the name. Pour the butter through a fine sieve into a small bowl. Wipe the pan and melt the remaining butter in it. Fry the brains, whole or cut in 1.25 cm (½ in) thick slices, until golden on all sides. Transfer the brains to a serving dish and keep warm.

Wipe the pan again and add the remaining tablespoon of vinegar and the browned butter. Stir well together on a low heat and season to taste with salt and freshly ground black pepper. Stir the capers, if used, and the parsley into the sauce and pour it immediately over the brains.

Serve with crusty bread as a first course, or with a crisp leafy salad or a crunchy vegetable like deep fried cour-gettes (see page 150) as a main dish.

There is little to choose between the flavours of calves' and lambs' sweetbreads. Larger calves' sweetbreads are better for frying in slices, but for serving in a creamy sauce, lambs' are just as good.

Sweetbreads in a Cream Sauce

SERVES 3–4

570 g (1¹/4 lb) sweetbreads
1 tablespoon lemon juice or wine
* vinegar*
600 ml (1 pint) creamy milk
1 onion, peeled and quartered
1 bay leaf
1 blade of mace
30 g (1 oz) butter
30 g (1 oz) plain flour
150 ml (¹/4 pint) dry white wine,
* reduced to 2 tablespoons by fast*
* boiling*
salt and freshly ground black
* pepper*
freshly grated nutmeg
1–2 tablespoons brandy (optional)

Put the sweetbreads in cold salted water with the lemon juice or vinegar and soak them for at least an hour. If they are frozen, soak them until they are completely thawed. Drain them and put them in a pan with the milk, onion, bay leaf and mace. Bring slowly to the boil, cover the pan and simmer very gently until they are just cooked – about five minutes for lambs' sweetbreads, 20 minutes for calves'. They are sufficiently cooked when they lose their pink blush and are firm to touch. Drain the sweetbreads. Strain and reserve the milk.

Put the sweetbreads in cold water until they are cool enough to handle, then pull away any membrane not required to hold them together. Lambs' sweetbreads are quite small, but calves' should be separated into bite-sized pieces for this dish.

Melt the butter in a pan and stir in the flour. Cook the *roux* on a low heat for a minute or two, then gradually add the reserved milk, stirring constantly, to make a smooth sauce. Stir in the wine and season to taste with salt, pepper and nutmeg. Add the sweetbreads to the sauce, and a tablespoon or two of brandy if you fancy. Cook for a minute or two more on a low heat and serve very hot with creamed potatoes, or, if you prefer a contrast of texture, in a puff pastry shell.

9

Poultry

Chickens, like boxers, are graded by size. And that, as far as many people are concerned, is all the choice there is. A spring chicken is technically speaking a three-month-old bird weighing around 1.25 kg (2½ lb). A poussin is younger and smaller, and Sunday lunch is likely to be a standard broiler tipping the scales at about 1.8 kg (4 lb).

The taste of factory-farmed poultry is invariably compared unfavourably with remembered farmyard birds, but a growing number of people are too young to know for sure. Now I come to think of it, what does a modern chicken look like before it is plucked? Surely not as pretty as a speckled *Scots dumpy* or as grand as Queen Victoria's *light brahmas*, or many more of the old poultry breeds which survive only through the efforts of the rare breeds societies.

Now that chicken is one of the cheapest meats and available all year round it is easy to forget that it was once an occasional treat. Free range chickens are the treat today. Since they are also more expensive they are almost certain to be advertised as such, and because they have matured more slowly, they should be tastier than battery birds.

The next best bet are fresh chickens hanging up in the butcher's or poulterer's shop. Hanging does improve the flavour of chicken and you can be pretty sure that any bird sold chilled in a polythene bag has not been hung.

Chilled fresh chickens will usually have a less pronounced flavour than birds which have been hung, but should be succulent and tender. Frozen chickens need careful, thorough thawing, preferably in the refrigerator, if they are to be worth eating.

The slightly resinous taste of pine nut kernels combined with thyme and rosemary flavour this easy dish. Spring chickens or poussin are so young and tender that they are easily split in halves. Place them breast up on a chopping board. Cut cleanly down one side of the breast bone. Then using poultry shears or hefty kitchen scissors snip the wishbone and cut through the bones of the back just to one side of the spine. If you prefer to use chicken pieces, wings with a good portion of breast meat are the best choice. Portions weighing about 225 g (8 oz) raw are the ideal size.

Poussin aux Pignons

SERVES 4

2 poussin weighing 450 g (1 lb), or
   more, each
55 g (2 oz) butter
1 clove garlic, crushed
1 teaspoon dried rosemary leaves
1/2 teaspoon dried thyme
salt and freshly ground black
   pepper
3 tablespoons pine nuts

Split each poussin as explained above.

Spread half the butter over the base of a shallow ovenproof dish big enough to hold the chicken pieces in one layer with a little space between them. Rub each portion on all sides with the garlic and spread the skin sides with the remaining butter. Sprinkle the dish with half the herbs and place the chicken pieces in it. Sprinkle them with the remaining herbs and season well with salt and pepper.

Bake the chicken in a preheated hot oven (220°C/425°F, gas mark 7) for 35–45 minutes depending on the size of the pieces. About 15 minutes before serving sprinkle the pine nuts over the chicken and baste the pieces with the pan juices.

Serve very hot with a dish of thinly sliced potatoes and a little onion baked in milk or stock, or with ribbon noodles.

Baby chickens weighing about 450 g (1 lb) each are too young to have a very pronounced flavour of their own. A carefully seasoned stuffing will improve their taste without overpowering it.

Stuffed Poussin

SERVES 4

4 fresh poussin, about 450 g (1 lb)
   each

For the stuffing:
225 g (8 oz) calves' sweetbreads
55 g (2 oz) butter
225 g (8 oz) minced veal
55 g (2 oz) onion, finely chopped
55 g (2 oz) open mushrooms, finely
   chopped
55 g (2 oz) fresh breadcrumbs
4 tablespoons finely chopped
   parsley

Soak the sweetbreads in several changes of cold water, then put them in a pan and cover with cold water. Bring slowly to the boil, then simmer for 10 minutes. Transfer the sweetbreads to a bowl of cold water. When they are cool enough to handle pull away the thin surface membranes and any tubes. Chop the sweetbreads finely.

Melt half the butter in a small frying pan until it foams, then add the veal. Fry the veal, without allowing it to brown very much, until it is almost cooked, then add it to the chopped sweetbreads. Add the onion to the pan and fry until it is tender, but not browned. Add the mushrooms and fry until they too have softened. Mix the meats, onion, mushrooms, breadcrumbs, parsley and egg

130

1 egg
salt and freshly ground black
 pepper

For the gravy:
3 tablespoons medium sherry or dry
 Madeira
1 teaspoon cornflour
salt and freshly ground black
 pepper

and season to taste with salt and pepper.

Stuff the birds with this mixture and truss them neatly. Spread the remaining butter on them and roast in a preheated moderate oven (180°C/350°F, gas mark 4) for one hour, or a little longer, basting them frequently with the butter and pan juices.

Remove the poussin from the roasting tin and keep them warm. Skim some of the fat from the pan juices and add 120 ml (4 fl oz) of water. Bring to the boil and scrape up the sticky bits from the tin. Add the sherry or Madeira and continue boiling until the liquid has reduced by half. Blend the cornflour with a little cold water, stir it into the gravy and continue cooking gently for two or three minutes. Season the gravy with salt and pepper to taste and strain through a fine sieve.

Arrange the poussin on warmed serving plates after removing the trussing strings. Top with a little of the gravy and serve the rest separately.

Devilled chicken was a popular Victorian dish made with leftover poultry.

SERVES 4

Devilled Chicken

4 or 8 chicken joints, cooked or
 partly cooked
110 g (4 oz) butter, softened
1 tablespoon dry mustard
2 tablespoons dry breadcrumbs
1 tablespoon Worcestershire sauce
1 tablespoon sweet chutney or
 spiced apple cheese (see page
 246)
salt and cayenne pepper

Line a grill pan with greased foil and arrange the chicken pieces in it.

Mix together all the remaining ingredients. Spread the devilled butter on the chicken pieces and grill under a medium heat so that the meat heats through thoroughly, or finishes cooking as the sauce browns. Baste the chicken from time to time as it grills.

Serve very hot with crusty bread or baked potatoes and a salad.

Stoved howtowdie is a very old Scottish recipe for pot roasting a chicken with a frugal oatmeal stuffing. Be sure to use oatmeal and not the rolled oats widely sold for making porridge outside its native land. In Victorian days the traditional garnish for *stoved howtowdie* was *drappit eggs*, spinach topped with poached eggs and grilled bacon.

Stoved Howtowdie

SERVES 4

55 g (2 oz) chicken fat or butter
1 small leek, finely sliced
170 g (6 oz) medium oatmeal
salt and freshly ground black
   pepper
1.35 kg (3 lb) roasting chicken
30 g (1 oz) butter
12 small onions, peeled
freshly grated nutmeg
thyme or lemon thyme
150 ml (¼ pint) stock or water

Melt the chicken fat or butter in a pan, add the leek and fry until it is soft, but not browned. Stir in the oatmeal and cook for a few minutes, stirring constantly, then season it generously with salt and pepper. Stuff the chicken with this mixture and truss it in the usual way.

Choose a pot or flameproof casserole which will hold the chicken without too much room to spare. Melt the butter in the pot, add the chicken and brown it on all sides. Add the onions and sprinkle the bird with a little of the nutmeg and thyme. Pour in the stock or water and bring to the boil. Reduce the heat to a simmer, cover the pot tightly and cook the chicken very slowly for 1½–2 hours.

When it is cooked, arrange the chicken on a warmed serving dish and arrange the onions round it. Reduce the gravy by fast boiling, check the seasoning and serve it with the chicken.

Anyone who has not tasted chicken cooked with forty cloves of garlic understandably finds it difficult to believe that the dish is not poisonously strongly flavoured with the stuff. But provided it is made with plump fresh garlic and not acrid cloves which have been stored too long, the result is especially tasty and not at all pungent.

Chicken with Forty Cloves of Garlic

SERVES 4

1 chicken weighing 1.35–1.6 kg
   (3–3½ lb), and its liver
1 bay leaf
1 sprig of parsley
salt and freshly ground black
   pepper
2 tablespoons olive oil
30 g (1 oz) butter
40 plump cloves garlic, peeled
4 thick slices white bread, crusts
   removed

Wipe the chicken inside and out and reserve the liver. Put the bay leaf and parsley in the chicken and season the interior with salt and pepper before trussing it.

Heat the oil and butter in a heavy flameproof casserole large enough to hold the chicken without too much room to spare. Add the chicken and brown it lightly on all sides, making sure that the butter does not burn. Add all the garlic cloves and a generous seasoning of salt and pepper. Cover the casserole tightly and cook in a preheated cool oven (140°C/275°F, gas mark 1) for about two hours, or until the chicken is tender and its flesh is almost falling from the bones.

Transfer the chicken to a serving dish and keep it warm while you prepare the garnish.

Skim two tablespoons of fat from the casserole and heat it in a small saucepan. Roughly chop the reserved chicken liver and sauté it in the fat until just firm.

Take the cooked garlic from the casserole and mash it with the liver, pressing it through a wire sieve to make a smooth purée.

Divide each slice of bread into two triangles. Toast the bread lightly or fry it in a mixture of olive oil and butter until golden brown. Divide the garlic and liver purée between the triangles of toast and arrange them round the chicken. Serve very hot with plainly baked or mashed potatoes, or with ribbon noodles. The skimmed pan juices may be served separately as a rich gravy.

The crisp skin of a well-roasted duck is so delicate that why anyone should think it embellished by a sweetish orange or cherry sauce is beyond me. A sharp sauce made with bitter oranges or sour cherries is, of course, another matter and excellent served with, as opposed to on the duck.

The idea of boiling a duck lacks immediate appeal, though Chinese cooks, who know more than most about duck, crisp and otherwise, dry salt and boil the birds for serving cold. A similar technique is attributed to Wales where boiled salted duck may be served hot, traditionally with an onion sauce, or cold with salad. Cold is very good indeed. Leaving the duck to cool in the stock ensures that the flesh is succulent. The skin, predictably in this case, is not the best part and can be discarded.

Salt Duck

SERVES 4

1 duck weighing 1.8–2.3 kg (4–5 lb)
110 g (4 oz) sea salt

Remove the giblets and dry the duck. (Fry the liver in butter and serve it on toast as a snack or starter, and use the giblets for stock.)

Place the duck in a deep dish and rub it all over, inside and out, with the salt. Cover the dish and stand it in a cool place, or refrigerator, for three days, turning the duck every 12 hours.

Rinse the duck in cold water and place it in a heavy pot or flameproof casserole. Cover it with boiling water, bring to the boil and skim, then simmer very gently for about two hours, or until the duck is plump and tender. Skim off the fat and leave the bird to cool in its stock.

Skin and carve the duck and serve it with a salad of orange segments and watercress sprigs, with fresh ripe figs, or with slivers of melon sprinkled with lemon juice. If you cannot resist potatoes, fry chunks of boiled potato in the duck fat skimmed off earlier. The salty stock may be used like bacon stock, for a pea or lentil soup.

Casseroled duck with olives is the ideal dish to make with the pieces left over from the recipe which follows it. If it is being made in advance for reheating, the olives are best added at the reheating stage.

Duck with Olives

SERVES 4

2 tablespoons olive oil
4 duck legs, or 1 duck cut in four
　pieces
1 clove garlic, peeled
salt and freshly ground black
　pepper
1 tablespoon plain flour
150 ml (¼ pint) duck or chicken
　stock
150 ml (¼ pint) dry white wine
bouquet garni of parsley, lemon
　thyme and a bay leaf
20 small green olives, stoned

Heat the oil in a heavy, flameproof casserole. Prick the fatty areas of the duck, piercing the flesh underneath a little as possible. Rub the duck with the cut garlic and season it with salt and pepper. Add the duck to the hot oil and brown it on all sides, sealing the flesh on a high heat, then reducing it quickly and allowing the duck to brown slowly so that its own fat melts and runs out.

Remove the duck with a slotted spoon and keep warm. Skim all but two tablespoons of fat from the casserole and stir in the flour. Gradually add the stock, stirring constantly, to make a smooth sauce. Stir in the wine and adjust the seasoning.

Return the duck to the casserole, add the bouquet garni, cover the casserole and cook on a low heat for about 1½ hours, or until the duck is tender.

While the duck is cooking, pour boiling water over the olives and leave them to stand. When the duck is ready, drain the olives and add them to the casserole. Serve immediately with creamed potatoes or a mixture of creamed potato and swede.

The ducks fattened in France for their livers have particularly meaty breasts which are fried and served rosy, like steaks, sometimes with a sauce of green peppercorns and cream, or with apple fried in butter. Good apples for this purpose are sharp Bramley Seedlings or the sweeter Cox's Orange Pippin. The breast meat of ordinary domestic ducks, though smaller, may be treated the same way.

Use the legs and carcasses for a casseroled dish which can be frozen, or at least refrigerated for a day or two. Alternatively, use the meat and liver in a terrine.

The duck's skin adheres closely to the flesh, so cut off the legs and wings at the joints and remove the skin from the breast meat before cutting the flesh carefully away in one piece from each side.

Duck Breast with Fried Apple

SERVES 4

55 g (2 oz) butter
4 Bramley Seedlings, or large
　Cox's Orange Pippin apples,
　cored and sliced

Melt half the butter in a heavy frying pan or sauté dish, add the apples and sauté gently, turning the slices once, until they are tender and just beginning to turn gold. Lift the apples from the pan with a slotted spoon and arrange

4 duck breasts, skin removed
salt and freshly ground black
* pepper*

them on a serving dish. Keep warm in a low oven.

Add the remaining butter to the pan and increase the heat. Season each duck breast with salt and pepper and fry quickly on each side to seal the meat. Reduce the heat and continue cooking until the meat is cooked. It should still be a little pink in the middle. Carve the duck diagonally in fairly thick slices. Arrange the meat on the bed of apples and serve immediately.

This dish really needs no more accompaniment than a sprig of watercress; but if you feel that the plates will look too bare, serve a lightly cooked green vegetable or creamed potatoes.

Like duck, goose is a bony, fatty bird, only more so and bigger. It has the same advantage, that the meat is self-basting and unlikely to be dry, and because goose is a larger bird it is easier to roast out the fat leaving the flesh moist and the skin crisp and glossy brown.

I have cooked fresh geese and also carefully thawed frozen geese and would be lucky to tell the difference. So now I would not hesitate to buy a frozen bird when that is a convenient course.

When choosing a goose allow at least 450 g (1 lb) cleaned weight per person. A 3–3.5 kg (7–8 lb) bird serves six without a great deal to spare, and cold goose eats so well that there is no risk of unwanted leftovers in ordering a larger one.

On the other side of the Channel and deep into eastern Europe, roast goose is still the traditional centrepiece of the Christmas meal in many places. In Denmark it often has an apple and prune stuffing, in northern France a stuffing of apples and black pudding, in Czechoslovakia sauerkraut, and in Poland and Ireland potato and onion. In Britain, where goose was all the rage until turkeys cornered the Christmas market on price grounds (they could never touch goose for flavour) sage and onion usually flavours the stuffing.

Having tried them all over the years, my favourite stuffing is the simplest possible mixture of mashed potato with onion and celery. The result is a blending of robust, homely tastes which is completely satisfying. Make a good gravy and serve the stuffing as a vegetable. Offer something sweet with goose – redcurrant jelly, apple sauce or a small baked apple – and a salad or green vegetable.

SERVES 6–8

Roast Goose with Potato Stuffing

1 goose weighing 4–5 kg (9–11 lb)
2.3 kg (5 lb) potatoes
30 g (1 oz) butter
450 g (1 lb) onions, finely chopped
4 sticks of celery, finely chopped
salt and freshly ground black
* pepper*

Remove the giblets from the goose and use them to make stock for the gravy. Pull away any large lumps of fat inside the goose and reserve them to render for dripping. Cut off the wing tips and the next section of the wing and add these to the stockpot.

Peel and boil the potatoes until tender, then drain and dry them well. Mash them thoroughly. Melt the butter in a small pan and add the onions. Cover the pan and allow the onions to sweat on a low heat until they are tender. Mix the onions, potatoes, celery and a generous seasoning of salt and pepper.

Stuff the goose with this mixture, remembering that the bird will shrink in the oven so should not be filled too full. Truss it neatly and prick the skin lightly with a fork or skewer on the legs, back and lower breast.

Set the goose on a rack in a roasting tin. Roast in a preheated moderately hot oven (200°C/400°F, gas mark 6) for 15 minutes. Turn the bird over onto its breast, reduce the temperature to moderate (160°C/325°F, gas mark 3) and roast for two hours. Turn it onto its back again for the final two hours of cooking time (total roasting time about 4¼ hours). The goose is cooked when the juices run pale gold. Test with a skewer inserted into the leg close to the body. Rest the goose in a warm place for 10–15 minutes before carving it.

The following recipe is in the continental tradition, combining sharp cooking apples with raisins for sweetness and chopped nuts for texture. It is a mixture which complements the rich texture and flavour of goose.

SERVES 6–8

Goose with Fruit and Nut Stuffing

1 goose, 3.5–4.5 kg (8–10 lb)
  trussed weight

For the stuffing:
140 g (5 oz) seedless raisins
45 g (1½ oz) butter
1 goose liver, roughly chopped
1 large onion, finely chopped
110 g (4 oz) fresh white
  breadcrumbs
3 medium cooking apples, peeled
  and chopped
55 g (2 oz) blanched almonds,
  coarsely chopped
3 tablespoons chopped parsley
1 teaspoon dried marjoram or
  oregano
salt and freshly ground black
  pepper

Pull out any lumps of fat still inside the goose and dry it well inside and out.

Put the raisins in a bowl and cover them with boiling water. Set them aside to plump up.

Melt the butter in a pan, add the liver and fry until it is just firm. Take the liver from the pan and set it aside to cool. Fry the onion in the remaining butter until it is soft, but not brown.

Chop the liver finely and put it in a large bowl with the onion and butter. Add the breadcrumbs, apples, almonds, drained raisins and herbs and season generously with salt and pepper. Mix these ingredients well and check the seasoning.

Stuff the goose loosely with this mixture. Truss it neatly and prick the flesh on the legs, sides and lower breast before roasting. Place the goose, breast side up, on a rack in a shallow roasting tin and roast in a preheated moderately hot oven (200°C/400°F, gas mark 6) for 15 minutes. Turn the bird onto its breast, reduce the temperature to moderate (160°C/325°F, gas mark 3) and cook for two hours. Turn the goose breast side up again and roast for another 2–2½ hours at the same oven temperature. Basting is unnecessary, but save the goose fat dripping for other dishes.

Your goose is cooked when the juices run a pale golden colour. Test with a skewer inserted into the leg close to the body. Rest the goose in the oven with the door open and the heat turned off for about 15 minutes before carving it.

To make thin gravy, skim the fat from the juices left in the roasting tin. Pour into the tin about 300 ml (½ pint) of stock made by boiling the goose giblets with an onion, a carrot, a bay leaf and a few black peppercorns – or stock or water mixed half and half with red or white wine. Stir the mixture with a wooden spatula or spoon, scraping up the crusty bits. Strain the resulting gravy base into a small saucepan and taste it. If the flavour is weak, reduce the liquid by fast boiling. Now season to taste with salt and freshly ground black pepper.

To make thick gravy, first make thin gravy and remove it from the heat. Make a *beurre manié* by blending 1½ tablespoons of plain flour with a tablespoon of softened butter. Stir small lumps of the paste into the hot gravy, return it to the heat and cook very gently until the gravy is thick and smooth.

There is no denying the economic sense of turkeys when there are many mouths to feed. The amount of meat on the birds, even the pocket-sized ones, is quite surprising. In fact, when one meets the oven-ready variety it is a puzzle to work out where the centre of gravity was in life and how they got about without tipping onto their beaks.

A perfectly roasted turkey is rare, and the larger the bird the more difficult this seems to achieve. The legs always need more cooking than the delicate white breast meat which dries out so quickly if overdone. Slow roasting, frequent basting, and covering the turkey with muslin for most of its time in the oven really does keep the white meat succulent.

Turkeys should be properly hung to develop their full flavour – a process sometimes skimped with frozen birds. This is one of the reasons that fresh turkeys so often taste better than frozen ones. The way to get the best from a frozen bird is to thaw slowly and carefully in the refrigerator – at least 48 hours for a large bird, 24 for a small one.

The simplest special occasion recipe for turkey that I know has no stuffing. Constant basting with honey and butter make it crisp and dark chestnut coloured on the outside, while underneath the flesh is very moist and white. The method, still used in the north of England, was brought to Britain by the Romans who cooked flamingoes, herons and other large birds in this way.

Honey Basted Turkey

SERVES 10–12

1 turkey, 4.5–5.4 kg (10–12 lb)
   trussed weight
salt and pepper
225 g (8 oz) runny honey
110 g (4 oz) butter

Dry the turkey inside and out and cut off the wing tips for the stockpot. Season the inside with salt and pepper. Sew or skewer the large cavity firmly to prevent juices escaping, then tie the legs together with string and tie the string round the parson's nose. Pull the neck skin gently down under the back and fasten it with metal skewers or wooden cocktail sticks. Set the turkey on a rack in a shallow roasting tin.

Melt together the honey and butter and paint it all over the bird several times until it is well coated.

Roast in the middle of a preheated hot oven (220°C/425°F, gas mark 7) for 30 minutes only, basting once. Reduce the temperature to moderate (160°C/325°F, gas mark 3) and continue roasting for about 3½ hours more, basting the bird at 30-minute intervals. If the turkey was put in the oven straight from the refrigerator it will take at least an extra 30 minutes to cook. To test whether the bird is cooked, insert a skewer into the thickest part of the leg near the body. It is ready when the juices run clear.

Rest the turkey in the oven with the door open and the heat turned off for about 15 minutes before carving it.

A good stuffing gives a lift to the taste of roast turkey as well as helping to keep it moist. When calculating the roasting time, remember that this is based on the stuffed weight of the bird at room temperature. Add extra time if the turkey has come straight from the fridge.

SERVES 10–14

Roast Turkey with Christmas Stuffing

1 fresh turkey, 3.4–4.5 kg
(8–10 lb) dressed weight

For the stuffing:
1 turkey liver
85 g (3 oz) shallots or onions,
  finely chopped
225 g (8 oz) minced pork, lean and
  fat
225 g (8 oz) minced veal
85 g (3 oz) ham, preferably Parma
  type, finely chopped
170 g (6 oz) dried fruit, peaches,
  prunes and apple, roughly
  chopped
340 g (12 oz) chestnuts, cooked
  and roughly chopped
3 tablespoons olive oil
85 g (3 oz) fresh brown or white
  breadcrumbs
85 g (3 oz) celery, finely chopped
2 tablespoons freshly grated
  Parmesan cheese

Roughly chop the turkey liver and put it in a bowl with the shallots or onions, minced pork and veal, ham, dried fruit and chestnuts. Mix lightly and thoroughly together.

Heat the oil in a large frying pan, add the stuffing mixture and sauté it gently for about 10 minutes. Remove from the heat and stir in the breadcrumbs, celery, cheese and sherry. Add the thyme and marjoram and season to taste with the nutmeg, salt and pepper. Leave until cold.

Stuff the turkey with this mixture, dividing it between the main cavity and the breast flap, and truss the bird securely. Set the turkey on a rack in a shallow roasting tin. Cut a double thickness of muslin large enough to cover the turkey and wring it out in water. Then dip it in the melted butter and drape it over the bird. Roast in a preheated moderate oven (160°C/325°F, gas mark 3) for 3¾–4½ hours, basting the turkey every 30 minutes with the remaining melted butter and the wine. Remove the muslin for the last 30 minutes of cooking time. To test whether the turkey is fully cooked, insert a skewer into the thickest part of the leg near the body. If the juices run clear it is ready.

When the turkey is ready, transfer it to a serving dish. Rest it in the oven with the door slightly ajar and the heat

138

3 tablespoons dry sherry
1 scant teaspoon dried thyme
1 scant teaspoon dried marjoram
freshly grated nutmeg
salt and freshly ground black
  pepper

To baste:
85 g (3 oz) butter, melted
6 tablespoons dry white wine

turned off for about 20 minutes before carving.

Skim the fat from the juices in the roasting tin and add giblet stock to make the accompanying gravy.

With such a richly stuffed turkey there is no need to serve bacon-wrapped chipolatas and bread sauce unless there would be family uproar at their absence. Roast potatoes, crisp and golden are too good to miss out, but a purée of leeks (see page 155) makes a change from sprouts.

10

Fair Game

There is no doubt about it that practice makes perfect when it comes to dinner parties. Well, if not perfect, then at least relaxed, and as much fun for the cook as for the guests.

I have my misgivings, like everyone else, when the main dish is a recipe I have not tried before, and wish at the last moment I had stuck to something I can cook with my eyes shut. But of course there is no dish quite as ideal as that. No amount of preparation and cooking in advance, and no amount of planning lets anyone off taking pains on the night.

The art, and it is one, is to keep the workload down to pleasurably manageable proportions. Aplomb is an invaluable ingredient. If the welcome is warm, the drinks generous, the company good, and the food hot or whatever it should be, who needs culinary fireworks?

When I particularly want to enjoy my guests I keep it simple. In winter this usually means roast game which can be popped into the oven when people arrive. Between dashing home from work, preparing fresh vegetables or salad, laying the table and having a bath, there is not much time for spud bashing.

Eating game, not shooting it, is my bag. Not that I disapprove in the least of popping off at birds or beasts. It is as good an excuse as any other for long walks in the fresh air. But the great advantage that the shooters have – those interested in eating their prey – is knowing when it was shot, how long it has hung, and whether it is young, old, or middling. For those of us who generally encounter the oven-ready bird, these are matters of trust. Weighty matters too, given the cost per pound of such seasonal and sought-after delicacies.

Pheasants are the most economical of the game birds as well as being the most widely available. Even a small hen pheasant will feed two people well, and a cock is enough for three, perhaps four. It is becoming quite difficult to buy birds which have been hung long enough to develop their flavour fully, so if you want them at all 'high' it will be necessary to order them well in advance.

Roast Pheasant

SERVES 4

110 g (4 oz) butter
2 shallots or 1 small onion, finely chopped
2 small eating apples, peeled and diced
salt and freshly ground black pepper
2 young pheasants, about 680 g (1½ lb) each dressed weight
2 thin slices of pork back fat
1 bunch of watercress

For the gravy:
150 ml (¼ pint) good game or chicken stock (see page 233)
2 tablespoons rowan, bitter orange or redcurrant jelly (see pages 245 and 242)
salt and freshly ground black pepper

Melt half the butter in a small saucepan, add the shallot or onion and cook it on a low heat until it is soft, but not browned. Add the apples and cook for a moment longer, then season with salt and pepper.

Stuff the pheasants with the apple and onion mixture. Place a slice of the pork fat on the breast of each bird and truss them neatly with string. Spread the remaining butter on the birds and put them in a shallow roasting tin. Roast in a preheated moderately hot oven (200°C/400°F, gas mark 6) for about 50 minutes, or until the pheasants are tender, basting them once or twice during cooking. Remove the pork fat for the final 10 minutes of the cooking time.

Remove the trussing string and put the pheasants on a serving dish. Rest them in the oven with the door slightly open and the heat turned off.

To make the gravy, skim the fat from the roasting tin and add the stock. Heat the mixture on top of the stove, scraping up the pan juices with a wooden spoon. Stir in the rowan, bitter orange or redcurrant jelly until it has melted, then season the gravy to taste with salt and pepper. Strain and serve in a warmed jug.

Remove the pheasants from the oven and garnish the dish with sprigs of crisp, peppery watercress. Serve immediately.

Pheasant with Cream and Apples

SERVES 4

2 young pheasants trussed with fat bacon for roasting
85 g (3 oz) butter
salt and freshly ground black pepper
2 shallots, peeled
450 g (1 lb) Cox's Orange Pippin apples
6 tablespoons game stock or water
4 tablespoons Calvados or cognac
150 ml (¼ pint) double cream

Put a small knob of butter, salt and pepper and a shallot inside each pheasant and place them in a roasting tin. Roast in a preheated very hot oven (220°C/425°F, gas mark 7) for about 45 minutes, or until cooked. The exact time will depend on the size of the birds and on whether you like them a little pink, or well done. Tip the juices from inside the birds into the roasting tin and set it aside. Rest the birds in a warm place until you are ready to carve them.

While the pheasants are resting, peel, core and thickly slice the apples. Melt the remaining butter in a frying pan,

141

add the apples and sauté until they are tender and beginning to brown a little, but still holding their shape. Transfer them to a serving dish, spread them evenly over the base and keep warm.

Carve the pheasants, taking thick slices from the breasts and severing the legs neatly. Arrange the meat on the fried apples, cover the dish and keep warm. Use the carcasses and barding bacon for stock or discard them.

Skim the fat from the juices in the roasting tin and stir in the stock or water. Cook on a high heat, scraping up the crusty bits, until the liquid has reduced by half. Add the Calvados or cognac and reduce again. Add the cream and reduce the sauce, stirring constantly, until it has thickened slightly. Strain the sauce over the pheasant and apples and serve immediately. Serve with a few sprigs of peppery watercress and new or small main-crop potatoes peeled after cooking in their skins.

With young grouse which are sure to be plump and tender, fast roasting in a hot oven (220°C/425°F, gas mark 7) is by far the best method of cooking them. Old birds need long, slow cooking, and this is a safer method too of dealing with any of uncertain age and tenderness.

Grouse with Chestnuts

SERVES 2–4 .

450 g (1 lb) fresh chestnuts
30 g (1 oz) butter
3 tablespoons peanut oil
110 g (4 oz) fat bacon, diced
110 g (4 oz) shallots or onion, finely chopped
2 grouse, trussed with fat bacon
2 tablespoons cognac
150 ml (1/4 pint) game or chicken stock
150 ml (1/4 pint) red wine
bouquet garni of parsley, celery, bay leaf and a sprig of thyme
salt and freshly ground black pepper

Using a sharp knife, slit the shiny brown skin of each chestnut on the domed surface. Place them in a single layer, flat side down, on a roasting tray. Pour in 300 ml (1/2 pint) of water and roast them in a preheated moderately hot oven (200°C/400°F, gas mark 6) for about 10 minutes. Peel the chestnuts as soon as they are cool enough to handle and set them aside.

Heat the butter and oil in a heavy flameproof casserole, add the bacon and sauté until it is crisp and golden. Remove the bacon, add the shallots or onion and cook until soft, but not browned. Remove the shallots, add the grouse and brown them quickly on all sides. Drain off all but a tablespoon of the fat, return the bacon to the casserole and sprinkle with the cognac. Light the cognac and, when the flames die down, return the shallots to the casserole and add the stock, wine, bouquet garni, salt and pepper. Cover the casserole and simmer on a low heat until the birds are tender. Add the chestnuts and continue cooking until they too are tender.

To serve, lift out the grouse and remove the trussing strings and barding bacon. Cut off the legs and carve the breast meat in one section for each side. Return the meat to the casserole and heat it through again, before serving with baked or fluffy mashed potatoes.

There are two schools of thought about partridge with lentils, most recipes insisting that the lentils should be puréed. As the lentils called for in this dish are the brown ones that still have their skins on, I think it is a pity to obliterate their texture. Visually too, texture is important, and they certainly look better whole.

Partridge with Lentils

340 g (12 oz) brown lentils
2 partridges, dressed and trussed
salt and freshly ground black
  pepper
30 g (1 oz) butter
2 tablespoons olive oil
110 g (4 oz) unsmoked fat streaky
  bacon or belly of pork, preferably
  in one piece
1 medium onion, chopped
150 ml (¼ pint) dry white wine
150 ml (¼ pint) chicken or game
  stock
1 peeled onion stuck with 3 cloves
3 cloves garlic, peeled
bouquet garni of parsley, thyme,
  celery and bay leaf

At least 12 hours before serving the dish, cover the lentils with cold water and leave them to soak.

If the partridges have been trussed with fat or bacon, remove it. Wipe the birds and season them inside and out with salt and pepper. Truss them again, if necessary.

Take a heavy pan which has a tightly fitting lid and is large enough to hold the birds side by side without too much room to spare. Heat the butter and oil in the pan. Dice the bacon or pork, add it to the pan and cook on a low heat until the fat begins to run. Increase the heat, add the partridges and brown them on all sides. Take them out and keep warm while you fry the onion until it is transparent and just beginning to brown.

Return the partridges to the pan, add the wine and simmer until it has reduced by half. Add the stock, cover the pan and simmer for 45 minutes to one hour, depending on the size and age of the birds.

Cook the lentils as soon as the partridges are simmering with the lid on. Drain the lentils and wash them in cold running water. Put them in a pan with the remaining ingredients and add cold water to a depth of 2.5 cm (1 in) above the lentils. Bring to the boil, cover and cook on a low heat until the lentils are tender, but not disintegrating. If they are ready before the partridges, drain and keep warm in the serving dish, discarding the onion, garlic and bouquet garni.

When the partridges are tender, lift them onto a chopping board and cut them in halves. Arrange the birds on top of the lentils in a serving dish. Skim some of the fat from the juices remaining in the pan and pour the liquid over the dish. Serve very hot.

Roe deer in the form of best venison is another of those home-grown delicacies which are becoming hard to find in British shops because the French are prepared to pay higher prices for the pleasure of eating them. Superior flavour is the claim you will hear most often for this smallest of the common native species. Fallow deer, the Bambi-spotted inhabitants of parks, are the type most readily available as venison, and larger red deer are now being farmed.

In so far as fashion affects a foodstuff as traditional as venison, the trends are predictable. Small joints of meat are preferred to very large ones, and the meat is sold fresher. Well-hung venison is becoming difficult to obtain.

A haunch of venison makes a rich and festive roast. Lard it all over hedgehog fashion with strips of pork fat for succulent meat and a merry-England appearance. For tenderness roast it pink like beef.

Order or choose a haunch which is the right size for your meal, allowing a minimum of 225 g (8 oz) raw weight, including bone, per person. Also buy raw pork back fat for the lardons. It is worth insisting on back fat because belly fat is softer and breaks up too easily. Ask the game dealer to cut out the pelvic bone as this will make the leg easier to carve. And if you have a *manche à gigot*, the carving accessory which screws onto the bone of a trimmed shank to hold it securely, then ask him to trim the shank too.

Venison is so lean and close-textured that larding really is advisable if the meat is to be succulent. Use a larding needle (the kind with jagged hinged jaws at the blunt end is easiest) and thin strips of pork fat 5 mm (barely ¼ in) thick. Then with the rounded side of the haunch upwards, and starting at the end furthest from the shank, make a shallow stitch about 2.5 cm (1 in) long, along the grain of the meat. Each stitch is a shallow U-shaped loop, trimmed neatly a little above the surface. Insert rows of these stitches at 1.25 cm (½ in) intervals over the surface of the haunch.

Roast Haunch of Venison

SERVES 10–12

4.5 kg (10 lb) haunch of venison
pork back fat for lardons
4 tablespoons good olive oil
300 ml (½ pint) white wine
freshly ground black pepper
1 teaspoon dried thyme
salt

Lard the meat as detailed above, then rub it all over with about half the olive oil. Set the meat in a large dish and pour on the wine. Sprinkle with the pepper and thyme. Cover the meat and leave it in a cool place to marinate, turning it occasionally, for up to 24 hours.

Salt the meat and place it, rounded side up, on a rack in a roasting tin. Roast in a preheated hot oven (220°C/425°F, gas mark 7) for 15 minutes to seal. Reduce the temperature to moderate (180°C/350°F, gas mark 4) and continue roasting for a further 1½ hours, basting with the marinade for the second half of the cooking time. To calculate the cooking time for a joint of a different size, allow 10 minutes for each 450 g (1 lb) in total, that is including the 15 minutes at the higher temperature. Cooked for this length of time the meat will be rare and very tender. Add five minutes more per 450 g (1 lb) for medium to well done meat. Rest the haunch for 10 minutes before carving.

Deglaze the roasting pan with white wine or stock to make a simple gravy, or add redcurrant jelly and cream to the pan juices for a richer sauce.

A rich gratin of potatoes or a mixture of other root vegetables goes well with venison, as do chestnuts and various fruits. Small baked apples filled with redcurrant jelly just before serving taste as good as they look if you use small Cox's Orange Pippins.

Picturesque, even gruesome terminology governed the art of carving in medieval England. For each bird or beast there was a correct procedure to be observed by the carver in a noble household. His harsh duties were to display that crane, dismember that heron, unbrace that mallard, wing that partridge, disfigure that peacock and so on. By contrast, the term for dealing with the humble rabbit sounds relatively gentle. He had only to unlace that coney.

Rabbits are believed to have been brought to Britain by the Romans, who reared them in hare gardens called *leporaria*. By Henry VIII's time, wild rabbits were such popular game with the poor that they required protection, and close seasons for their sale were proclaimed in 1529 and 1551.

Thus encouraged the rabbits lived to breed another day and early cookery books are full of ingenious ways of preparing them for table. None is more so than Richard Bradley's ruse to make a pheasant of a rabbit. In his *Lady's Director* of 1732 Professor Bradley, the Cambridge botanist, explains how it is 'trussed in such a manner that it will appear like a pheasant, and eat like one, with its sauce. This is called by the topping poulterers, a Poland-Chicken, or a Portugal-Chicken. But it is most like a pheasant, if it is larded.'

Country cooks have always, often from necessity no doubt, made much of rabbit. Queen Victoria's chef, Charles Elmé Francatelli, can be found commending rabbit to townsfolk. In his *A Plain Cookery For The Working Classes*, we have the royal chef explaining how to make a rabbit pudding.

The rabbits on sale in towns today are usually bred in captivity. They may lack the flavour of rabbits which have nibbled thyme in the wild, but are likely to be young, plump and tender.

Rabbit Braised in Cider

SERVES 6

55 g (2 oz) butter
110 g (4 oz) fat streaky bacon, diced
450 g (1 lb) button onions, peeled
55 g (2 oz) plain flour
salt and freshly ground black pepper
2 teaspoons dry mustard powder
2 plump rabbits, jointed
2 large cloves garlic, finely chopped
600 ml (1 pint) very dry cider
bouquet garni of parsley, thyme and bay leaf
225 g (8 oz) button mushrooms

Melt half the butter in a heavy, flameproof casserole, add the bacon and fry it gently until lightly browned. Remove it with a slotted spoon and set aside. Add the onions to the casserole and brown them on all sides. Set them aside with the bacon.

Mix together the flour, salt, pepper and mustard in a paper or plastic bag. Put the rabbit pieces in the bag and shake them until they are well-coated with seasoned flour. Add the rabbit pieces to the casserole and brown them quickly on all sides. Add the garlic when the rabbit is nearly browned.

Return the bacon and onions to the casserole and add the cider, bouquet garni and salt and pepper to taste. Bring to the boil on top of the stove, then cover the casserole closely and transfer it to a preheated cool oven (140°C/275°F, gas mark 1) and cook for 1½–3 hours, depending on the tenderness of the rabbit.

When the rabbit is almost tender, sauté the mushrooms in the remaining butter and add them to the casserole. Cook for another 10 minutes before serving with new or creamed potatoes. A fresh herb dressing made by mixing together six tablespoons of finely chopped parsley and two teaspoons of finely grated orange zest makes an interesting addition to this dish. Sprinkle it on the meat after serving.

145

Wild quail are not fair game in this country. The birds sitting in demure rows on the game dealer's slab will be farmed, though whether they should be classed as tame game or exotic poultry is just the kind of subject which, in a well ordered world, is saved for discussion over a glass of good sherry.

Quail are too small to carve. You deal them, like cards, at least two apiece. This has a special appeal for timid or lazy cooks and those inclined to gaze too long upon the decanters. 'You mean they make a great three-martini-dinner' said a sharp American friend. I do.

Farmed quail are not usually hung and their flavour, although as delicate as their appearance, is at the same time distinctively gamey. The birds I buy are fresh, plucked, cleaned and ready to cook. The heart and liver, which are usually left inside, are best removed if the recipe involves splitting and flattening the quail. Grilling, roasting, sautéing and barbecuing are all suitable treatments for quail. They are so small that they take only minutes to cook so need never be spoiled when guests are late.

One of the most attractive ways of serving quail, and it tastes as good as it looks, is to flatten them and push a spoonful of moist stuffing under the skin which covers the breast. Opened out and stuffed like this the quail lose their pathetically sparrow-like appearance.

Stuffed Roast Quail

SERVES 4

8 plump quail
30 g (1 oz) butter
1 small onion, finely chopped
55 g (2 oz) open mushrooms, finely chopped
30 g (1 oz) fresh white breadcrumbs
55 g (2 oz) Parma ham, finely diced
2 tablespoons finely chopped parsley
1/2 teaspoon finely chopped fresh tarragon, or a pinch of dried tarragon
salt and freshly ground black pepper
2 tablespoons double cream

Using poultry shears or kitchen scissors, cut each quail along its spine from neck to tail. Pull away the heart and liver if they are still inside. Place the quail, breast upwards, on a wooden board and press with the ball of the hand to flatten it a little. Carefully loosen the skin over the breast to make a pocket for the stuffing. Lastly make a small slit in the skin at the end of the breast furthest from the neck and tuck the ends of the legs through this hole. As the birds have been flattened the bones of the legs should cross neatly and stay in place. Prepare the remaining quail in the same way.

To prepare the stuffing, melt the butter in a small pan, add the onion and cook until tender, but not browned. Add the mushrooms and stir on a low heat until they release their juices, then increase the heat and cook the mixture until it is almost dry. Add the onion and mushrooms to the breadcrumbs, ham, parsley and tarragon. Season to taste with salt and pepper and stir in the cream. Mix well to blend and use this mixture to stuff the quail.

Set the birds well apart on a buttered baking tray, tucking the skin of the neck flaps under them. Brush them with melted butter and roast in a preheated moderately hot oven (200°C/400°F, gas mark 6) for 15–20 minutes, basting once or twice during cooking.

Almost any fresh vegetable could be served with the quail but they do look pleasingly theatrical arranged round the perimeter of a bubbling dish of dauphinoise potatoes.

146

11

Vegetables

A disposable shrink-wrapped box held the most perfect *mange tout* peas I have seen. They were like babies' toes, immaculate and miniature. March had just blown into Britain and the label showed that the infant green pods had flown all the way from Guatemala. They were not dear, and they tasted pretty good too, but it did seem odd that it could be worth someone's while to grow, harvest and package sugar peas, then fly them halfway round the world to sell for the price of a few lemons.

Of course Guatemalan *mange tout* are no stranger really than the Californian asparagus we are accustomed to seeing in January. There are slender Kenyan green beans the year round, midwinter courgettes from Spain, fennel from Israel, and peppers and aubergines from goodness knows where's sunnier climes. Some weeks it seems that the only home-produced vegetables are the sprouts and swedes and cabbages.

The choice of fresh vegetables has never been wider or, taken in the round, better. But there have been casualties. Peas that taste as sweet as the ones my granny grew in her Scottish garden have virtually disappeared from the shops at any time of year. It is more economic for farmers to grow the heavy croppers that freezing and canning manufacturers want for their tins and packets. To taste peas that are tiny and tender and sweet, or pungent tomatoes, newly dug potatoes or freshly picked spinach, you must grow them yourself.

The ways in which we cook vegetables are more varied too than they were even 10 years ago, and more respectful of their character and vitamins. Those that are not eaten raw are more often steamed or stir-fried than boiled.

Once tried, stir-frying is an irresistible method of cooking many vegetables. Not only do they keep their colour and flavour and a bite of crispness, but a minimum of their nutritional value is lost in the cooking process. The method is splendidly quick and its few principles easily mastered.

An iron wok, the traditional basin-shaped Chinese cooking pot, is the ideal utensil for the job because it has the right heat-conducting characteristics and its deep sloping sides allow fairly large quantities of ingredients to be stirred and tossed in a small amount of oil without being projected onto the kitchen walls. That said, a wok is not essential. An iron frying or paella pan will do quite well.

Peanut oil (groundnut oil or *huile d'arachide* on some labels) stands up best to the high temperatures generally used for stir-frying. Corn oil is also suitable, but olive oil and butter have too low a smoking point for this method.

A wide variety of vegetables is suitable for stir-frying. Beansprouts, spring onions and Chinese leaves are predictable candidates. Less obviously suitable choices include any vegetables which can be cooked lightly and quickly when cut into pieces of appropriate shape and uniform size.

Stir-fried Spring Onions

SERVES 2

170 g (6 oz) spring onions
2 tablespoons peanut oil
1 tablespoon soy or tamari sauce
freshly ground black pepper to taste

Trim both ends of the spring onions and discard any floppy or discoloured outer layer. Cut them in halves, and if the white ends are the thickness of a pencil or fatter, slit them again lengthwise. Wash and thoroughly dry them.

Heat the pan until it is very hot and add the oil which should look shimmery at once. Before it starts to smoke (if it does start again with slightly less heat and fresh oil), add the spring onions all at once. Fry them for about two minutes, lifting and turning constantly to prevent them sticking and burning. Add the soy sauce and pepper and continue stirring and lifting until the spring onions are just cooked and most of the liquid has evaporated.

Serve immediately with almost any plainly roasted or grilled meat. Stir-fried spring onions are especially delicious with roast lamb.

Chinese oyster sauce, which does indeed include oysters, or at any rate extracts from them, tastes more like a cross between Bovril and Marmite than anything much to do with shellfish, and it is curious that it goes as well as it does with lettuce or Chinese leaves. If you have not already met it in a restaurant, it is worth an inexpensive trial from most suppliers of oriental foodstuffs.

Stir-fried Lettuce

SERVES 2

1 large cos lettuce, or half a head of
    Chinese leaves
2 tablespoons peanut oil
2 tablespoons dry sherry
4 tablespoons oyster sauce (see
    above)

Cut the tough base from the lettuce or Chinese leaves and discard any damaged outer leaves. Cut it in 2.5 cm (1 in) wide strips across the leaves. If necessary, wash it and dry very thoroughly. (Small cos lettuces may be quartered lengthwise instead of being cut in strips.)

Heat the pan until it is very hot and add the oil which should look shimmery at once. Before it starts to smoke, add the chopped leaves all at once. Fry them for two or three minutes, lifting and turning constantly to prevent them sticking or burning. Sprinkle with the sherry and stir-fry for another 30 seconds or so. Add the oyster sauce, stir briefly to coat the leaves and serve immediately. This one is especially good with roast chicken.

The best thing about beansprouts is their crunch. They also have the merit of being a much better source of vitamins than their pallid appearance suggests, and they are cheap. Add a few more interestingly flavoured crisp vegetables like celery and red peppers and you have a kind of hot, crunchy salad.

Stir-fried Winter Salad

SERVES 2

225 g (8 oz) beansprouts
2 sticks of celery
1 small red or green pepper
1 small leek, or 4 spring onions
1 clove garlic
3 tablespoons peanut oil
1 teaspoon sugar
1/2 teaspoon salt
1 teaspoon vinegar

Wash and thoroughly dry the beansprouts. Pick out any which are badly damaged and discard any bean skins sticking to them. If the sprouts are more than about 5 cm (2 in) long, cut them in halves. Finely slice the celery, cutting it diagonally across the stalk like French bread. Cut the pepper in halves, discard the seeds and slice the flesh into narrow strips. Slit the leek in halves lengthwise, wash and thoroughly dry it, and cut into narrow diagonal strips. If you are using spring onions chop them in very short lengths. Peel the garlic and chop it very finely. Mix together all the vegetables, except the garlic.

Heat the pan until it is very hot and add the oil which should look shimmery at once. Before it starts to smoke, add the chopped garlic and stir it briefly before tipping in all the vegetables. Fry them for three to four minutes, lifting and turning constantly to prevent them sticking or burning. Sprinkle the mixture with the sugar, salt and vinegar, mix well and serve immediately.

Who was not told in childhood that spinach is good for you? Did it really curl hair and build strong muscles or was it, like bread before cake, in some way good for one's character? Wash fresh spinach in plenty of cold water to rid it completely of tooth-cracking grit and nip off the stalks where they join the leaves.

Stir-fried spinach is very quickly prepared, and with its Chinese flavour, goes especially well with plainly roasted pork or duck.

Stir-fried Spinach

SERVES 3–4

3 tablespoons vegetable oil
1 clove garlic, crushed with 1 teaspoon salt
680 g (1½ lb) fresh spinach, washed
55 g (2 oz) butter
1 teaspoon caster sugar
3 tablespoons soy sauce

Heat the oil in a very large saucepan or wok, add the garlic and salt and fry very briefly on a high heat. Add the spinach all at once and fry it, stirring constantly, on a high heat for two to three minutes, or just until the leaves have wilted completely. Add the butter, sugar and soy sauce and stir the spinach, still on a high heat, for another two minutes. Serve immediately.

Stir-fried Lettuce with Ginger

SERVES 4

2 lettuces, preferably cos or Webb's Wonder
2 tablespoons peanut oil
1 clove garlic, very finely chopped
2.5 cm (1 in) green ginger, peeled and very finely chopped
2 tablespoons dry sherry
1 tablespoon soy sauce

Trim the lettuces of damaged leaves and wash them by dunking them, head first, into several changes of cold water. Drain and dry them well, then cut into quarters.

Heat a wok or large frying pan until it is very hot and add the oil which should look shimmery at once. Before it starts to smoke, add the garlic and ginger, and immediately afterwards the lettuces. Fry them for two or three minutes, lifting and turning constantly to prevent them sticking or burning.

Sprinkle the sherry and soy sauce over the lettuce and continue stir-frying for 30 seconds or so to coat the leaves. Serve immediately.

Golden sticks of deep fried courgette, crisp on the outside, tender and juicy in the middle, are one of the pleasures of American steakhouse meals where deep fried zucchini are served either as a first course, or as a vegetable.

Deep Fried Zucchini

SERVES 4

110 g (4 oz) plain flour
2 tablespoons olive oil
120 ml (4 fl oz) water
2 egg whites, beaten until stiff

Sift the flour into a bowl, add the oil and water and stir to a smooth, thick batter. Rest the batter in the refrigerator for an hour or two, then just before using it, fold in the stiffly beaten egg whites.

6–8 medium-sized courgettes
oil, preferably peanut, for deep
  frying
salt

Wash and dry the courgettes. Trim off the stalks and cut them lengthwise into sticks about twice the thickness of a pencil. Dry them thoroughly, dip them in the batter and deep fry (see page 229) them for three or four minutes in the oil heated to about 180°C/350°F. At this temperature a 2.5 cm (1 in) cube of day-old bread will fry crisp and golden in about 90 seconds. Fry the courgettes a few at a time and dry them on absorbent kitchen paper. Sprinkle them with salt and serve immediately.

Field mushrooms, the wild version of the cultivated mushroom, and ceps *(boletus edulis)*, which look on top like shiny buns and underneath have a honeycomb of tiny tubes, are the only ones I trust myself to pick, apart from the wonderfully flavorous morel which wears its honeycomb pattern on the outside and appears, unpredictably, in spring and early summer.

Cultivated button mushrooms sold all year round do not have as much flavour as their wild brethren. The flat, open mushrooms are sometimes cheaper than buttons and, for taste, a great improvement on them.

The flavour of an open mushroom grilled with garlic, parsley and butter is so splendid, and superior to snails given the same treatment, that I would never now dream of bothering to cook that delicacy known in the Mendips as *wallfish*. Which is not to say that there is no occasion when they are a real treat as long as someone else has fiddled over them.

Recipes in which mushrooms predominate tend to be simple. The ingredients which enhance them, worked out long ago, are hard to improve on, and apparent innovations are often traceable to other cuisines. Mushrooms cooked gently in butter are so easily prepared that instruction would seem superfluous if it were not from the hand of Eliza Acton whose *Modern Cookery for Private Families* was first published in 1845.

'MUSHROOMS AU BEURRE *(Delicious)* Cut the stems from some fine meadow mushroom-buttons, and clean them with a bit of new flannel, and some fine salt; then either wipe them dry with a soft cloth, or rinse them in fresh water, drain them quickly, spread them in a clean cloth, fold it over them, and leave them for ten minutes, or more, to dry. For every pint of them thus prepared, put an ounce and a half of fresh butter into a thick iron saucepan, shake it over the fire until it *just* begins to brown, throw in the mushrooms, continue to shake the saucepan over a clear fire that they may not stick to it or burn, and when they have simmered three or four minutes, strew over them a little salt, some cayenne, and pounded mace; stew them until they are perfectly tender, heap them in a dish, and serve them with their own sauce only, for breakfast, supper, or luncheon.

'Nothing can be finer than the flavour of the mushrooms thus prepared; and the addition of any liquid is far from an improvement to it.

'They are very good when drained from the butter, and served cold, and in a cool larder may be kept for several days. The butter in which they have stewed is admirable for flavouring gravies, sauces, or potted meats. Small flaps, freed from the fur and skin, may be stewed in the same way; and either these, or the buttons, served under roast poultry or partridges, will give a dish of very superior relish.'

In one of her inimitable footnote observations, Miss Acton adds: 'Persons inhabiting parts of the country where mushrooms are abundant, may send them easily, when thus prepared, to their friends in cities, or in less productive counties. If poured into jars, with sufficient butter to cover them, they will travel any distance, and can be re-warmed for use.'

Winter vegetables lack the glamour of summer salad stuffs. An earthy heap of swedes does not galvanise the culinary imagination like a green patchwork of herbs and leafy things. Perhaps this is why the time-consuming task of washing and trimming salads never seems to count as work in the same way that peeling or scraping root vegetables does.

Yet a little care with worthy winter roots and cabbages pays dividends. Casseroled, braised or stuffed, these are much more interesting dishes than any emerald green pods, stalks or seeds from frozen packets. They also make a pleasingly well-done change for those who are not convinced that they really enjoy their vegetables *al dente*.

Hard varieties of cabbage – green, white or red – are much the better for slow, careful cooking. The addition of a little fat, butter, bacon dice, chicken, duck or goose dripping is an improvement. Caraway seeds, if you like the taste of them are an excellent addition, as are juniper berries. Or give the cabbage a sweet sour flavour with a little vinegar and sugar.

Braised Red Cabbage

SERVES 6

900 g (2 lb) red cabbage
55 g (2 oz) butter or dripping
1 tablespoon sugar
1 teaspoon salt
6 tablespoons water
4 tablespoons wine vinegar
1 crisp eating apple
4 tablespoons redcurrant jelly
freshly ground black pepper

Quarter the cabbage, cut away the central stalk and shred the leaves finely.

Mix the fat, sugar, salt, water and vinegar in a heavy ovenproof casserole and bring to the boil on top of the stove. Add the cabbage, toss well to coat the pieces on all sides and bring to the boil again. Cover the casserole, transfer it to a preheated moderate oven (160°C/325°F, gas mark 3) and cook for about two hours, or until the cabbage is tender. Check from time to time that the cabbage is not drying out, and add a little more water if necessary.

Grate the apple and stir it into the cabbage, together with the redcurrant jelly and pepper. Return the cabbage to the oven for another 30 minutes or so before serving with roast meat, poultry or game. Braised cabbage re-heats well.

Cabbage with Juniper

SERVES 4–6

225 g (8 oz) belly of pork
1 kg (2¼ lb) red cabbage
1 medium onion, thinly sliced
24 juniper berries, bruised
salt and freshly ground black pepper
150 ml (¼ pint) dry red or white wine, or stock

Trim the pork of rind and bone and cut it in 1.25 cm (½ in) dice. Put the meat in a heavy ovenproof casserole and cook on a low heat, stirring from time to time, until most of the fat has melted and the pork is golden brown.

Remove the outer leaves and hard core from the cabbage and slice it finely. Add it to the casserole with the onion, juniper berries, salt and pepper and stir until the cabbage is well coated with fat. Add the wine or stock, cover the casserole and bake in a preheated cool oven (150°C/300°F, gas mark 2) for about 2½ hours, or until the cabbage is very tender. Check during the cooking that the dish does not dry too much, and add more liquid if necessary.

Cabbage with juniper reheats very well (you may even think it improved), and the recipe can also be made with hard white cabbage.

Braised Lettuce

SERVES 4

85 g (3 oz) bacon fat or butter
2 teaspoons sugar
salt and freshly ground black
  pepper
16 small white onions, peeled
4 lettuces, preferably cos or Webb's
  Wonder
2 bay leaves

Melt half the fat in a heavy pan and add half the sugar and a little salt and pepper. Add the onions and cook, uncovered, on a low heat, stirring occasionally, until they are at least half cooked and are coated with a buttery caramel glaze. Keep warm.

Trim any damaged leaves from the lettuces and wash them well by dunking them, head first, in several changes of cold water. Drain them and cut in halves, slicing from crown to base.

Melt the remaining fat in another large pan and add the lettuces, the remaining sugar and a little salt and pepper. Cook the lettuces until they are wilted and slightly coloured, then remove them from the pan. When they are cool enough to handle, roll them up in neat packets and arrange these round the edge of the pan. Put the onions in the middle, add the bay leaves, cover the pan and simmer on a low heat until the onions are fully cooked.

When the onions and lettuce are ready, boil off any excess liquid quickly. Remove the bay leaves and serve immediately. Snippets of crisply fried bacon make an excellent garnish for this dish.

White turnips, like their golden Swedish cousins, have a taste one likes or loathes. It is not a flavour that can be disguised or modified much. A creamy white sauce which contrasts pleasantly with the bitterness of turnips is conventional. Less widely known is the combination of turnips with oranges.

Turnips with Oranges

SERVES 4–6

12 young white turnips
2 medium oranges
salt
55 g (2 oz) butter
freshly ground black pepper

Peel the turnips carefully to retain their attractive shape. Finely grate the zest from one of the oranges and set it aside. Squeeze the juice from both and put it in a pan with the turnips and a little salt. Cover the pan and simmer on a low heat until the turnips are tender – about 25 minutes depending on their size.

Drain the turnips and arrange them in one layer in a flameproof dish which can go from oven to table. Dot each turnip with the butter and sprinkle with a little finely grated orange zest and plenty of pepper. Pop the dish under a hot grill for a moment or two to melt the butter and crisp the orange zest. Serve immediately.

Turnips with oranges are very good with roast beef or duck.

'The Jerusalem's dead' sang Albert Chevalier on the music hall boards at the turn of the century. What he was singing about was not a catastrophic drop in demand for the artichokes on his cart, but the demise of the donkey which had been pulling it. And that, in the roundabout rhyming slang of London's street traders, is the connection. For 'choke' rhymes with moke, the gypsy name for donkey, which the Cockneys adopted.

There are a variety of theories about how the Jerusalem artichoke came by its name which, historians of these matters agree, has nothing at all to do with the Holy Land. The most plausible and widely accepted explanation is that it is a corruption of the Italian *girasole* artichoke. *Girasole* because the top of the plant looks like a sunflower, and its edible tubers taste not unlike globe artichokes. In the south of France and nearby parts of Italy it goes under the jolly name *topinambur*.

The phantom Middle Eastern connection persists nonetheless and almost any recipe for a soup based on Jerusalem artichokes has been called Palestine soup for the past hundred years or more.

Jerusalem artichokes can be cooked in most of the ways used to prepare potatoes. They make interesting chips, excellent creamy gratins, and delicately flavoured soufflés and purées. They may also be braised or sautéed, whole or in pieces, and respond well to additions of cream, butter, lemon juice, tomato or cheese.

Choose artichokes much as you would potatoes, picking firm specimens in, if possible, the most easily peeled shapes. Knobbliness is the big snag with artichokes and some cooks prefer to blanch them before attempting to take the peel off. A growing number of cooks do not peel artichokes at all. They just scrub them well. Once peeled, raw artichokes quickly blacken unless put immediately into cold water acidulated with a drop or two of vinegar or lemon juice.

Sliced artichokes baked in cream, with a hint of garlic and cheese, make an excellent vegetable dish to serve with almost any plainly roasted or grilled meat or fish. The sauce invariably separates, but this cannot spoil the flavour.

Strongly flavoured alpine cheese like Swiss Gruyère or French Beaufort are especially good in this gratin, but strong Cheddar is in no way inferior.

Gratin of Artichokes

SERVES 4

1 clove garlic, peeled
45 g (1½ oz) butter
450 g (1 lb) Jerusalem artichokes
salt and freshly ground black pepper
freshly grated nutmeg
55 g (2 oz) Gruyère or Beaufort cheese, finely grated
300 ml (½ pint) creamy milk
300 ml (½ pint) single cream

Rub a shallow ovenproof dish with the cut clove of garlic then butter the dish generously. Peel or scrub the artichokes, slice them thinly and arrange them in the dish in overlapping layers. Season each layer lightly with salt, pepper and nutmeg and sprinkle it with a little of the cheese. Pour in the milk, then the cream and dot the top with a little more butter.

Bake in a moderately hot oven (200°C/400°F, gas mark 6) for about 15 minutes. Reduce the temperature to moderate (180°C/350°F, gas mark 4) and continue cooking until most of the liquid has been absorbed and the artichokes are creamy and tender. Serve from the baking dish.

For a Mediterranean flavour which is particularly good with grilled or roasted veal or lamb, sauté artichokes in a fruity olive oil, with a hint of garlic and a few ripe tomatoes.

Topinamburs Provençal

SERVES 4

450 g (1 lb) Jerusalem artichokes
salt
3 tablespoons olive oil
1 large clove garlic, finely chopped
225 g (8 oz) ripe tomatoes, peeled
*   and deseeded*
freshly ground black pepper

Peel or scrub the artichokes. Parboil them in salted water and drain them while they are still firm. Cut in slices about 7 mm (¼ in) thick. Heat the oil in a heavy pan, add the artichokes and garlic and cook on a low heat, stirring constantly, until the slices of artichoke are coated with oil on all sides.

Chop the tomato flesh and add it to the pan. Season with the pepper and continue cooking on a low heat, stirring from time to time, until the artichokes are tender. If they dry too much before they are quite cooked, add a little water or wine and continue cooking until they are tender.

Purée of Leeks

SERVES 8

1.8 kg (4 lb) leeks
55 g (2 oz) butter
salt and freshly ground black
*   pepper*
6 tablespoons single cream

Top and tail the leeks and slit them in halves lengthwise. Wash out any earth and shake them dry. Slice the leeks very finely across the length.

Melt the butter in a large, heavy-based saucepan and add the leeks. Cook them, uncovered, on a very gentle heat, stirring from time to time, until they are very tender.

To make a really smooth purée blend the cooked leeks in a food processor or blender, or work them through the coarse disc of a *mouli légumes*.

Season the purée to taste with salt and pepper and stir in the cream. Keep the purée warm or reheat it in the top of a double boiler, or in a covered bowl on top of a pan of simmering water.

Gratin of Carrots

SERVES 4

680 g (1½ lb) carrots, scraped
110 g (4 oz) butter
1 clove garlic, very finely chopped
1 tablespoon lemon juice
salt and freshly ground black
*   pepper*
150 ml (¼ pint) double cream
30 g (1 oz) white breadcrumbs

Grate the carrots using a medium blade. Melt half the butter in a large frying pan, add the carrots and garlic and fry gently on a low heat, turning frequently, until the carrots are almost tender, but not browned. Stir in the lemon juice and season to taste with salt and pepper.

Transfer the fried carrots to a buttered gratin dish and pour over the cream. Heat the remaining butter in the frying pan until it foams, then add the breadcrumbs and fry until they are crisp and pale gold. Sprinkle the breadcrumbs over the carrots and bake in a preheated moderately hot oven (190°C/375°F, gas mark 5) for about 30 minutes. Serve hot.

Hot potatoes bring out the flavour of cold meats and are ideal buffet fare. Jacket potatoes are not easy to eat standing up or from a plate perched on your knee. And sauté potatoes, while delicious, need last-minute preparation. The ideal potato dishes for buffets are recipes of sliced or grated potatoes cooked in stock, milk, or cream. The Swedish dish called 'Jansson's temptation' includes anchovy fillets and goes very well indeed with most cold meats and, of course, with the many pickled herring specialities of Scandinavia. Swedish anchovies are pickled like herrings and the 'right' kind for this dish; but it is very good too with the salted anchovies available everywhere.

Janssons Frestelse

SERVES 8 OR MORE

1.8 kg (4 lb) potatoes
450 g (1 lb) onions
12 anchovy fillets
30 g (1 oz) butter
350 ml (12 fl oz) single cream

Peel the potatoes and grate them coarsely. Peel the onions and slice them into thin rings. Chop the anchovy fillets into small pieces.

Butter a gratin or oven-to-table baking dish and cover the base with a layer of potato. Cover with a layer of onion rings and anchovies and another layer of potato. The number of layers will depend on the size of the dish, and the top layer should be potato.

Pour over half the cream and dot the dish with the remaining butter.

Bake in a preheated moderately hot oven (200°C/400°F, gas mark 6) for 20 minutes. Pour over the remaining cream and bake for another 30 minutes, or until the potatoes are tender. Keep warm in a low oven until needed, or cool and reheat, adding a little more liquid if the dish becomes too dry.

Soufflé Potatoes

SERVES 12

12 large baking potatoes
110 g (4 oz) butter, melted
250 ml (8 fl oz) double cream
6 eggs, separated
salt and freshly ground black
   pepper

Scrub the potatoes, dry them thoroughly and prick the tops in two or three places with a fork. Arrange them on a baking sheet and bake in a preheated hot oven (220°C/425°F, gas mark 7) for about 1½ hours, or until tender.

Cut a lid lengthwise off each baked potato and scoop the flesh into a bowl. Add the melted butter and cream and mix well before beating in the egg yolks and seasoning to taste with salt and pepper. Whisk the egg whites until stiff and fold them into the creamed potato.

Divide the mixture between the potato shells and return them to the oven to cook for about 15 minutes, or until the filling is puffy and golden. Serve immediately.

Freshly made potato *latkes* are the traditional Jewish accompaniment to salt beef and are very good with almost any meat, hot or cold.

Potato Latkes

SERVES 4–6

900 g (2 lb) potatoes, peeled weight
2 large eggs, beaten
4 tablespoons self-raising flour
salt and freshly ground black
 pepper
oil for frying

Grate the potatoes very, very finely and drain the pulp in a sieve for about 10 minutes. Mix the potatoes with the eggs, flour, salt and pepper.

Fry tablespoons of the mixture in 1.25 cm (½ in) of hot oil for about 5 minutes on each side. The *latkes* should be a rich brown and crisp on the outside, soft and cooked in the middle. Drain them on kitchen paper and serve very hot.

Green flageolet beans are the one storecupboard vegetable that might pass for fresh if one did not know that they are sold dried. They also come cooked, in tins. In France they are often served with roast lamb, but are equally good with beef or pork. They can be served quite plain, moistened with just a little butter or roasting juices, salt and pepper. Or they can be dressed up with garlic, snippets of crisp bacon, or a creamy sauce. The following recipe uses the beans in their dried form, but of course you can start with tinned beans. Rinse them well.

Flageolet Beans with Cream

SERVES 4–6

340 g (12 oz) dried flageolet beans
unsalted stock or water
6 rashers smoked streaky bacon
15 g (½ oz) butter
1 large onion, finely chopped
salt and freshly ground black
 pepper
2 egg yolks
150 ml (¼ pint) double cream

Cover the beans with cold water and leave them to soak overnight.

Next day, drain the beans and put them in a pan with sufficient stock or fresh water to cover them. (Adding salt at this stage could toughen the beans which is why the recipe calls for unsalted stock. Salt should always be added to dried beans only when they are tender.) Bring to the boil, cover the pan and simmer until the beans are tender. Drain and set them aside and keep warm.

Cut the bacon in small snippets. Melt the butter in a pan, add the bacon and fry on a low heat until its fat begins to run, but do not let it brown. Remove the bacon, leaving the fat in the pan, and set it aside. Add the onion to the pan and fry until it is tender, but not browned. Return the beans and bacon to the pan and season to taste with salt and pepper.

Beat together the egg yolks and cream in a small bowl. Off the heat stir the cream into the bean mixture and mix well. Reheat, if necessary, but do not let the dish boil now or the eggs will curdle. Serve immediately.

Pease pudding has been made since the Middle Ages and is still traditionally served with boiled bacon or roast pork. Boiling it in a cloth was the original cooking method, but now it is more usually steamed in a covered basin or baked. The texture can range from a light creamy purée to a solid pudding which can be turned out and cut in wedges. This recipe produces a pudding which is just firm enough to turn out.

Pease Pudding

SERVES 4–6

450 g (1 lb) dried peas, whole or split
1 medium onion, roughly chopped
1 teaspoon dried mint (optional)
55 g (2 oz) butter
1 large egg, beaten
salt and freshly ground black pepper

Cover the peas with cold water and leave them to soak overnight.

Drain the peas and put them in a pan with the onion, and mint if you like it. Cover with cold water, bring to the boil, and simmer, covered, until the peas are tender. Drain well, then purée the peas and onions by pressing them through a sieve, or using a food processor. Add the butter and egg and mix well. Season to taste with salt and pepper.

Turn the pea purée into a well-buttered pudding basin and cover it with buttered foil, tied on tightly. Set the basin in a large saucepan and pour in boiling water to come halfway up the sides of the basin. Cover the pan and simmer for about one hour, or until the pudding is firm.

To serve, turn out the pudding onto a heated plate and cut it in wedges.

The most striking attribute of saffron is its ability to tint foods and fabrics jazzy shades of yellow from palest primrose to deep orange or, in the case of Indian rice dishes, these and every shade between.

The taste and smell of saffron echo the warm, flowery sweetness of the colour. And luckily, at £200 a pound, too much of this good thing makes food taste bitter not better.

As every schoolchild knows, saffron is the dried stigmas of crocus flowers. We all know that the flowers grow well in Britain because Saffron Walden in Essex – *walde* was Anglo-Saxon for field – took its name from the local crocus growing industry. But any window-box gardeners dreaming of saffron self-sufficiency should note two facts. It takes 70,000 to 80,000 flowers to make one pound of saffron; and *Crocus sativus*, the right kind, must on no account be confused with the poisonous autumn flowering meadow or autumn crocus *Colchicum autumnale*, which is not a true crocus but a member of the lily family.

Two more facts, which have no relevance but great appeal, are that the Romans enjoyed a massage with saffron-scented oil after a bath, and that in thirteenth century England saffron cost 15 very old shillings a pound.

Saffron is an essential ingredient of classic dishes as different as Spanish *paella*, French *bouillabaisse* and Cornish saffron cake. It is as important an element of a *risotto alla milanese* as Italian *arborio* rice and fresh Parmesan cheese.

Milanese Risotto

about 1 litre (1³⁄4 pints) light chicken stock
55 g (2 oz) butter
2 tablespoons olive oil
2 tablespoons finely chopped shallot or onion
340 g (12 oz) arborio rice
2 packets of saffron (about ¹⁄2 teaspoon)
salt and freshly ground black pepper
30 g (1 oz) Parmesan cheese, freshly grated

Heat the stock and keep it simmering steadily. In a heavy-based pan or casserole heat together half the butter and all the oil, add the shallot or onion and sauté until it is transparent. Add the dry rice and stir it around until each grain is coated. Dissolve the saffron in the stock. Pour about 150 ml (¹⁄4 pint) of the simmering stock over the rice and cook, stirring constantly, on a medium heat.

Add another ladleful of stock and cook, stirring constantly, until that too has been absorbed. Continue adding liquid and cooking almost dry until each grain of rice is swollen and tender, but still has a little bite in the centre. The special texture of risotto is its moist creaminess, which is achieved by adding the liquid a little at a time and the constant stirring which prevents the rice sticking to the pan.

When the rice is tender, season it to taste with salt and pepper and stir in the remaining butter and Parmesan. Rest the risotto off the heat for a minute or two before serving it on its own as a first course, or with *osso bucco* (see page 114), a meltingly tender dish of casseroled shin of veal.

Your risotto may not need the full litre of stock, or it may absorb a little more. The exact amount will depend on the age of the rice and the speed at which it is cooked.

Good, long grain rice like Indian *basmatti* has an interesting and delicious flavour of its own. Cooked simply with a little butter, and water of course, it is a perfect accompaniment to delicately flavoured stews and casseroles as well as curries and other highly flavoured dishes. A saffron flavoured and lightly spiced pillau can be served with plainly roasted or grilled meat, or with fish.

Pillau

450 g (1 lb) basmatti *or long grain rice*
30 g (1 oz) clarified (see page 227) or fresh butter
6 whole cloves
6 whole cardamom pods
10 cm (4 in) cinnamon stick, broken in pieces, or ¹⁄2 teaspoon ground cinnamon
about 450 ml (³⁄4 pint) cold water
1 packet of saffron
salt to taste

Wash the rice in cold water and leave it to soak while you prepare the spices.

Melt the butter in a heavy saucepan with a well-fitting lid, and add the cloves, cardamoms and cinnamon. Stir the spices for a moment or two on a medium heat, making sure they do not burn. Drain the rice and add it to the spiced butter. Stir the rice in the fat until it is well coated, then add the cold water. Dissolve the saffron in a little hot water. Bring the rice to the boil, stir in the saffron and salt, reduce the heat to very low and cover the pan. Cook the rice for about 10 minutes, or until all the water is absorbed and each grain is tender and separate.

If all the water is absorbed before the rice is tender, add

more water by sprinkling it over the top of the rice with your hand. Cover the pan and continue cooking until the rice is ready. *Basmatti* will take only about 10 minutes; other kinds of long grain rice need longer cooking.

Fluff up the rice with a fork and serve on a heated dish. Well-browned rings of fried onion make an attractive decoration scattered over a pillau.

Lemon flavoured rice is particularly good and goes well with roast chicken, veal or pork and with fish.

Lemon Rice

SERVES 4–6

340 g (12 oz) basmatti *rice*
30 g (1 oz) clarified (see page 227)
  or fresh butter
350 ml (12 fl oz) cold water
4 whole cardamom pods
finely grated zest and juice of 1
  lemon
1 teaspoon salt
freshly ground black pepper

Wash the rice in cold water and drain it well. Melt the butter in a heavy pan which has a tightly fitting fit. Add the rice and stir over a low heat, mixing until each grain is coated with butter. Add the cold water, cardamoms, lemon juice and salt and bring to the boil. Reduce the heat, stir once and cover the pan. Cook the rice for about 10 minutes, or until all the water is absorbed and each grain is tender and separate.

If all the water is absorbed before the rice is tender, add more water by sprinkling it over the top of the rice with your hand. Cover the pan and continue cooking until the rice is ready.

When the rice is cooked sprinkle the lemon zest over it and fold it in lightly with a fork, fluffing up the rice at the same time. Season with the pepper and serve hot.

12

Salads

There is no reason why ravishingly pretty salads that taste as stunningly lively and fresh as they look cannot be produced every day of the year. Just think of some ingredients there are to choose from. Take leaves. There are the floppy butterhead lettuces with varieties like Continuity and Bibb, and crisp lettuces like the long-leafed cos or tightly curled Iceberg and Webb's Wonder. The various forms of chicory offer slightly bitter-tasting leaves which are more robust than lettuce but not nearly as tough as cabbage, and most types are available right through the worst winter months. There are pale spears of Belgian chicory, raggedy frizzy leaves of curly endive, and less crinkly heads of escarole or Batavian endive. The star of this breed, the beautiful red leafed radicchio makes any salad look dressed up. Hard cabbages are marvellous for coleslaw of course, but spring greens have salad duties too, together with young spinach, Chinese greens, sorrel, corn salad or lamb's lettuce, watercress and young dandelion leaves. Then there are all the fresh herbs: the parsley, chives, mint, coriander, basil, savory and chervil, and others more difficult to find unless you grow them yourself. And all these before straying into the realms of edible flowers, the daisy and marigold petals, primroses and nasturtiums.

Onions and all their tribe are essential salad ingredients, and of the root vegetables, raw beetroot and parsnip are as good and as useful as carrots and celeriac. Crisp bulbs of Florence fennel with its clean aniseed taste, and indispensably useful celery are stalks to eat raw. Like ripe tomatoes, avocados, sweet peppers and cucumbers they need almost no preparation.

Partly cooked French beans and florets of cauliflower, not raw but still crisp, are lovely in salads, as are all kinds of sprouted seeds from beansprouts and alfalfa to mustard and cress.

Making good salads is an art. It is a cultivated flair for making felicitous combinations of taste and texture and dressing them with care. And as with every art form there are ground rules which may be followed or broken. Like – leafy salads almost always benefit from the inclusion of something crisp or crunchy, be it bacon bits, nuts, croûtons, or thin slices of apple. Or – tender leaves and shoots need light dressing made with fragrant cold pressed oils, while the mustardy vinaigrettes, blue cheese dressings and hearty mayonnaise-based sauces are best with tougher customers like cabbage and endive.

None of us needs much help to make splendid summer salads, and so a good proportion of the recipes and ideas in this chapter are for salads which can be made in winter, or at any time of year with ingredients from the storecupboard as well as from the garden or greengrocer.

I made this Christmas salad to serve with a roast goose which had been stuffed with a mixture of potato, onion and celery. The stuffing made one vegetable and this glamorous salad the second one. It was the simplest Christmas dinner imaginable and one of the best.

Christmas salad is a festive looking mixture of dark pink radicchio, deep green watercress and pale chicory, with apple and nuts for taste and texture, and a well-flavoured dressing made with walnut oil and raspberry vinegar. Nut oils can be overpowering when used neat in salad dressings, so I use between half and two-thirds of almost tasteless peanut oil with walnut or hazelnut oil. This salad can also be served with cheese. Try it with a creamy piece of Stilton.

Christmas Salad

SERVES 6–8

1 clove garlic, peeled
1 large or 2 small heads of
   radicchio
2 spears of chicory
1 bunch of watercress
1 crisp Cox's apple
2 tablespoons shelled, coarsely
   chopped pecans or walnuts

For the dressing:
4 tablespoons peanut oil
2 tablespoons walnut oil
1–1½ tablespoons raspberry
   vinegar
salt and freshly ground black
   pepper

Rub the salad bowl with the cut clove of garlic and discard it. Tear any large leaves of radicchio into two or three pieces and put all the radicchio in the bowl with the separated leaves of chicory and top sprigs of the watercress. Quarter and core the apple and cut it in thin, moon-shaped slivers, with or without the skin. Add these to the salad together with the nuts. Mix together all the dressing ingredients and pour over the salad. Toss well and serve immediately.

A niçoise salad can be a meal in itself or served as a first course. It is a cheerful sight in winter as well as in summer.

Salad Niçoise

SERVES 4

1 clove garlic, peeled
1 large lettuce, or other salad
* greens*
225 g (8 oz) tomatoes, cut in
* wedges*
1 small tin of red kidney beans, or
* other cooked beans*
1 small tin of new potatoes, or
* leftovers*
4 hard boiled eggs, quartered
1 large tin of tuna, drained and
* flaked*
1 small tin of anchovies, drained
small black olives
2 spring onions, chopped, or 1
* small onion, cut in thin rings*

For the dressing:
6 tablespoons fruity olive oil
1–2 tablespoons wine vinegar or
* lemon juice*
1 teaspoon made mustard
salt and freshly ground black
* pepper*

Rub a big bowl or dish with the cut clove of garlic. Tear or roughly chop the lettuce or salad greens and put them in the bowl with the tomatoes. Rinse the beans and potatoes in cold water and strew them on the salad, chopping the potatoes if they are large. Add the hard boiled eggs and tuna fish. Decorate the dish with the anchovies, olives and onion.

To make the dressing, put all the ingredients in a jar and shake well. Just before serving pour the dressing over the salad, and let the first person to be served turn the salad in the dressing.

Who doesn't remember the childish taunts and threats that accompanied picking dandelions? In France the diuretic attributes of the dandelion are acknowledged by adults too. They call this dish *salade de pissenlits au lard*. Pick tender young dandelion leaves in spring for this salad. By midsummer they are too bitter.

Hot Bacon Salad

SERVES 4

1 small head of escarole, or 450 g
* (1 lb) tender young dandelion*
* leaves*
1 clove garlic (optional)
110 g (4 oz) piece of smoked,
* streaky bacon*
freshly ground black pepper
1 tablespoon wine vinegar

Wash the escarole or dandelion leaves and dry thoroughly. Rub the salad bowl with the cut clove of garlic, if using. Tear the escarole or dandelion leaves into smallish pieces and throw them into the bowl.

Remove the rind and cut the bacon into small dice. Put the bacon, without additional fat, into a heavy frying pan and cook on a low heat until the fat runs and the bacon is crisp. Remove the bacon with a slotted spoon and keep it warm. Add the pepper and vinegar to the hot fat in the pan and stir well.

Mix the bacon and hot bacon fat dressing with the salad in the bowl and toss well. Serve immediately.

Hot croûtons of fried bread or slices of hard boiled egg are sometimes added to this salad.

Savoyard Salad

SERVES 2

½ a head of escarole
1 head of chicory
110 g (4 oz) Gruyère cheese, diced
2 tablespoons walnut halves
4 tablespoons walnut or olive oil
1½ tablespoons wine vinegar
½ teaspoon mustard powder
salt and freshly ground black
    pepper
2 tablespoons oil for frying
1 thick slice day-old white bread,
    cubed

Wash and dry the escarole and tear it into smallish pieces. Trim the chicory and cut it in 1.25 cm (½ in) chunks. In a bowl mix together the escarole, chicory, cheese and walnuts.

Make the dressing by shaking together in a jar the walnut or olive oil, vinegar, mustard, salt and pepper.

Just before serving, heat the oil in a pan, add the cubes of bread and fry until they are crisp and golden. Scatter the croûtons on the salad, toss in the dressing and serve immediately.

Coleslaw, or slaw as it is termed in fast food places, is one of the most economical salads to make all year round, and variations on the basic hard cabbage, carrot, onion and mayonnaise recipe are too numerous to list. Finely grated raw parsnip, beetroot or celeriac are good additions in winter. Red cabbage, grated apple, chopped nuts and a few currants ring the changes at any season. Mayonnaise, whether home made or a brand made with the right ingredients, is the most usual dressing. Cut it half and half with sour cream or natural yogurt for a lighter and less fattening taste. Less expensive in cost and calories are plain seasoned yogurt or sour cream, or a light vinaigrette.

Winter Coleslaw

SERVES 4

225 g (8 oz) hard white cabbage
110 g (4 oz) raw beetroot
110 g (4 oz) raw carrot
110 g (4 oz) raw parsnip
2 tablespoons currants
3 or more tablespoons sour cream
salt and freshly ground black
    pepper

Shred or grate the cabbage. Peel the beetroot and scrape the carrot and parsnip, and grate them finely. Mix the vegetables with the currants and cream. Add salt and pepper and mix well together. Chill before serving.

In Naples the eel or carp traditionally served on Christmas Eve is accompanied by this delicious cauliflower salad.

Cauliflower and Olive Salad

SERVES 6 OR MORE

1 large cauliflower
2 cloves garlic
18 small black olives
1 tablespoon capers
4 tablespoons olive oil
1 tablespoon lemon juice
1 teaspoon caster sugar
1 teaspoon made mustard
salt and freshly ground black
*   pepper*

Cut off the leaves and tough central stalk of the cauliflower and break the head into florets. Bring a large pot of salted water to the boil, drop the florets into it and cook until the cauliflower is barely tender. It should still have a bite of crispness. Drain.

Rub the serving bowl or dish with one cut clove of garlic. Put the cooked cauliflower in the bowl and sprinkle with the olives and capers.

To make the dressing, blend or shake together in a jar the oil, lemon juice, sugar, mustard, salt and pepper, with one clove of pressed or finely chopped garlic to taste. Pour the dressing over the cauliflower and mix well.

If chopped or crushed garlic in any salad dressing is too much of a good thing, use oil flavoured subtly with garlic. Soak three bruised cloves of garlic in about 250 ml (8 fl oz) of olive oil. Keep the oil in a stoppered jar for several days, then discard the garlic and use the oil as needed.

An unusual combination of flavours – artichoke, potato and fennel – makes an interesting salad to serve with cold beef or ham.

Italian Salad

SERVES 4

2 cooked artichoke hearts, sliced
4 small boiled potatoes, diced
1 small fennel heart, thinly sliced
110 g (4 oz) small firm
*   mushrooms, thinly sliced*
2 tablespoons mayonnaise
2 tablespoons single cream
salt and freshly ground black
*   pepper*
2 hard boiled eggs, quartered
1 teaspoon capers
1 tablespoon chopped parsley

Mix together the artichoke hearts, potatoes, fennel and mushrooms in a bowl. Mix the mayonnaise with the cream and season it to taste with salt and pepper. Pour the thinned mayonnaise over the vegetables and toss lightly together.

Pile the mixture in a serving bowl and decorate it with the eggs, capers and parsley.

Oranges star in several Mediterranean salads which are refreshing and light to serve in winter as first courses or with rich meats like goose, duck or pork, either hot or cold.

The Greek hors d'œuvre salad of sliced oranges, onion rings and black olives is a particular favourite of mine. The Sicilians have another good salad of cucumber and oranges. When fresh mint is hard to come by substitute fresh chives, coriander leaves or parsley.

Orange and Olive Salad

SERVES 6

6 juicy, thin skinned oranges
1 small, mild onion
110 g (4 oz) small black olives,
  preferably Niçoise
salt
cayenne pepper
4 tablespoons olive oil

Use a very sharp knife to peel the oranges, taking off the pith and membrane at the same time. Cut them in thin slices. Remove any pips and arrange the orange slices in a shallow dish. Peel the onion and either chop it finely or slice it in thin rings. Sprinkle the onion over the oranges. Niçoise olives are too difficult to stone, but if you are using any other kind, stoning them is an optional refinement. Scatter them over the oranges and onion.

Salt the mixture lightly because the olives will already be salty. Sprinkle with a little cayenne and dribble the oil over the surface. Serve immediately.

Orange and Cucumber Salad

SERVES 4–6

2 small, juicy oranges
1 cucumber
a few red radishes (optional)
1 tablespoon lemon juice
3 tablespoons olive oil
salt to taste
cayenne pepper
fresh mint, chives, coriander or
  parsley, finely chopped

Peel the oranges, removing all the pith, and cut them into the thinnest possible slices. Peel the cucumber and cut it in very thin round slices. Wash the radishes, if you are using them, and cut them in thin slices too. Arrange the sliced fruit and vegetables in a shallow bowl or dish. Put the lemon juice, oil and salt in a jar and shake well together. Pour the dressing over the salad, then sprinkle with a little cayenne and one of the fresh herbs. Serve immediately.

Orange and watercress is a salad combination which is always successful. It calls for crisp, really leafy watercress, dark green and peppery, not bunches of roots and stalks. Lamb's lettuce is one of those luxury salad stuffs that never seems to be available the day one has set one's heart on serving it. Like watercress, it is only worth buying if it is really fresh. The stalks will be crisp, but the pretty rounded leaves always flop over like puppies' ears. If nut oils are not available for the dressing use a light olive oil.

Orange and Watercress Salad

2 or 3 bunches of watercress
110 g (4 oz) lamb's lettuce
(optional)
2 small oranges

For the dressing:
1 tablespoon sherry or cider vinegar
1 tablespoon walnut or hazelnut
oil
2 tablespoons peanut oil
salt and freshly ground black
pepper

Wash and carefully pick over the watercress and lamb's lettuce, if using, and shake them dry. Arrange them in sprigs in a salad bowl or shallow dish. You may like to rub the bowl with a cut clove of garlic first.

Use a very sharp knife indeed to cut the oranges in halves lengthwise, then, without removing the skin, into neat segments. Cut the zest and pith off each segment. This is a much easier way of producing neatly trimmed segments of orange than peeling the fruit first and cutting out the segments. Scatter the pieces of orange over the salad. Put all the ingredients for the dressing in a jar and shake them well together. Pour over the salad, toss and serve immediately.

Courgette and radish salad looks attractive and goes well with cold roast beef or pork.

Courgette and Radish Salad

SERVES 4

4 small courgettes
1 bunch of red radishes
4 tablespoons olive oil
1¹/₂ tablespoons wine vinegar
salt and freshly ground black
pepper
3 tablespoons chopped parsley or
chives

Wash and trim the courgettes and radishes. Slice them as thinly as you can.

Mix the oil, vinegar, salt and pepper. Pour the dressing over the vegetables, stir, and marinate the salad in the refrigerator for an hour.

Just before serving, mix two tablespoons of the parsley or chives into the salad and sprinkle the remainder on top.

Chicory and apple salad is good with cold ham or chicken and an ideal accompaniment to cottage cheese.

Chicory and Apple Salad

SERVES 2

1 large or 2 small heads of chicory
1 crisp apple
2 tablespoons lightly toasted
peanuts
2 tablespoons mayonnaise
1 tablespoon fresh lemon juice

Trim the chicory and cut it in 1.25 cm (½ in) slices. Core and coarsely chop the apple. Put the chicory, apple and peanuts in a bowl.

Mix together the mayonnaise and the lemon juice, add to the salad ingredients and mix well. Serve immediately, or chill for an hour before serving.

Tinned lentils or beans make excellent storecupboard salads to serve with cold meats or continental sausages. Rinse the lentils or beans in cold water, drain and mix with some of the thick, slightly mustardy dressing in the *salade niçoise* recipe (see page 163).

Beanz meanz . . . well, never mind the consequences, they make a jolly good salad. Pad this one out with chopped Frankfurter sausage and it makes a meal.

Mixed Bean Salad

SERVES 6

225 g (8 oz) cooked red kidney
  beans
225 g (8 oz) cooked white haricot
  or cannellini beans
225 g (8 oz) green flageolet beans
1 small onion, finely chopped
4 tablespoons olive oil
2 tablespoons lemon juice, or wine
  or cider vinegar
salt and freshly ground black
  pepper
1/2 teaspoon made mustard
1 tablespoon chopped parsley

Freshly cooked beans are best tossed in the dressing while warm. Tinned beans should be well washed and drained.

Mix together the beans and onion in a large bowl. Blend the oil, lemon juice or vinegar, salt, pepper and mustard. Mix the dressing with the beans and chill the salad for an hour or two. Top with the parsley just before serving.

Pasta salad is an idea which seems at first glance to have more economic than gastronomic appeal. Like most salads, cold pasta dishes are much the better for last-minute assembly and, unusually, much the worse for being chilled. Not quite warm is about the right serving temperature for the delicious chicken and pasta salad here. Fresh herbs make all the difference to this dish, so if the ones I use are not available, experiment with others.

Chicken and Pasta Salad

SERVES 4

2.25 litres (4 pints) chicken stock
  or water
170 g (6 oz) medium-sized pasta
  shells or bows
2 tablespoons olive oil
1 tablespoon lemon juice
1 clove garlic, crushed
salt and freshly ground black
  pepper
1 tablespoon chopped lemon thyme,
  basil, tarragon or parsley
170 g (6 oz) cooked chicken,
  chopped
6 tablespoons good mayonnaise

Bring the stock or water to the boil in a large saucepan and throw in the pasta. Bring the liquid back to the boil, reduce the heat and cook the pasta, uncovered, until it is just tender, but still has a little bite.

Drain the pasta and, while it is still hot, mix it with a dressing made by shaking together in a jar the oil, lemon juice, garlic, salt, pepper and herbs.

When the pasta has cooled to lukewarm, mix it with the chicken and mayonnaise. Serve with lots of crisp green salad stuffs.

Celeriac is usually blanched before being used in salads.

Celeriac Salad

SERVES 4–6

450 g (1 lb) raw celeriac
4 tablespoons real mayonnaise
4 tablespoons double cream,
    whipped to soft peaks
1 tablespoon fresh lemon juice
1 teaspoon dry English mustard
salt and freshly ground black
    pepper

Bring about 600 ml (1 pint) of water to the boil in a medium-sized saucepan. Peel the celeriac and cut it in thin slices. Immediately drop the slices into the boiling water and blanch them for three minutes. Drain and dry the softened celeriac and cut the slices into narrow *julienne* strips.

Mix the mayonnaise, cream, lemon juice, mustard, salt and pepper. Add the celeriac and fold it into the dressing. Chill the salad for an hour or more before serving.

Commercially bottled beetroot often has such a gaspmakingly harsh pickling liquid that the colour of the beetroot is the only good or natural thing left. In this salad recipe the sweet, earthy flavour of fresh beetroot is complemented by the other ingredients. If fresh thyme is not available, try a teaspoonful of finely grated orange zest.

Beetroot and Thyme Salad

SERVES 4–6

450 g (1 lb) freshly cooked beetroot
1 teaspoon fresh thyme leaves
3 tablespoons olive oil
1 tablespoon wine vinegar or
    orange juice
salt, sugar and freshly ground black
    pepper to taste

Peel the beetroot and grate or dice the flesh finely. Sprinkle with the thyme. Combine the remaining ingredients. Pour the dressing over the beetroot and mix lightly. Chill the salad for an hour or so before serving.

Raw Beetroot Salad

SERVES 4–6

450 g (1 lb) raw beetroot
1 tablespoon wine vinegar
4 tablespoons light vegetable oil
1 teaspoon sugar
salt and freshly ground black
    pepper to taste

Wear rubber gloves to prevent the beetroot staining your hands while you peel them with a sharp knife. Grate the raw beetroot very finely.

Mix together the remaining ingredients. Stir the dressing into the grated beetroot and chill the salad for an hour or more before serving.

Cucumber Salad

1 medium-sized cucumber
2 tablespoons salt
2 tablespoons wine or cider vinegar
6 tablespoons light olive oil
½ teaspoon dry English mustard
½ teaspoon sugar
freshly ground black pepper

Cut the cucumber into 7 cm (3 in) lengths and peel each section. Using an apple corer or small knife, remove the seedy centre to leave thick pipes of cucumber flesh. Slice the cucumber into rings about 3 mm (⅛ in) thick – the exact thickness is not crucial. Sprinkle the sliced cucumber with the salt and set it aside to drain for 30 minutes.

Mix the vinegar, oil, mustard, sugar and pepper. Drain the cucumber rings and pat them dry. Toss them in the dressing to coat each slice. Chill the salad for two or three hours before serving.

Sliced raw mushrooms served with two dressings, vinaigrette and sour cream, make a very simple first course. You may, if you prefer, marinate the mushrooms in the oil and lemon dressing and serve them topped with sour cream. The mushrooms for this dish should be very fresh, very crisp, and tightly shut.

SERVES 4–6

Mushroom Salad

450 g (1 lb) button mushrooms
6 tablespoons olive oil
2 tablespoons fresh lemon juice
salt and freshly ground black
    pepper
½ teaspoon Dijon mustard
    (optional)
150 ml (¼ pint) sour cream, or
    half and half whipped double
    cream and natural yogurt

Wipe the mushrooms, remove the stalks and slice the caps as thinly as you can.

Mix the oil, lemon juice, salt, pepper and mustard, if you like it. Serve the sliced mushrooms in a large bowl, the cream in a small one, and the vinaigrette in another.

Recipes for some of the marvellous salads served in the Cranks chain of vegetarian restaurants are in the *Cranks Recipe Book*. Here is an unusual one.

Creamy Paprika Dressing

MAKES ABOUT 300 ml (½ pint)

1 teaspoon raw brown sugar
2 teaspoons paprika
1 teaspoon salt
4 tablespoons cider or wine vinegar
1 free range egg
200 ml (⅓ pint) oil

Combine the sugar and seasonings. Add the vinegar and egg. Beat well. Add the oil, one teaspoon at a time, until about one quarter has been used. Slowly add the remaining oil, beating well between each addition.

Alternatively, use the liquidiser or food processor method. Break the egg into the goblet and add the sugar, paprika, salt and vinegar. Blend for 10 seconds. With the machine switched on, slowly feed in the oil. As the oil is added the dressing will become thick.

Beanshoot Salad

SERVES 4–6

55 g (2 oz) whole peanuts
1 tablespoon oil
½ teaspoon salt
55 g (2 oz) carrots
2 bananas
225 g (8 oz) fresh beanshoots
creamy paprika dressing (see above)

Put the peanuts, oil and salt in a small ovenproof dish. Mix well, then roast in a preheated moderately hot oven (200°C/400°F, gas mark 6) for about 10 minutes, or until golden. Leave until cold.

Grate the carrots and slice the bananas, then combine them with the peanuts and beanshoots. Toss in sufficient dressing to moisten.

13

Puddings

Ice cream is the most evocative of puddings. It brings back summer holidays and the bicycle bell call of the hokey-cokey man with his tricycle cart, and rushing down the garden path with grandpa's big mug to have it filled for the ice cream sodas which were invariably constructed in tall sundae glasses.

First there were cones, and when one was old enough to be trusted with them, sliders or wafers which had to be licked round the edges and the wafers squeezed together to prolong the pleasure. Then there was Cornish ice cream so yellow and sweet and rich that the grown ups said we would be sick, but we never were.

Dainty ices eaten with small spoons in pavement cafés seemed the height of student sophistication. Later still came confirmation of the curious, if vulgar truth, that few puddings, even ices, are not improved by the right booze . . . lemon sorbet laced with a shot of iced vodka.

Elaborate iced puddings, crenellated, complicated and decorated to the teeth, were fashionable among Victorian and Edwardian hostesses, and one can see why. However fussed over, ice cream is always somehow light-hearted and it demands a minimum of last-minute attention.

Mousses, creams and jellies are equally obliging, as are light, uncooked cheesecakes, and traditional trifles. Nowadays it is not exotic fruits or out of season strawberries which cause a sensation at table, but old fashioned hot puddings, or something really flashy like a hot liqueur flavoured soufflé.

Chocolate mousse in its many forms, from pale airy confections to dark and wickedly rich goo, is such a perennially popular pudding that one meets it almost too frequently. Butterscotch mousse is a worthy rival.

Butterscotch Mousse

SERVES 6

55 g (2 oz) butter
170 g (6 oz) soft brown sugar
600 ml (1 pint) fresh milk
¼ teaspoon salt
2 large eggs, separated
5 tablespoons water
1 tablespoon gelatine granules

Melt the butter in a heavy-based saucepan and stir in the sugar. Cook on a medium heat until the mixture begins to brown and give off a rich smell of butterscotch. Remove from the heat immediately and stir in the milk and salt. Continue stirring until the butterscotch has dissolved completely.

Beat the egg yolks and strain the butterscotch mixture into them. Stir well, then return the mixture to the pan and cook it over a gentle heat, without allowing it to boil, until it has thickened slightly. Set it aside to cool.

Put the water in a small pan and sprinkle the gelatine on top. When it has softened, heat it gently, without boiling, until the crystals have melted completely. Stir the dissolved gelatine into the butterscotch custard and leave the mixture in a cold place until it is just beginning to set.

Whisk the egg whites until they hold stiff peaks and fold them into the custard. Divide the mousse between six individual dishes or glasses and chill well before serving with small, very crisp biscuits.

(This mousse should have an even honeycomb texture throughout. If it sets in two layers, one solid and one airy, the flavour will not be spoiled. It just means that the meringue has been added when the custard base was still too runny.)

I have a particular affection for rosemary. It is an obligingly untemperamental herb which will grow from a sprig stuck in the ground, survives our winters, and grows like mad so that one can hack off handfuls to throw on a barbecue and the trimming only encourages it.

A few sprigs of rosemary will scent a jar of caster sugar for sprinkling on pies or using in custards or creams in the same way as vanilla sugar. Or you can infuse the rosemary in cream for a speedier result.

Rosemary Creams

MAKES 6

2 sprigs of rosemary about 10 cm
(4 in) each
300 ml (½ pint) double cream
300 ml (½ pint) milk
55 g (2 oz) sugar
2 large eggs

Bruise the rosemary and put it in a heavy pan with the cream and milk. Heat to just below boiling point then remove from the heat at once and leave it to infuse for an hour or so.

Strain the cream into a bowl and add the sugar and eggs. Beat well. Divide the cream between six custard cups or ovenproof ramekins and set them in a larger ovenproof tin or dish. Pour in boiling water to come halfway up the sides of the small dishes and bake them in a preheated cool oven (140°C/275°F, gas mark 1) for 30 minutes, or until the creams have just set. Serve them warm, cool or chilled with thin sweet biscuits.

Crème brûlée is a classic dinner party pudding. Its success, I think, depends on the childish delight each of us takes in bashing through the brittle coat of caramel to get at the rich custard underneath.

Crème Brûlée

SERVES 8

4 egg yolks
2 tablespoons caster sugar
600 ml (1 pint) double cream
1 vanilla pod, or ¼ teaspoon
    vanilla essence
8 tablespoons Demerara sugar

Combine the egg yolks and caster sugar and whisk until the mixture is pale and fluffy.

Put the cream in a pan with the vanilla pod and bring slowly to the boil. Fish out the vanilla pod (wash and dry the pod, which will live to serve another day). If using vanilla essence add it after the cream has boiled and cooled a little.

Whisk the cream into the egg mixture. Rinse the pan and strain the custard into it through a fine sieve. Heat gently, stirring constantly – do not allow the mixture to boil – until it will coat the back of a wooden spoon.

Pour the custard into eight or more small ramekins or custard pots, filling them almost to the brim. Stand the dishes in an ovenproof tin or dish and pour in boiling water to come halfway up their sides. Bake in a very cool oven (120°C/250°F, gas mark ½) for about 40 minutes, or until the custards have set firm.

Allow them to cool, then chill them for at least four hours.

To caramelise the tops, remove the grill pan from the grill and heat the grill to very hot. Take the grilling rack out of the pan and fill the pan with ice. Set the chilled custards on the ice and sprinkle with the Demerara sugar. Cook quickly under the grill until the sugar melts and bubbles. Cool quickly and chill again before serving.

The custards may be made the day before serving, but the caramel topping will dissolve if it is made too far ahead.

Compot Creams

SERVES 6–8

225 g (8 oz) dried fruit: apricots,
    peaches, pears and apples
85 g (3 oz) Demerara sugar

Cover the fruit with cold water and leave it to soak for several hours or overnight.

Put the fruit and its soaking water in a pan with the

150 ml (¼ pint) double cream
150 ml (¼ pint) soured cream
1 teaspoon dried cinnamon

sugar and bring to the boil. Cover the pan and simmer until the fruit is tender. Drain the fruit and return the liquid to the pan. Reduce the syrup by fast boiling to about two tablespoons. Cut the fruit into 1 cm (⅓ in) cubes and pour the reduced syrup over it. Chill well.

Whip the double cream until it holds soft peaks. Fold in the soured cream, fruit, syrup and cinnamon. Mix well and chill thoroughly before serving with unfilled brandy snaps.

Alternatively, purée the fruit before adding it to the cream and use the mixture to fill brandy snaps.

Almost any pudding flavoured with chocolate will be greeted with applause, none more enthusiastically than little pots of rich dark chocolate mousse.

Chocolate Pots

SERVES 4–6

110 g (4 oz) dark dessert chocolate
120 ml (4 fl oz) double cream
3 large eggs, separated
1 teaspoon finely grated orange zest
2 tablespoons brandy, whisky or
    orange liqueur

Break the chocolate into a bowl or the top of a double boiler and add the cream. Melt the chocolate over hot but not boiling water.

Beat the egg yolks in another bowl and, still beating, pour in the melted chocolate. Whisk the mixture over the hot water until it is thick and smooth, then stir in the orange zest and brandy, whisky or orange liqueur. Remove from the heat. Whisk the egg whites until they hold a stiff peak and fold them into the chocolate mixture. Divide the mousse between four or more individual pots or glasses and cool until set.

Hot Chocolate Soufflé

SERVES 4

6 sponge finger biscuits
4 tablespoons whisky, brandy or
    rum
55 g (2 oz) cocoa powder
85 g (3 oz) caster sugar
1 teaspoon ground cinnamon
6 whites of large eggs

Break the biscuits into quarters and put them in a small bowl with the whisky, brandy or rum.

Sift together the cocoa, sugar and cinnamon.

Whisk the egg whites in a large bowl until stiff and fold in the cocoa mixture. Spoon a third of the meringue into a buttered and sugared soufflé dish of about 900 ml (1½ pints) capacity. Add half the sozzled biscuits and another third of the meringue. Add the remaining biscuits, followed by the last of the meringue.

Stand the soufflé dish in a larger ovenproof container and pour in cold water to come halfway up the side of the soufflé dish. Bake in a preheated moderate oven (160°C/325°F, gas mark 3) for about 45 minutes, or until well risen. Serve immediately with pouring cream flavoured with a little whisky, brandy or rum.

A *marquise au chocolat* can best be described as resembling frozen fudge, and it should therefore be served in modest slices. It is very rich and very satisfying. Whipped cream flavoured with a little orange liqueur is a particularly good accompaniment.

Marquise au Chocolat

225 g (8 oz) dark semi-sweet
   chocolate
110 g (4 oz) unsalted butter
2 large eggs, separated
85 g (3 oz) icing sugar

Break the chocolate into a bain marie, or into a bowl which will stand over a pan of simmering water, and add the butter. Melt them together, stirring constantly, until the mixture is smooth.

In another bowl, beat together the egg yolks and sugar until the mixture is pale and fluffy. In a third bowl whisk the egg whites to a stiff meringue.

Quickly mix together the melted chocolate and the egg yolk mixture, and lightly fold in the meringue. Immediately spoon the mixture into a small brick-shaped freezer container (a loaf tin is ideal), cover with foil and freeze until firm.

Unlike most ice creams which freeze very hard, this mixture is so rich that it should never become too hard to slice straight from the freezer. When it is firm, turn it onto a chilled serving plate and serve immediately.

Chocolate *roulade* looks like a Swiss roll but the texture is quite different. It has a crisp crazy-paving coat, and moist cake and cream centre.

Chocolate Roulade

SERVES 8 OR MORE

3 large eggs, separated
170 g (6 oz) caster sugar
450 ml (¾ pint) double cream
2 tablespoons brandy
30 g (1 oz) plain flour
45 g (1½ oz) cocoa powder
¼ teaspoon salt
55 g (2 oz) granulated sugar

Combine the egg yolks with half the caster sugar and whisk until the mixture is pale and light. In another bowl, whip 120 ml (4 fl oz) of the cream until it is thick, then beat in the brandy. In yet another bowl whisk the egg whites until they are frothy, then add the remaining caster sugar and whisk to a firm meringue. Add the meringue to the egg yolk and cream mixtures and fold lightly to mix. Sift together the flour, cocoa and salt and fold into the egg mousse.

Spoon the mixture into a large Swiss roll tray which has been well oiled. Sprinkle the top with the granulated sugar and bake in a preheated cool oven (150°C/300°F, gas mark 2) for about 30 minutes, or until the top is firm. Cool the roulade in its tin and fill it as soon as it has cooled.

Whip the remaining cream until it is firm, adding a little brandy or orange liqueur if you like. Turn the roulade out of its tin on to a sheet of greaseproof paper. Spread it evenly with the cream and, using the paper to help roll it, roll up tightly. Chill well before serving.

Chocolate roulade is best made the day before it is to be eaten, and it freezes well.

A sufficiency of ice cream rates high as a holiday priority with children. If you have not already won the special popularity accorded to makers of the very rich, very easy hot chocolate sauce made by melting Mars bars in evaporated milk, the hols are the time to go for it.

Very Gooey Chocolate Sauce

SERVES 4

1 Mars bar, sliced
1 small can of unsweetened
  evaporated milk

Put the slices of Mars bar in a small saucepan with the evaporated milk and heat together very gently, stirring constantly, until the sauce is thick and smooth. Serve with vanilla ice cream.

In many places espresso coffee is served with a shaving of lemon zest to fold above the cup, shooting a mist of lemon oil onto the surface of the coffee. The same combination of flavours makes an austere jelly to serve on its own or with a sumptuous cloud of sweetened whipped cream flavoured with vanilla. Deadly earnest slimmers could substitute artificial sweetener for all but 30 g (1 oz) of the sugar. A small proportion of real sugar greatly improves the flavour of almost any food or drink sweetened with saccharin.

Espresso Jelly

SERVES 4–6

600 ml (1 pint) freshly made
  espresso or strong black coffee
thinly pared zest of 1/2 a lemon
110 g (4 oz) sugar
15 g (1/2 oz) gelatine crystals

Mix the hot coffee, lemon zest and sugar. Stir until the sugar has dissolved, then leave until cold. Remove and discard the zest.

Put two or three tablespoons of cold water in a small saucepan and sprinkle the gelatine on top. Leave it for a few minutes to soften, then heat gently, stirring constantly, until the crystals have melted completely.

Mix together the gelatine and coffee and pour into a decorated jelly mould which has been dipped in cold water. Alternatively, divide the jelly between four to six tall wine glasses. Chill before serving.

Serve a chilled, coffee flavoured custard sauce with vanilla, praline or chocolate ice cream. Use the coffee custard as a change from chocolate sauce with profiteroles, with nut filled pancakes, hot chocolate soufflés, mousses and creams.

Chilled Coffee Sauce

MAKES ABOUT 600 ml (1 pint)

4 egg yolks
170 g (6 oz) caster sugar
pinch of salt
150 ml (¼ pint) double strength black coffee
300 ml (½ pint) creamy fresh milk
¼ teaspoon vanilla extract

Beat together the egg yolks, sugar and salt until the mixture is very pale and the whisk leaves a trail. Whisk in the coffee and milk and transfer the mixture to the top of a double boiler set over simmering water, or to a heavy-based saucepan. Cook on a gentle heat, stirring constantly, until the custard coats the back of a wooden spoon. Remove from the heat and stir the sauce from time to time as it cools. Add the vanilla extract and chill well.

Suet puddings of any description were always greeted with loud cries of 'ah duff' when I was a child and I assumed it was one of those idiotic family traditions. However, *The Shorter Oxford Dictionary* knows all about duff being a flour pudding boiled in a bag. Cloths have given way to pudding basins now, thank goodness, and duff is the lighter for it.

Why Sussex pond pudding is attributed to that county is not clear. The pond is obvious as soon as you cut into the rich suet crust and find a whole lemon surrounded by buttery syrup which quickly makes a puddle if not exactly a pond. It is a fresh tasting duff.

Sussex Pond Pudding

SERVES 4–6

225 g (8 oz) self-raising flour
¼ teaspoon salt
110 g (4 oz) shredded suet
about 120 ml (4 fl oz) iced water
110 g (4 oz) butter, diced
1 large lemon
110 g (4 oz) Demerara sugar

Sift the flour and salt into a bowl. Add the shredded suet and mix lightly with a fork to distribute it evenly. Make a well in the centre of the flour and add the water, a little at a time, to make a soft dough. You may not need all the water and a knife is the best instrument for the mixing. Knead the dough lightly on a floured surface until it is free of cracks and roll it out to a thickness of about 7 mm (¼ in).

Cut a quarter segment from the dough and set it aside for the lid. Use the remaining dough to line a well-buttered pudding basin of 900 ml (1½ pints) capacity. Dampen the edges of the join to make a seal.

Put half the butter in the bottom of the basin. Prick the lemon all over with a skewer and sit it upright in the butter. Cover with the sugar and remaining butter. Roll out the remaining dough for a lid. Dampen the edges and press it gently into place. Cover the basin with a layer of greaseproof paper and foil which have been folded together to make a 2.5 cm (1 in) pleat across the diameter of the basin and tie on tightly with string.

Stand the basin in a saucepan and pour in boiling water

to come one-third of the way up its sides. Cover the pan tightly and simmer the pudding for 3½ hours. Top up the water level from time to time using boiling water and never allowing the water to go off the boil.

Rest the pudding for a moment or two before turning it onto a deep plate. Make sure each serving includes a slice of the lemon as well as a spoonful of syrup.

It is whole lemons again which give Ohio Shaker lemon pie its unique character.

Ohio Shaker Lemon Pie

SERVES 4–6

2 lemons
225 g (8 oz) sugar
340 g (12 oz) plain flour
½ teaspoon salt
170 g (6 oz) butter, chilled
1 egg yolk
iced water to mix
4 eggs, beaten
sugar to dredge

Cut the lemons, skin and all, into paper-thin slices. Discard any pips. Mix the lemon slices with the sugar and set them aside for at least two hours or, better still, overnight.

Sift the flour and salt into a mixing bowl. Cut the butter into dice and toss them lightly in the flour. Rub in the fat, using your fingertips or a pastry blender, until the mixture resembles fine breadcrumbs. Mix the egg yolk with six tablespoons of the iced water and sprinkle it over the flour mixture. Mix lightly together, adding a little more water if necessary to make a firm dough. Press the dough lightly into a ball, wrap in greaseproof paper and refrigerate it for at least 30 minutes.

Roll out the pastry thinly on a floured surface. Cut one circle of pastry about 5 cm (2 in) larger than a 20 cm (8 in) pie plate, and another circle for the lid. Line the pie plate with the larger piece of pastry. Put the beaten eggs, lemon slices and their syrup in a bowl and fold them lightly together. Fill the pie with this mixture, dampen the edges of the pastry and top with the lid. Crimp the edges of the pie and cut two or three slits in the top to let out steam. Dredge the lid with sugar.

Bake in a preheated hot oven (230°C/450°F, gas mark 8) for 15 minutes. Reduce the temperature to moderate (180°C/350°F, gas mark 4) and bake for another 30 minutes, or until a knife inserted into the centre comes out clean. Serve hot, warm or cold.

Bread and butter pudding need not be stodgy. This recipe, from Chef Anton Mosimann of London's Dorchester Hotel, is as popular as it is light.

Bread and Butter Pudding

SERVES 4

250 ml (8 fl oz) milk
250 ml (8 fl oz) double cream
pinch of salt
1 vanilla pod
3 eggs
110 g (4 oz) sugar
3 small bread rolls
30 g (1 oz) butter
1 tablespoon sultanas or currants,
    soaked in water
1½ tablespoons apricot jam
a little icing sugar

Put the milk, cream, salt and vanilla pod in a pan and bring to the boil. Mix the eggs and sugar in a bowl. Remove the vanilla pod from the hot cream and pour it into the egg mixture, stirring briskly. Strain this custard through a sieve. Cut the rolls in thin slices, discarding the top and bottom crusts, then butter them.

Arrange the slices in an ovenproof dish and sprinkle them with the sultanas or currants. Add the custard and dot with any remaining butter. Set the pudding dish in a baking tin and pour in boiling water to come halfway up the sides of the dish. Bake in a cool oven (140°C/275°F, gas mark 1) for about one hour, or until the pudding is just firm.

Spread the apricot jam over the top of the pudding and dust lightly with the icing sugar. Place the pudding under the grill to set the glaze and brown it lightly. Serve the pudding hot, warm or cold with cream.

In the days when Lent was more rigorously observed than is generally the case now, eggs and butter were forbidden throughout the fast. Then Shrove Tuesday, with its pancakes and races, was a final fling, an occasion for working off high spirits as well as surplus stores.

Pancakes were about in medieval England and by the seventeenth century elaborate recipes were in circulation. Rebecca Price, wife of a country squire in the reign of Charles II, copied out this recipe given her by a Mrs Whitehead:

'Take a pinte of creame and the yolks of ten eggs; and ye white of two; foure spoonfulls of sack; and 2 of rose water, a little nutmeg grated; beat all these together with a little flower very thine; the pan must first be rubbed with a little butter, and after dried with a cleane cloath; before you put in your stuff; make your pan very hott otherwise they will heave too light; and not bake so well; you may frye ym with butter, or without'.

Half a pint of milk and one egg seems rather a comedown after such richness.

Pancakes

MAKES 12

110 g (4 oz) plain white or
    wholemeal flour
¼ teaspoon salt

Sift the flour and salt into a bowl and make a well in the centre. Add the egg and half the milk and mix from the centre, gradually drawing in the flour to make a smooth,

1 large egg, beaten
300 ml (½ pint) milk
1 tablespoon oil, preferably
    sunflower or peanut

thick batter. Add the remaining milk and oil and beat lightly until the batter is smooth again.

Beating the batter develops the gluten in the flour, making the mixture elastic and unwilling to run smoothly over the pan. Because wholemeal has less gluten than white flour, a batter made with it can be used immediately.

Batter made with white flour should be rested for about 30 minutes. Either type may be thinned by adding more milk to make thinner pancakes.

To cook the pancakes, use a small heavy pan of about 15 cm (6 in) diameter. An omelette pan is best if you do not have a pancake pan. Heat the pan well and grease it lightly. Pour about two tablespoons of batter into the centre of the pan and quickly swirl it to cover the base by tipping the pan. Cook the pancake until the underside is golden, then turn it over and cook until the other side is golden too. Cook the remaining batter in the same way.

Stack the pancakes on a covered plate over a pan of hot water to keep warm. To serve, sprinkle them with lemon juice and sugar and roll them up, or fill them.

Apple and Honey Pancakes

SERVES 6

450 g (1 lb) crisp dessert apples,
    preferably Cox's Orange Pippins
55 g (2 oz) butter
6 tablespoons honey
1 tablespoon lemon juice
12 freshly made pancakes (see
    facing page)
2 tablespoons icing sugar

Peel, core and quarter the apples and cut them into thick slices. Melt the butter in a frying pan until it foams, then add the apples. Fry gently until they are tender and just beginning to brown. Add the honey and lemon juice and cook for a moment longer.

Divide the apple mixture between the pancakes. Roll them up and dust the tops with the icing sugar. Serve hot or warm, just as they are, or with plain yogurt or cream.

Lemon Cheese Pancakes

SERVES 4

225 g (8 oz) yogurt curd or cream
    cheese (see page 66)
1 egg, separated
55 g (2 oz) sugar
3 drops of vanilla essence
1 tablespoon finely grated lemon
    zest
8 freshly made pancakes (see
    facing page)
2 tablespoons icing sugar

Mix the cheese, egg yolk, sugar, vanilla essence and lemon zest and beat well. Whisk the egg white until it holds firm peaks and fold it into the cheese mixture.

Divide the lemon cheese between the pancakes and roll them up. Arrange them on a warm serving dish or dishes and dust with the icing sugar. Pop the pancakes into a preheated very cool oven (110°C/225°F, gas mark ¼) for about five minutes to warm the filling a little. Serve immediately.

Crêpes are a splendidly useful standby for unexpected guests or well-nigh instant family meals. I like to keep a stack of these lacy home-made pancakes in the freezer, but frozen crêpes are also sold by some freezer centres, and I have recently seen plastic packs of large Breton crêpes which keep for months in the storecupboard. Frozen crêpes thaw in moments if spread on a flat surface at room temperature, and all types can be used for sweet or savoury fillings. Any variation on the crêpes Suzette theme is a sure winner. The flames and flavours are irresistible.

Crêpes Suzette

SERVES 6 OR MORE

110 g (4 oz) plain flour
¼ teaspoon salt
3 eggs, beaten
250 ml (8 fl oz) milk
*3 tablespoons melted butter or
 peanut oil*
85 g (3 oz) unsalted butter
85 g (3 oz) caster sugar
*juice and finely grated zest of 2
 large oranges*
3 tablespoons cognac
*3 tablespoons orange Curaçao,
 Cointreau or Grand Marnier*

Sift the flour and salt into a bowl and make a well in the centre. Add the eggs and a little of the milk and mix from the centre, gradually drawing in the flour to make a thick, smooth batter. Add the remaining milk, a little at a time, stirring constantly until the batter has the consistency of single cream. The batter should be beaten as little as possible, as overbeating will result in tough crêpes. Rest the batter for one to 24 hours in the refrigerator. Just before using the batter, stir in the melted butter or oil.

Heat a small, heavy crêpe or omelette pan on a medium heat and grease it very lightly with a piece of crumpled kitchen paper wiped on a knob of butter. Pour in just enough batter to coat the base of the pan (usually two or three tablespoons), swirl it to the edges of the pan and cook until the underside of the pancake is golden. Run a knife or spatula round the edge of the pancake to loosen it, and turn it over carefully. Cook until the second side is lightly coloured. Cook the remaining batter in the same way.

To keep the pancakes warm, stack them on a plate over a pan of simmering water with a leaf of greaseproof paper between each one. To freeze the crêpes, simply wrap the stack loosely in foil and freeze in the usual way.

The first one or two crêpes in any batch seldom turn out perfectly. One always seems to waste a couple while adjusting the heat correctly and working out exactly the right quantity of batter to use for each pancake.

A very large frying pan or a big, oval gratin dish made of enamelled cast iron is the best implement for the next phase of the recipe.

Melt the butter in the pan on a low heat and stir in the sugar. Cook gently together until the mixture begins to give off just the faintest whiff of caramel. Be careful not to let it darken too much or the sauce will be bitter. Stir in the orange juice and finely grated zest.

Now you need to work fast and methodically or the sauce will be soaked up by the first crêpes before the last few are in the pan. Take the first crêpe and place it, prettiest side down, in the pan. Fold it in half, then in half again to make a wonky triangle and move it to the side of the pan. Repeat the operation until all the crêpes have been used up. If the first pan is certain to become too crowded to work in, lift each folded crêpe into a second pan as soon as it is done.

Mix together the cognac and orange liqueur in a small pan and warm them gently. Pour the liquid over the crêpes, stand back and set light to it immediately. Serve as soon as the flames die down.

For the base of an uncooked cheesecake I use a Victoria sandwich mixture.

Basic Uncooked Cheesecake

MAKES A DEEP 18 cm (7 in) CAKE

1 sponge base 1 cm (¹/₃ in) thick
340 g (12 oz) fresh cream cheese
3 large eggs, separated
170 g (6 oz) caster sugar
¹/₂ teaspoon vanilla essence
250 ml (8 fl oz) double cream
5 tablespoons lemon juice
2 tablespoons water
15 g (¹/₂ oz) gelatine crystals

Take an 18 cm (7 in) loose-bottomed cake tin about 7.5 cm (3 in) deep and line it with greaseproof paper. Drop in the sponge base.

In a large bowl beat together the cheese, egg yolks, half the sugar, vanilla essence and cream. Put the lemon juice and water in a small pan and sprinkle the gelatine on top. Leave it for a minute or two to swell and soften, then heat gently until the gelatine has melted completely, but do not allow it to boil. Beat the gelatine into the cheese mixture.

Whisk the egg whites until they hold a soft peak, add the remaining sugar and continue whisking until they hold a firm peak. Fold the meringue into the cheese mixture and mix carefully until it is well blended.

Spoon the cheese mixture into the prepared tin, level the top and chill for at least two hours before serving.

There is a purist view of strawberries, quite widely held, that they are best eaten with sugar and cream and that any other treatment of them is a gastronomic equivalent of sacrilege. For perfect berries it is the perfect treatment. But for ripe fruit which is misshapen, a little biffed, or otherwise disqualified for such artless presentation, a recipe or two may come in handy.

Strawberry Cheesecake

SERVES 6–8

55 g (2 oz) butter
170 g (6 oz) shortcake biscuit
  crumbs
120 ml (4 fl oz) fresh orange juice
1 sachet of gelatine crystals
225 g (8 oz) ripe strawberries
2 eggs, separated
110 g (4 oz) caster sugar
225 g (8 oz) ricotta or cream cheese
juice of ½ a lemon
250 ml (8 fl oz) double cream
whole strawberries to decorate

Melt the butter and stir in the crumbs. Press the mixture evenly over the base of a 20 cm (8 in) round loose-bottomed cake tin, preferably the type with expanding sides. Chill well.

Put the orange juice in a small pan and sprinkle the gelatine on top. Leave it for a minute or two to soften and swell, then heat gently until the gelatine has dissolved completely.

Rub the strawberries through a sieve, or process them briefly in a blender, and strain the purée.

In a large bowl beat together the egg yolks and sugar until the mixture is pale and fluffy. Add the cheese and beat until smooth. Beat in the gelatine mixture, strawberry purée and lemon juice. Whip the cream until it holds a soft peak and the egg whites to a stiff meringue. Fold them into the cheese mixture. Pour the filling into the prepared tin and chill until firm. Remove the cheesecake from the tin before decorating the top with a ring of halved strawberries.

Ideally strawberries Romanoff should be made with whole, perfect fruit. But it is also a lovely way to serve the good bits of slightly damaged fruit.

Strawberries Romanoff

SERVES 4

450 g (1 lb) ripe strawberries
3 tablespoons icing sugar
1 tablespoon rum
2 tablespoons Cointreau
150 ml (¼ pint) double cream
1 tablespoon kirsch

Hull, wash and dry the berries. Put them in a bowl with the sugar, rum and Cointreau and chill them for at least an hour.

About one hour before serving them, whip the cream until it holds a peak and stir in the kirsch. Fold the cream into the strawberries and chill again before serving.

A crisp pastry case filled with pastry cream topped with ripe strawberries takes a lot of beating in the popularity stakes. Flavour the pastry cream with Benedictine and taste France. It really is not necessary to glaze these tarts as shops do if they are to be eaten soon after being assembled.

Strawberry Tart

SERVES 6–8

225 g (8 oz) plain flour
1 tablespoon icing sugar
110 g (4 oz) butter, chilled
1 egg yolk
iced water to mix

For the pastry cream:
450 ml (³/4 pint) milk
5 cm (2 in) vanilla pod, split
 lengthwise
5 egg yolks
110 g (4 oz) caster sugar
2 tablespoons plain flour
1 tablespoon cornflour
15 g (¹/2 oz) butter
120 ml (4 fl oz) double cream
1–2 tablespoons Benedictine
 (optional)

To finish:
340 g (12 oz) strawberries
4 tablespoons redcurrant jelly
 (optional)

Sift the flour and sugar into a large bowl. Cut the butter into small dice and toss them in the flour. Rub in the fat, using a pastry blender or your fingertips, until the mixture looks like fine breadcrumbs.

Beat the egg yolk with four tablespoons of the iced water and sprinkle over the flour mixture. Mix lightly together, adding a little more water if needed. Press the dough lightly into a ball, wrap in greaseproof paper and a damp cloth and refrigerate it for 30 minutes.

Lightly butter a 25 cm (10 in) loose-bottomed flan tin. Roll out the dough thinly on a floured surface. Rest it for about 15 minutes before lifting it gently onto the tin and easing it into shape. Trim the edges and chill for another 10 minutes.

Just before baking line the shell with greaseproof paper or foil and weight it with dried beans. Set it on a baking sheet and bake in a preheated moderately hot oven (200°C/400°F, gas mark 6) for 10 minutes. Remove from the oven and take out the beans and lining paper. Prick the base with a fork, reduce the temperature to moderate (180°C/350°F, gas mark 4) and bake the shell for another 10 minutes. Cool it on a wire rack.

To make the pastry cream, put the milk and vanilla pod in a small pan, bring to the boil, remove from the heat and leave it to infuse, until cold if possible.

Combine the egg yolks and sugar in a bowl and whisk until light and fluffy. Gradually whisk in the flour and cornflour. Strain the milk and add it gradually to the egg mixture, whisking constantly.

Pour the mixture back into the pan. Bring to the boil on a moderate heat, stirring constantly. Cook gently for another three minutes or so, taking courage at the moment when the mixture looks like scrambled egg. Keep beating and it will smooth out.

Remove the pan from the heat and beat in the butter. Beat for a little longer until the mixture begins to cool, then cover and chill it.

Whip the cream until it holds a soft peak and beat it lightly into the custard. Add the liqueur and mix well.

Spread the pastry cream over the base of the pastry shell. Hull the strawberries and arrange them in circles on the custard, halving them if they are very large.

Heat the redcurrant jelly with two tablespoons of water until it melts. Glaze the fruit with the melted jelly.

An iced strawberry soufflé is an elegant summer pudding which can be made with the good bits of bruised or damaged fruit as long as the berries are ripe and well flavoured.

Iced Strawberry Soufflé

340 g (12 oz) ripe strawberries
110 g (4 oz) granulated sugar
2 large eggs, separated
110 g (4 oz) icing sugar
150 ml (¼ pint) double cream
1 tablespoon iced water

Turn the freezer to its coldest setting. Prepare a soufflé dish of 1.2 litres (2 pints) capacity with a paper or foil collar which stands at least 2.5 cm (1 in) above the rim of the dish.

Hull, wash and dry the strawberries. Rub them through a sieve, or process them lightly in a blender, and strain the purée. Add the granulated sugar and stir from time to time until it has dissolved, then refrigerate the purée for an hour or more to develop the flavour.

Put the egg yolks in a bowl and add half the icing sugar. Beat lightly together, then set the bowl over a pan of just-simmering water and continue beating. When the mixture is warm, but not hot, take the bowl off the heat and continue beating until the egg mousse is cool and has tripled its original volume. Chill the mousse thoroughly.

Whisk the egg whites in another bowl until they are foamy. Add the remaining icing sugar and continue beating until the meringue holds stiff peaks.

Whip the cream with the iced water until it forms soft peaks.

Mix the chilled strawberry purée and egg mousse. Add the meringue and the whipped cream and whisk them lightly together.

Turn the mixture into the prepared soufflé dish and freeze until firm. If your freezer runs at a very low temperature and the soufflé becomes very hard, ripen it in the refrigerator for about 15 minutes before serving. Remove the collar from the dish before ripening and serving the soufflé, which may be decorated with whipped cream and whole strawberries.

Hot Raspberry Soufflé

285 g (10 oz) ripe raspberries
255 g (9 oz) granulated sugar
5 whites of large eggs

Rub the raspberries through a sieve, or process the fruit lightly, and strain the purée.

Put the sugar in a heavy, medium-sized saucepan with 150 ml (¼ pint) of cold water. Heat gently until the sugar dissolves, then increase the heat and boil briskly to the small crack stage (141°C/285°F on a sugar thermometer). Add the fruit purée to the syrup and boil to the soft ball stage (115°C/240°F).

Whisk the egg whites until they hold stiff peaks. Pour the fruit syrup into the meringue and fold together.

Spoon the mixture into a buttered and sugared soufflé dish of about 900 ml (1½ pints) capacity. Bake in a preheated moderately hot oven (200°C/400°F, gas mark 6) for 15–20 minutes.

Serve immediately, on its own, or with pouring cream or vanilla ice cream.

Rhubarb and the milkman's horse will never be parted in my memory. The milkman's horse was the only one I was ever keen on. It was very big, I am sure it was, and dapple grey, and old, and I was too young to notice whether it was he or she.

It was always given its nose bag somewhere along our street, and generally did something else as well and we raced out with shovels to collect it for the rhubarb which, early in the year, flourished pink and pale green at the bottom of the garden under an upturned bucket with a rusty hole in the base. Everyone knew that manure was very good for rhubarb.

SERVES 4–6

Rhubarb Crumble

900 g (2 lb) rhubarb
170 g (6 oz) white or brown sugar
grated zest of 1 orange
170 g (6 oz) plain white or
  wholewheat flour
85 g (3 oz) butter

Wash and dry the rhubarb. Trim the ends of the stalks and cut them in 2.5 cm (1 in) lengths. Put them in a pie dish and sprinkle with half the sugar and the orange zest.

Sift the flour into a bowl, cut the butter into small dice and rub it into the flour until the mixture has the texture of fine breadcrumbs. Stir in all but a tablespoon of the remaining sugar. Spoon the crumble mixture over the rhubarb and press it down lightly. Sprinkle the remaining tablespoon of sugar over the top.

Set the dish on a baking sheet and bake the crumble in a preheated moderately hot oven (200°C/400°F, gas mark 6) for 45 minutes to one hour. Serve it hot or warm with cream or top of the milk.

Eve's pudding is another lovely, old fashioned recipe.

Eve's Pudding

SERVES 4

450 g (1 lb) cooking apples, peeled, cored and sliced
85 g (3 oz) Demerara sugar
1 teaspoon finely grated orange or lemon zest
55 g (2 oz) butter, softened
55 g (2 oz) caster sugar
85 g (3 oz) self-raising flour
1 large egg, beaten
a little milk

Butter a pie or soufflé dish of approximately 1 litre (1¾ pints) capacity and arrange the apple slices in the bottom. Sprinkle with the Demerara sugar and orange or lemon zest.

In a bowl cream the butter and add the caster sugar. Beat until the mixture is pale and fluffy. Beat in alternate spoons of sifted flour and egg until all of both have been incorporated. Stir in enough milk to make a mixture which will just drop from a spoon.

Spread the sponge mixture over the fruit. Bake in a preheated moderately hot oven (190°C/375°F, gas mark 5) for 35–45 minutes (depending on whether the dish is shallow or deep), or until the sponge is well risen and golden brown. Serve hot or warm with thin cream or top of the milk.

Apple macaroon is an absolutely delicious variation on apple pie. It has a sweet, crunchy macaroon topping instead of the usual pastry, and is equally good hot, warm, cold or chilled. Serve it with cream or natural yogurt.

Apple Macaroon

SERVES 4

450 g (1 lb) cooking apples, peeled and sliced
granulated or soft brown sugar to taste
2 egg whites
110 g (4 oz) caster sugar
55 g (2 oz) ground almonds

Put the apples in an ovenproof dish and sprinkle them with sugar. Whisk the egg whites until they are light, but not really stiff. Fold in the sugar and almonds and spread the mixture lightly over the apples. Bake in the centre of a preheated moderate oven (180°C/350°F, gas mark 4) for 50 minutes to one hour.

Golden Apple Pudding

SERVES 4–6

170 g (6 oz) fresh white breadcrumbs
170 g (6 oz) soft brown sugar
55 g (2 oz) butter
680 g (1½ lb) cooking apples, peeled, cored and sliced
1 tablespoon lemon juice

Mix the breadcrumbs and half the sugar. Melt the butter in a frying pan, add the crumb mixture and fry on a medium heat until the sugar has melted and most of the crumbs are crisp.

Put the apples in a saucepan, add the remaining sugar, lemon juice and a little water and cook on a low heat until the apples are tender. Taste them for sweetness and add more sugar if needed.

Arrange alternate layers of apple and crumbs in a serving dish, finishing with a good layer of the crumbs. Chill the pudding.

Habitués of Chinese restaurants will be familiar with the addictive powers of caramel coated, sesame sprinkled, oriental apple fritters.

Chinese Toffee Apples

6 crisp eating apples (about 680 g/1½ lb)
6 tablespoons plain flour
1 tablespoon cornflour
2 egg whites
vegetable oil for deep frying
110 g (4 oz) sugar
1 tablespoon sesame seeds

Peel, core and quarter the apples and dust the pieces lightly with a little of the plain flour. Sift the remaining flour and the cornflour into a bowl. Add the egg whites and stir to a thick, sticky batter.

Heat the oil to 190°C/375°F. Coat the apple quarters with the flour paste and deep fry them (see page 229), a few at a time, until they are golden brown. Rest the fritters on absorbent kitchen paper.

In a small saucepan heat the sugar with two tablespoons of water, stirring frequently until the sugar melts and the syrup is lightly caramelised. It should be a very pale golden brown to make a thin glaze. Dip the apple fritters in the caramel and sprinkle them with the sesame seeds.

Serve the fritters in small heaps on individual oiled dishes. Put a bowl of cold water on the table too so that everyone can dip their fritters into it, one at a time to harden the caramel. Alternatively, do this in the kitchen and serve immediately.

Beautifully ripe pears are so good as they are that there is little temptation to turn them into puddings. Rock-hard cooking pears and unripe dessert pears can be, with care, the basis of many good things. Softening them up and tinting them red in spiced wine is a treatment which has survived since Tudor days. Any leftover wine syrup can be used to start another batch of drunken pears or to make a delicately spiced pink syllabub.

Drunken Pears

1 litre (1¾ pints) red wine
110 g (4 oz) sugar
2 sticks of cinnamon
6 cloves
finely pared zest of 1 small orange or tangerine
6 hard but handsome pears

Put half the wine in a saucepan with the sugar, cinnamon, cloves and orange zest. Heat gently until the sugar has dissolved completely.

Using a very sharp stainless steel knife (carbon steel would blacken the fruit) peel the pears very carefully, leaving on the stems and preserving the shape of the fruit as well as possible.

Arrange the peeled pears standing upright in a pan or ovenproof casserole in which they fit fairly snugly together. A big soufflé dish may be just the thing. Pour in the spiced wine syrup and add enough of the remaining wine to cover the pears up to their stalks. Cover the pan or casserole and simmer the pears very gently on top of the stove or in a very cool oven (120°C/250°F, gas mark ½) until they are tender and almost translucent. This may take anything from one hour to as many as four, depending on the hardness and size of the pears. It is worth being patient though and working on a low heat so that the pears are perfectly tender without breaking up.

Serve the pears hot, warm or chilled with a little of their syrup and plenty of thick cream. You may like to reduce the syrup by fast boiling.

Clafoutis is a traditional French country pudding of dark juicy cherries baked in a rich batter that is not quite custard and not quite cake.

Clafoutis

SERVES 4–6

680 g (1½ lb) ripe black cherries
2 large eggs
85 g (3 oz) caster sugar
3 tablespoons plain flour
¼ teaspoon salt
150 ml (¼ pint) double cream
300 ml (½ pint) fresh milk
2 tablespoons kirsch (optional)

Stone the cherries and arrange them in the bottom of a well-buttered, shallow, ovenproof dish.

Put the eggs and sugar in a bowl and beat them well together until the mixture is thick and light. Add the flour and salt and beat until smooth. Gradually beat in the cream, milk and kirsch to make a light batter.

Pour the batter over the cherries and bake in a preheated moderately hot oven (190°C/375°F, gas mark 5) for about 45 minutes or until the *clafoutis* is golden brown on top, and set, but not too firmly. Serve it hot, warm or cold with a sprinkling of caster sugar on top and thin, chilled cream to pour over it.

Grape and almond tart is a moist flan which is best served cold because the filling firms up as it cools.

Grape and Almond Tart

SERVES 4–6

170 g (6 oz) shortcrust pastry (see
   page 185)
2 large eggs
110 g (4 oz) caster sugar
6 tablespoons ground almonds
2 tablespoons double cream
a few drops of vanilla essence
340 g (12 oz) seedless grapes

Line a 23 cm (9 in) flan tin or dish with the pastry and chill well. Cover the pastry shell with foil and weight it with dried rice or beans. Set on a baking sheet and bake in a preheated hot oven (200°C/400°F, gas mark 6) for 10 minutes if using a tin, 15 for a china dish. Remove from the oven and take out the rice and foil. Prick the base with a fork, reduce the temperature to moderate (180°C/350°F, gas mark 4) and bake the shell for another 10–15 minutes.

Whisk the eggs and sugar until thick and light. Beat in the almonds, cream and vanilla essence. Arrange the grapes on the baked pastry case and spoon the almond mixture over them. Return the tart to the oven and bake for 40–45 minutes, or until the top is golden and the filling just firm. Serve cold.

For the simplest of endings to an autumnal supper: stuffed figs. They take only moments to prepare.

Stuffed Fresh Figs

SERVES 4

8 ripe purple figs
110 g (4 oz) ground almonds
55 g (2 oz) caster sugar
1 tablespoon cream cheese
1 tablespoon fresh lemon juice
   (optional)
8 whole unblanched almonds

Wash and dry the figs. Slice each fig twice from the stem almost through to the base, so that the quarter segments can be opened like petals.

Mix the ground almonds with the sugar, cheese and lemon juice, if you are using it, to a stiff paste and put a spoonful in each opened fig. Top each blob of stuffing with a whole almond and serve the figs at room temperature.

There is no reason why home-made ices should be spoiled by gritty ice crystals. If the partially frozen ice is tipped into a bowl at half time and beaten vigorously till smooth, the texture when it is frozen firm will be like velvet. Fast freezing helps to eliminate the growth of big ice crystals, so always turn the freezer or ice compartment to its coldest setting at least one hour before putting in the ice cream container.

The following recipes can all be made successfully without special equipment, and all will freeze firm in the ice-making compartment of a refrigerator. Freezer owners will need to ripen rock-hard ices in the refrigerator before serving.

Fresh limes make a sharply refreshing sorbet. The recipe works equally well with lemons or two grapefruit substituted for the limes.

Lime Sorbet

MAKES ABOUT 1 litre (1¾ pints)

4 limes
1 orange
450 ml (¾ pint) water
225 g (8 oz) granulated sugar
2 egg whites
2 tablespoons icing sugar

Cut the zest from the limes and orange using a very sharp knife or potato peeler and taking care not to include the bitter white pith. Put the zest in a pan with the water and granulated sugar and heat slowly together until the sugar has dissolved completely. Increase the heat and boil the syrup for five minutes, then set it aside to cool.

Squeeze the juice from the fruit. Mix the syrup with the juice and strain the mixture. Pour it into a freezer tray, cover and freeze until the edges have set firm and the centre is still slushy.

Beat the egg whites until they are foamy, add the icing sugar and continue beating until the meringue holds a stiff peak.

Tip the partially frozen ice into a chilled bowl and beat it until smooth. Add the meringue and whisk lightly together. Return the mixture to the freezer and freeze until firm. (A second beating is occasionally necessary for ices frozen in the ice-making compartment of a small refrigerator.)

191

Hazelnut Ice Cream

MAKES ABOUT 1 litre (1¾ pints)

110 g (4 oz) shelled hazelnuts
4 egg yolks
170 g (6 oz) soft brown sugar
300 ml (½ pint) milk
250 ml (8 fl oz) double cream,
  chilled
2 tablespoons iced water

Toasting the hazelnuts improves and intensifies their flavour. Spread them on a baking sheet and roast in a preheated moderate oven (160°C/325°F, gas mark 3) for about 15 minutes, or until the centres are a pale biscuit colour. Cool the nuts then tip them onto a clean, dry tea towel and rub off the skins. Grind or chop them finely.

Beat the egg yolks and sugar together until the mixture is very pale and the whisk leaves a ribbon-like trail. Whisk in the milk and transfer the mixture to a saucepan. Cook the custard on a low heat, stirring constantly, until it thickens a little, just enough to coat the back of a wooden spoon. Cool the custard, stirring occasionally to prevent a skin forming, then chill it well.

Whip the cream with the iced water until it forms soft peaks. Mix the chilled custard with the hazelnuts and cream and beat them lightly together. Pour the mixture into a freezer tray, cover and freeze until it has the texture of stiff slush.

Turn the ice cream into a chilled bowl and beat it vigorously. Return it to the freezer tray, cover and freeze until firm.

Blackcurrant Sorbet

MAKES ABOUT 1 litre (1¾ pints)

450 g (1 lb) ripe blackcurrants
juice of 2 oranges
170 g (6 oz) caster sugar
2 egg whites
2 tablespoons icing sugar

Top and tail the blackcurrants. Purée the raw fruit either by processing it briefly or by pressing it through a coarse sieve. Then pass the purée through a fine sieve to catch the tiny blackcurrant pips.

Mix together the purée, orange juice and caster sugar and stir from time to time until the sugar has dissolved completely. Pour the purée into a freezer tray, cover and freeze until it has the texture of stiff slush.

Whisk the egg whites until they are foamy, add the icing sugar and continue whisking until the meringue holds stiff peaks.

Turn the blackcurrant ice into a chilled bowl and whisk it vigorously. Add the meringue and beat lightly together. Return the mixture to the freezer tray, cover and freeze until firm.

Peach Sherbet

1 kg (2¼ lb) ripe peaches
juice of 1 lemon
juice of 1 orange
170 g (6 oz) caster sugar

Peaches are easier to peel if you drop them into boiling water for 30 seconds or so, then the skins will slip off easily. Peel the peaches and remove the stones. Purée the flesh by processing it briefly or passing it through a sieve.

Mix together the purée, lemon and orange juices and sugar and stir from time to time until the sugar has dissolved completely. Pour the purée into a freezer tray, cover and freeze until it has the texture of stiff slush.

Tip the sherbet into a chilled bowl and beat it vigorously. Return the mixture to the freezer tray, cover and freeze until firm.

Raspberries make a particularly fine sorbet. A little kirsch added to the mixture is a pleasing addition. But beware of adding any alcohol to sorbets or ice creams if you are freezing them in the ice-making compartment of a small refrigerator as alcohol inhibits freezing. Freezers with three- or four-star ratings will cope.

MAKES ABOUT 1 litre (1¾ pints) # Raspberry Sorbet

450 g (1 lb) ripe raspberries
juice of 2 oranges
225 g (8 oz) granulated sugar
2 tablespoons kirsch (optional)
2 egg whites
2 tablespoons icing sugar

Rub the raspberries through a fine sieve to remove the seeds, or process them briefly in a blender, and strain the purée.

Mix the purée with the orange juice, granulated sugar and kirsch and stir from time to time until the sugar has dissolved completely. Chill the purée for an hour or more to develop the flavour. Turn the purée into a flat-bottomed plastic box or metal container, cover and freeze until the mixture has the texture of stiff slush.

Beat the egg whites until they are foamy, add the icing sugar and continue beating until the meringue holds stiff peaks.

Tip the partially frozen ice into a chilled bowl and beat it vigorously until smooth. Add the meringue and beat lightly together. Return the mixture to the freezer, cover and freeze until firm.

Strawberry Ice Cream

MAKES ABOUT 1 litre (1¾ pints)

340 g (12 oz) ripe strawberries
juice of 1 orange
juice of 1 lemon
170 g (6 oz) granulated sugar
450 ml (¾ pint) double cream
3 tablespoons iced water

Rub the hulled strawberries through a sieve, or process them briefly in a blender, and sieve the purée.

Mix together the purée, orange and lemon juices and sugar and stir from time to time until the sugar has dissolved completely. Chill the purée for an hour or more to develop the flavour.

Whip the cream with the iced water until it forms soft peaks. Mix the chilled purée with the whipped cream and whisk them lightly together. Turn the mixture into a flat-bottomed plastic box, cover and freeze until it resembles a stiff slush.

Tip the partially frozen ice into a chilled bowl and whisk it vigorously to break down any large ice crystals. Return the mixture to the freezer, cover and freeze until firm.

Strawberry Sorbet

MAKES ABOUT 1 litre (1¾ pints)

450 g (1 lb) ripe strawberries
170 g (6 oz) granulated sugar
juice of 1 orange
juice of 1 lemon
2 egg whites
2 tablespoons icing sugar

Rub the hulled strawberries through a sieve, or process them lightly in a blender, and strain the purée.

Mix together the purée, granulated sugar, orange and lemon juices and stir from time to time until the sugar has dissolved completely. Chill the mixture for an hour to develop the flavour fully. Turn the purée into a flat-bottomed plastic box or metal container, cover and freeze until the mixture is firm at the edges but still slushy in the middle.

Turn the partially frozen sorbet into a chilled bowl and beat it vigorously until smooth. Beat the egg whites until they are foamy, add the icing sugar and continue beating until the meringue holds stiff peaks.

Add the meringue to the partially frozen ice and beat lightly together. Return the mixture to the freezer tray and freeze until firm.

Pistachio kulfi (a delicately flavoured Indian ice cream) is easy to make and not nearly as sweet as commercial ice creams. Traditional recipes begin with pints of fresh milk which then have to be boiled down over several hours. Having done it I can report in all honesty that tinned, evaporated milk works just as well.

Pistachio Kulfi

SERVES 4–6

600 ml (1 pint) evaporated milk
4 tablespoons caster sugar
2 tablespoons finely chopped
  pistachio kernels (fresh, not
  salted)
1 teaspoon ground cardamom

Combine all the ingredients and stir until the sugar has dissolved completely. Pour the mixture into a flat-bottomed container, cover and freeze until it has the consistency of heavy slush. Tip it into a chilled bowl and beat the mixture vigorously to break up the ice crystals. Return it to the container and freeze until firm, beating once more if necessary. Ripen the ice in the refrigerator for 30 minutes or more before serving.

Shells of citrus fruits filled with sorbets made from the fresh juice are a delightful end to any meal. If you are serving them at home there is no need to bring them to table bullet-hard as far too many restaurants do. There is no fun in chipping away at a rocky ice, so ripen them in the refrigerator for 15–20 minutes before serving.

Clementines Givrées

SERVES 6

900 g (2 lb) clementines, satsumas,
  tangerines or other soft citrus
  fruit
juice of 1 lemon
285 g (10 oz) caster sugar

Pick out six well-matched fruits. Choose fruit which is neither too large nor too small to be filled with sorbet and pick out six good looking specimens. Cut a hat off each fruit at the end opposite the stalk and, using a teaspoon, carefully scoop out all the flesh into a bowl. Arrange the emptied shells on a lightly oiled tray and put them in the freezer.

Squeeze the juice from the remaining fruit, add the pulp taken from the shells already emptied and strain both into a bowl. Stir in the lemon juice and sugar and continue stirring until the sugar has dissolved completely.

Pour the fruit juice into a shallow container and freeze until it is firm. Tip it into a bowl and beat it well before piping the mixture into the frozen fruit shells. Return the filled shells to the freezer until needed, then ripen them in the refrigerator for a short while before serving.

This ice, made only of fruit juice and sugar, is smooth and dense. It may be lightened by folding in one or two beaten egg whites when the frozen sorbet is beaten before filling the shells. This substantially increases the volume of the mixture, and you will need to prepare more fruit shells.

Gooseberries have what advertising people would call an image problem. Well, they are not exactly glamorous, are they? What with their unflattering nicknames – goosegogs and hairy grapes – and their deceitful role in the reproduction of our species, gooseberries are hardly a subject of gastronomic reverence.

Early green gooseberries and elderflowers appear at the same time of year to make this lovely scented sorbet.

Gooseberry and Elderflower Sorbet

MAKES ABOUT 1 litre (1¾ pints)

1.35 kg (3 lb) green gooseberries
900 ml (1½ pints) water
4 elderflower heads
340 g (12 oz) sugar

There is no need to top and tail the gooseberries for this recipe. Wash them and put them in a pan with the water and simmer slowly until the fruit is very soft and pulpy. Strain the juice through a scalded jelly bag or clean tea towel as for the jelly (see page 244).

Tie the elderflower heads loosely in muslin and put them in a pan with the juice and sugar. Heat slowly until the sugar has dissolved, then bring to the boil and immediately turn off the heat. Leave the elderflowers in the syrup to infuse until it is quite cold, then remove them.

Pour the cold syrup into a metal or plastic freezer box and freeze until the mixture is like stiff slush. Turn it into a chilled bowl and beat it vigorously. Return it to the freezer and freeze until firm.

Cointreau Soufflé

SERVES 4

300 ml (½ pint) milk
3 large eggs, separated, and 2 additional whites
55 g (2 oz) caster sugar
finely grated zest of 2 oranges
30 g (1 oz) plain flour
4 tablespoons Cointreau
1 tablespoon icing sugar

Bring the milk to the boil and set it aside. Beat the egg yolks with half the caster sugar and the orange zest until the mixture is thick and pale. Whisk in the flour, followed by the hot milk. Pour the mixture back into the milk pan and bring it to a simmer, whisking constantly. Continue whisking and simmering for two minutes, then remove the pan from the heat and allow the custard to cool a little before stirring in the Cointreau.

Whisk the egg whites until they hold a stiff peak, then add the remaining caster sugar and whisk a little longer until the meringue is glossy. Fold a spoonful of the meringue into the custard until it is well blended, then lightly fold in the remainder.

Turn the mixture into a prepared soufflé dish of 1 litre (2 pints) capacity, or divide it between four 300 ml (½ pint) dishes. Dust with the icing sugar. Set the filled dish or dishes on a baking sheet and bake in the centre of a preheated hot oven (220°C/425°F, gas mark 7) for 12–15 minutes for the large soufflé, 8–10 minutes for the individual ones.

Claret Jelly

SERVES 4–6

pared zest and juice of 1 lemon
2 sachets of gelatine crystals
1 bottle drinkable claret
110 g (4 oz) sugar
10 cm (4 in) stick of cinnamon
2 cloves

Put four tablespoons of cold water in a small pan, add the lemon juice and sprinkle the gelatine on top. Leave it to soften.

Heat the claret slowly with the sugar, lemon zest, cinnamon and cloves, but do not allow it to boil. Add the softened gelatine and stir until the gelatine has melted completely. Strain the mixture through a fine sieve into a wetted jelly mould and leave it to set in a cool place.

Unmould the jelly and serve it on a candlelit table. Offer lightly whipped cream in a separate bowl.

Port-soaked French toast makes a quick, special pudding. This version probably originated in Portugal, although the recipe comes from Brazil where it is a popular festive pudding called *rabanadas*.

Rabanadas

SERVES 4

8 slices French bread about 2 cm
  (³/4 in) thick
3 tablespoons caster sugar
175 ml (6 fl oz) port
2 large eggs
55 g (2 oz) butter
1 teaspoon ground cinnamon

Arrange the slices of bread in one layer on a plate. Mix one tablespoon of the sugar with the port and pour it over the bread. Beat the eggs in a bowl and, when the bread has soaked up the sweetened port, dip each slice in egg to coat both sides.

Melt the butter in a large frying pan, add the soaked bread and fry on both sides until it is golden brown and crisp. Mix the remaining sugar with the cinnamon and sprinkle over the toast.

Those who do not know what goes into zabaglione are surprised that this warm, boozy froth contains only the yolks and not the whites of eggs. Marsala is the correct wine to use, but any sort of sherry produces a perfectly acceptable result.

Zabaglione

SERVES 4

4 egg yolks
4 tablespoons caster sugar
8 tablespoons dry Marsala or
  sherry

Combine the egg yolks and sugar in a fairly large, deep bowl and whisk until the mixture is pale and light. Place the bowl over a pan of hot, but not boiling, water and whisk in the wine. Continue whisking the mixture over this gentle heat until it froths and swells into a dense foam. Divide the zabaglione between four wine glasses and serve immediately with a crisp biscuit or wafer.

When I put this heady eighteenth century trifle recipe in *The Times* I assumed that its name, whim-wham, was an indication of its alcoholic smack. Readers of the paper had other ideas which they aired in the correspondence columns.

Miss Audrey Hogston

'Sir, I was delighted to see a recipe for "Whim Wham" on your cookery page. Not only did it sound delicious, but it reminded me that when, as a little girl, I asked my mother what was in the broth – or any similar dish – she would answer "Whim Whams and goose's bridles". I have often wondered whether this was a typical example of her nonsense or a "London" saying of which she had a remarkable fund.

Do any of your readers know the expression and is there any hope that we may shortly be given a recipe for goose's bridles?'

Miss Paula Neuss

'Sir, Perhaps I could try to shed some light on the "goose's bridles" in Audrey Hogston's mother's broth. No doubt "bridle" was originally "bride-ale", "an ale drinking at a wedding". At a goose's wedding there must, of course, be a gosling, who eventually became known as a "goose's bridle" because of the way he restrained his wife.

At her ale-dunking or tunning, Skelton's Elinor Rumming (who is dressed up "with a whim-wham/Knit with a trim-tram/Upon her brain-pan") would take anything in exchange for beer, including "two goslings". At the end of the dunking session, things got out of hand, and I expect Elinor's whim-wham fell into the beer along with the goslings (or goose's) bridles. Thus they became associated as ingredients in any brew or broth.'

Admiral Sir Frank Twiss

'Sir, I was intrigued to read Miss Audrey Hogston's letter about "Whim-whams" having learnt, and occasionally used, the expression "Whim-wham for a goose's bridle" since I was a midshipman.

In the course of instruction by the Commissioned Boatswain of a Battleship in 1928, I was warned that if a youngster asked a silly question deserving a silly answer he was likely to be dismissed with the words, "It's a whim-wham for a goose's bridle".

I have always supposed that this expression had a naval or seafaring ancestry.'

Mrs Patrick Young

'Sir, Whim whams for goose's bridles were invariably on the menu when, as children in Australia, we asked our family cook, "Doris, what's for pudding?" I always understood that Doris's family and the expression came from Cheshire.'

Whim-wham

30 g (1 oz) butter
110 g (4 oz) flaked almonds
1 tablespoon caster sugar
18 sponge finger biscuits
juice of 2 oranges or tangerines
120 ml (4 fl oz) sweet sherry
120 ml (4 fl oz) brandy
450 ml (¾ pint) double or
  whipping cream

Melt the butter in a heavy frying pan, add the almonds and fry on a medium heat until they are golden. Sprinkle them with the sugar and shake the pan over a low heat until it melts. Spread the almonds on a lightly greased plate to cool.

An hour or two before serving put the sponge fingers, broken in halves, into a large serving bowl. Mix the orange juice, sherry and brandy and pour into the bowl.

Just before serving, whip the cream until it holds soft peaks. Spoon the cream over the sponge fingers, which should by now have absorbed most of the liquid. Sprinkle the top with the fried almonds and serve at once.

The essential ingredients for a really good trifle are fresh fruit, real custard and plenty of cream. Within these limits sumptuous variations are possible. Raspberries, frozen in winter, are particularly good, and so are properly trimmed orange segments. Or use winter imports of exotic fruits to make a tropical trifle. Try fresh mango with pineapple, banana and orange.

Then there is the cake part, which can be bought trifle sponges, stale home-made sponge cake, sponge finger biscuits, macaroons, ratafias, or a mixture of any or all of them. The custard must be made with eggs, and the topping in this recipe is an everlasting syllabub which should keep in the fridge for a few days without separating. Though if you have not made this kind of syllabub before you may prefer not to risk keeping it.

Which leaves the matter of the booze. Sherry, or a mixture of sherry and brandy, is conventional. A little light rum in the tropical trifle can be recommended, and a dash of orange liqueur is good with almost any fruit base.

Orange and Syllabub Trifle

300 ml (½ pint) sweet white wine
6 tablespoons Cointreau, Grand
  Marnier or cognac
1 lemon
110 g (4 oz) light brown sugar
2 eggs
2 egg yolks
30 g (1 oz) caster sugar
2 teaspoons cornflour
600 ml (1 pint) milk
½ teaspoon vanilla essence
8 trifle sponges, or stale sponge cake
55 g (2 oz) ratafias
6 small oranges, peeled and cut in
  segments
300 ml (½ pint) double cream
slivered toasted almonds to decorate

Put the wine in a bowl with the liqueur or cognac. Add the juice of the lemon and a few strips of its thinly pared zest. Stir in the brown sugar and set the mixture aside while you make the custard.

Mix together in a bowl the eggs, egg yolks, caster sugar and cornflour. Heat the milk almost to boiling and pour it over the egg mixture, stirring briskly. Pour the mixture into the pan, or put it in the top of a double boiler, and heat gently, stirring constantly, until the custard has thickened. Cover the custard and set it aside to cool. When it is quite cold stir in the vanilla essence.

Break up the trifle sponges or cake and arrange them over the base of a large glass serving bowl. Scatter the ratafias between them. Chop the carefully trimmed orange segments into smallish pieces and add them to the bowl with any juice which is left.

Remove the lemon zest from the reserved wine and

liqueur mixture and pour half the mixture over the fruit and sponge. When the liquid has soaked in a little, spoon the custard over the fruit in an even layer. Leave the bowl in a cool place overnight.

To make the syllabub topping, add the cream to the remaining wine and liqueur mixture and whisk together until the cream holds soft peaks. Spoon it over the trifle and decorate the top with the almonds, or with fine slivers of orange zest which have been poached to remove the bitterness.

A red wine syllabub, pale pink and lightly spiced, makes a delicate alternative to plum pudding.

Christmas Syllabub

SERVES 6–8

250 ml (8 fl oz) red wine
6 tablespoons sugar
10 cm (4 in) stick of cinnamon
10 whole cloves
zest of 1 lemon
zest of 1 tangerine
450 ml (¾ pint) double cream, chilled

Put the wine, sugar, cinnamon, cloves and lemon and tangerine zest in a small saucepan and bring to the boil. Remove from the heat immediately and set aside for 24 hours.

Strain the wine into a large bowl and discard the zest and spices. Add the cream and, using a balloon whisk, whip the mixture until it holds soft peaks.

Divide the syllabub between six or eight glasses and chill it for two hours before serving with small, crisp biscuits.

In old engravings, especially Victorian ones, Christmas puddings are spherical, often on fire, and quite enormous. But before succumbing to the temptation of boiling the mixture in a cloth, wipe nostalgia from your eyes and pause for a moment to consider the density of a pudding as big as a beach ball which will hold its shape when let out of the bag.

I made a round Christmas pudding – once – using a curious old recipe that involved large quantities of biscuit crumbs and a miserly hand with the fruit. The result would probably have been lamentable however cooked, but my ignorance about preparing the cloth certainly did not improve matters. (In case anyone still wants to try it, the cloth should be scalded and the inside floured before the mixture is imprisoned in it and the pudding steamed.)

My favourite Christmas pudding recipe includes butter for flavour, nuts for texture, and breadcrumbs (instead of flour) for lightness. This pudding keeps just as well as more traditional recipes made with suet.

Christmas Pudding

MAKES ABOUT 20 SERVINGS

340 g (12 oz) currants
340 g (12 oz) seedless raisins
340 g (12 oz) sultanas
340 g (12 oz) fresh white breadcrumbs

Put all the dry ingredients in a large bowl and mix them well together. In a jug, whisk together the melted butter, cognac or whisky, milk and eggs. Pour the liquid into the dry ingredients and stir to mix very thoroughly. Allow the mixture, which is a fairly dry one, to stand in a cool place

110 g (4 oz) chopped nuts:
 almonds, hazels, pecans, or a
 mixture of these
110 g (4 oz) Demerara sugar
1 tablespoon finely grated orange
 zest
1 tablespoon finely grated lemon
 zest
1 teaspoon ground cinnamon
1 teaspoon freshly grated nutmeg
225 g (8 oz) butter, melted
175 ml (6 fl oz) cognac or whisky
150 ml (¼ pint) milk
4 large eggs

for about 12 hours before turning it into one very large or two smaller buttered pudding basins. Do not fill the basins to within more than 2.5 cm (1 in) of the rim, so leaving space for the mixture to rise and lighten. Cover the basins with buttered greaseproof paper and foil and tie this on very tightly with string.

Stand each basin in a saucepan and pour in boiling water to come about halfway up its sides. Bring back to the boil, reduce the heat to a gently bubbling simmer, cover the pans and steam the puddings for six hours regardless of size. Top up the level of water in the pans with *boiling* water as necessary.

Allow them to cool, then remove the buttered paper and foil and re-cover the basins with fresh papers, not buttered this time. Before steaming the puddings a second time for serving, cover them the same way as for the initial cooking and steam for at least two hours.

Christmas pudding improves in flavour if stored in a cool, dry place. Adding extra brandy or whisky after the first steaming, when the pudding is quite cold, and again before it is reheated on Christmas Day, is an optional refinement. I recommend it.

To serve the pudding, turn it onto a heated serving plate and pour about two tablespoons of heated brandy over it. Light the warm brandy at once and take the pudding to the table with blue flames of burning spirit licking over it. Be careful in the merriment of the occasion not to overdo the ignition act. The result could be a nasty case of cook flambé.

SERVES 6–8

110 g (4 oz) unsalted butter,
 softened
225 g (8 oz) dark brown Barbados
 sugar
½ teaspoon grated nutmeg
3 tablespoons dark rum

Westmorland Rum Butter

Beat the butter in a bowl until it is light and fluffy but has not oiled. Gradually beat in the sugar, nutmeg and rum. Transfer the mixture to one or more small bowls and refrigerate until firm. Use as required.

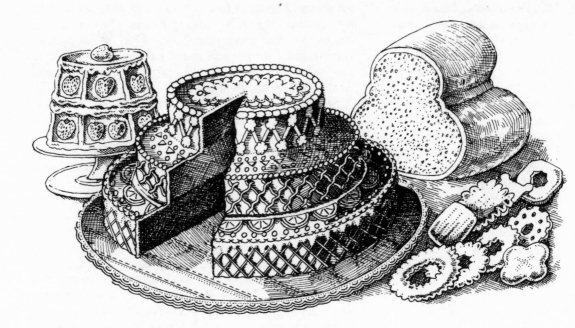

14

Breads, Cakes and Biscuits

Baking bread at home is a uniquely satisfying occupation. There is the moment when the warm, yeast scented dough becomes satiny with kneading, the pleasure of seeing it rise as it should, the marvellous baking smell from the oven. And, of course, when the time comes to eat it, the peculiar pride that results from making something so basic and so delicious.

With cunning, and forethought, and overnight doughs which can be left to their own devices for hours on end, it is perfectly possible to bake one's own bread regularly while putting in a full working week away from home. But few of us do, perhaps because the process is essentially an unhurried one, to be enjoyed for its own sake, not rushed or slotted into some break-neck timetable of super-efficiency.

Quicker by far for those who have to earn a crust, and for everyone who cannot see the point of baking bread when there is a decent baker round the corner, are the yeastless breads that can be mixed and thrown into the oven on the spur of the moment. Some of the most successful of these quick soda or baking powder-raised breads are fortified with protein and ideal for packed and picnic lunches. Because the fillings – ham, cheese, nuts or fruit – are baked in, there is nothing to go soggy between home and the races, school, the office or wherever.

Both traditional yeast-raised and quick soda breads rise more impressively if they are baked under cover. When the dough is put straight into a hot oven its expansion is soon inhibited by the hard crust which is quickly formed at high temperatures. By covering the bread with an inverted earthenware bowl (or tin in the case of soda bread) the dough creates a steamy atmosphere in which it can rise freely. Then, when the bread has reached its full potential, the cover is removed and baking continued until the loaf is cooked and a good crust formed.

When the qualification 'about' prefaces an ingredient it is usually because the right amount is going to be a matter of taste. In bread recipes, 'about' invariably refers to the quantity of liquid required and that, of course, is a matter of hard-won judgement. Descriptions of how kneading turns an unresponsive lump of flour and water into a supple, silky dough, can only say that it is so. Experienced fingers know so and work confidently with doughs that novice breadmakers are tempted to abandon as too sticky or too tough. But as everyone who has made bread a few times learns, the chances of baking good bread are very high indeed. It is only consistent perfection which comes a little harder.

My husband once baked a perfect Coburg loaf. Under its thin, golden crust the bread was light, evenly textured and tender. It was a very moreish loaf indeed and neither of us has ever been able to make another to equal it. We have not succeeded in matching precisely enough the materials, conditions and timing which accounted for that peerless loaf. But all this failure proves is the abiding truth that yeast-raised bread dough has a life of its own which no human will can fully control.

A Coburg is a round, usually white loaf which has been baked without a tin and has a wide cross cut in the top which opens in the oven to form crusty peaks. If the top is cut with a lattice of squares then the loaf is known as a rumpy. If it is baked without cuts at all it is a cob, and with one slash it may be called a Danish cob.

Crusty White Coburg

MAKES 1 LOAF

400 g (14 oz) strong, unbleached white flour
2 teaspoons salt
¼ teaspoon dried yeast and a pinch of sugar, or 8 g (¼ oz) fresh yeast
about 250 ml (8 fl oz) warm water

Mix together the flour and salt and sift them into a large bowl. Warm the flour in a low oven for a few minutes while preparing the yeast. Sprinkle the dried yeast and sugar on a little of the warm water (the temperature to aim for is 37°–38°C/98°–100°F). Mix well and leave until the mixture begins to froth and the granules of yeast have dissolved completely. If you are using fresh yeast, mix the yeast with a little of the water to make a smooth, runny cream.

Make a well in the warm flour and pour in the yeast mixture and most of the water. Mix to a soft dough, adding the remaining water if needed. Do not knead the dough at this stage. Just cover it and leave it in a warm place to rise.

When the dough has doubled its bulk, which will take between one and two hours, knock it down and knead it until it is smooth and supple. Form the dough into a ball and set it on a floured baking sheet. To prevent the loaf spreading too flat in the oven, tuck the edges of the ball of dough underneath it as if they were a loose bedcover.

Cover the dough and leave it to rise again until it has doubled its bulk once more. Cut a cross in the centre of the loaf with a very sharp knife. As soon as the cuts open,

203

which should be immediately or in a few minutes, cover the loaf with a large bowl or casserole and bake in a preheated hot oven (230°C/450°F, gas mark 8) for 20 minutes. Reduce the temperature to moderately hot (200°C/400°F, gas mark 6), remove the cover and continue baking the loaf for about 20 minutes, or until it sounds hollow when tapped on the base.

Bread baking produces such lovely smells that it is almost worth doing for that reason alone. What could be nicer for a late breakfast or brunch than freshly made granary rolls? Mix the dough the night before and leave it to rise slowly overnight. If you want to start from scratch in the morning, double the quantity of yeast for a quicker rise.

Granary flour, sometimes called meal, includes a proportion of malted grain and can be found in health food shops.

Granary Rolls

MAKES 10

1/4 teaspoon dried granular yeast
1/4 teaspoon sugar
300–350 ml (10–12 fl oz) warm water
450 g (1 lb) granary flour
110 g (4 oz) strong white flour
1 tablespoon salt
2 tablespoons lightly flavoured olive oil

Mix the yeast and sugar in a cup with four tablespoons of the warm water and stir well. The water should be about 43°C/110°F. At this temperature the yeast will be reactivated quickly, but as too great a heat will kill it, it is better, if you cannot measure the temperature, to err on the cool side. Leave the mixture to stand in a warm place for a few minutes until the yeast has dissolved completely and the liquid starts to froth.

In a large bowl mix the granary flour, strong white flour and salt. Make a well in the centre. Stir the yeast liquid and pour it into the well with the remaining water and the oil. Mix to a soft dough.

Turn the dough onto a floured surface and knead it lightly for a minute or two. Form it into a ball. Wash the bowl and oil it lightly. Return the dough to the bowl, cover it with plastic food wrap and leave it to rise overnight in a cool place.

By morning the dough should be well risen. Punch it down and knead it again lightly. Divide it into 10 pieces, roll each into a ball, and arrange them on an oiled baking sheet – well separated for crisp rolls, closer together for soft-sided ones. Cover the tray lightly and stand it in a warm place for about an hour, or until the rolls have almost doubled their bulk.

Bake the rolls in a preheated moderately hot oven (200°C/400°F, gas mark 6) for 15–20 minutes. Cool the rolls on a wire rack and serve while still warm.

Once upon a time continental breakfast meant the real thing. It was, and in the right places still is, a basket of buttery croissants and brioches served with bowls of fragrant French coffee.

Now, it too often means undistinguished rolls which were never intended for the breakfast table, mini packs of melted butter, preserves, portion packed for your inconvenience, and rotten coffee.

Croissants have survived the translation of continental breakfast into an international institution remarkably well. Good croissants turn up on supermarket shelves as well as in the better bakeries, and hotels the world over attempt them with varying degrees of success.

Brioches are not so well travelled. Could it be that the colloquial meaning of *faire une brioche*, to make a blunder, is more widely understood than one might have supposed? The expression is said to stem not from any tricky culinary procedure but from an ancient practice of fining musicians for playing out of tune and spending the cash thus exacted on brioches. But that is an unlikely tale if ever I heard one. More likely, brioches are seen less often because the recipe is less easily fudged. There is no escaping the quantities of eggs and butter they call for.

The basic recipe which follows will make at least a dozen individual brioches; the exact number will depend on the size of the tins. Traditionally, special fluted tins with steeply sloping sides are used. Dariole moulds or popover pans are handy substitutes.

Basic Brioche Dough

MAKES 12 OR MORE

2 tablespoons water
2 teaspoons sugar (optionally more)
15 g (½ oz) fresh yeast, or 1 scant teaspoon granulated dried yeast
450 g (1 lb) strong white bread flour
1 teaspoon salt
6 large eggs, lightly beaten
225 g (8 oz) lightly salted butter, softened
1 egg yolk beaten with 2 tablespoons water to glaze

Heat the water to lukewarm (about 43°C/110°F) and add a pinch of sugar and the yeast. Whisk the mixture lightly and set it aside in a warm place for about five minutes, or until the yeast has dissolved and frothed up.

Sift the flour, salt and remaining sugar into a warm bowl. Make a well in the centre and add the beaten eggs and the yeast mixture. Using your hand or a wooden spoon, incorporate the flour into the liquid to make a well-blended dough. Add the butter and work it in thoroughly with your hands. At this stage the dough is impossibly soft and tacky and appears quite unworkable. Let nothing you dismay. It will calm down during two rising periods. Cover the bowl with a damp cloth or plastic food wrap and leave it to rise for at least two hours, probably longer, but until it is light and airy.

Knock the air out of the dough and transfer it to a clean bowl. Cover it again and chill overnight. It will rise again very slowly in the refrigerator, and it is this slow rising which gives the bread its distinctive, fine texture.

Brush the moulds generously with melted butter and set them on a baking sheet.

Turn the dough onto a lightly floured surface and knead it briefly with well-floured hands. Take a piece of the dough which will half-fill one of the moulds, and pinch off a quarter to make the traditional top-knot which gives *brioches à tête* their name. Roll the larger piece into a ball and place it in a mould. Roll the smaller piece into another ball. Using scissors, snip a cross on top of the larger ball, and press the smaller one into the cross. When all the dough has been shaped, cover the brioches lightly and leave them to rise again until they have almost doubled their bulk. Do not be tempted to hurry the rising in too warm a spot which would cause the butter to leak from the dough.

Brush the tops of the brioches with the egg yolk and water glaze and bake in a preheated moderately hot oven (200°C/400°F, gas mark 6) for 15–20 minutes, or until they are well-risen and golden.

Turn the brioches out of their tins as soon as they are cooked and cool them on a wire rack. Serve hot or warm with butter and jam.

Lunch in one of the Cranks chain of vegetarian restaurants is my idea of a real treat. A bowl of mixed salad and one of their cheese baps makes a very satisfying meal.

The baps are served split, buttered and filled with mustard and cress.

Cranks' Cheese Baps

MAKES 6

15 g (½ oz) fresh yeast
1 teaspoon honey
300–350 ml (½–⅔ pint) warm
   water
450 g (1 lb) wholemeal flour
1 teaspoon sea salt
1 free range egg, beaten
255 g (9 oz) Cheddar cheese,
   grated

Mix the yeast and honey in a small bowl with 150 ml (¼ pint) of the warm water. Leave in a warm place for about 10 minutes to froth.

Mix the flour with the salt. (In very cold weather, warm the flour slightly.) Pour the yeast mixture into the flour, add the egg and gradually add the remaining water, mixing well by hand. Knead the dough for about five minutes. Cover with a cloth and leave in a warm place for about one hour to double in size.

Knock down the dough and knead it lightly. Roll out on a lightly floured surface to a rectangle 38 × 25 cm (15 × 10 in). Sprinkle a third of the cheese over the centre one-third of the dough. Fold the left-hand third of the dough over the cheese. Sprinkle another third of the cheese over the double thickness of dough, then fold the right-hand side of the dough over to cover the cheese completely. Roll out and cut out 10 cm (4 in) rounds. Place on a floured baking sheet and brush lightly with milk. Sprinkle with the remaining cheese and leave for another 30 minutes or so to rise again.

Bake in a preheated moderately hot oven (200°C/ 400°F, gas mark 6) for about 25 minutes. Cool the baps on a wire tray.

The foods of Hallowe'en are cheap, simple, and invariably home made. Barm brack, a cake or tea bread enriched sometimes with fruit, sometimes with caraway, and raised with yeast, is traditional in Ireland. Caraway and candied peel flavour the seed cake made in Wales. In Scotland there is iced fruit cake or gingerbread. Other Irish favourites are boxty bread made with the addition of potato and bacon fat, and colcannon, a dish of potato and kale. Pumpkin pie, which must be well spiced to succeed, is the choice in America.

Barm Brack

MAKES 1 LOAF

225 g (8 oz) raisins
110 g (4 oz) currants
200 ml (¹/₃ pint) water
110 g (4 oz) sugar
15 g (¹/₂ oz) fresh yeast, or 1
   teaspoon granular yeast
570 g (1¹/₄ lb) strong or plain flour
1 teaspoon salt
1 teaspoon ground mixed spice
55 g (2 oz) butter, chilled
55 g (2 oz) candied peel, chopped
   (optional)
1 large egg

Put the raisins and currants in a bowl, cover with cold tea and leave them to soak for several hours, or overnight.

Heat the water to lukewarm (about 43°C/110°F) and mix a quarter of it in a small bowl with a teaspoon of the sugar and all the yeast. Leave it to stand until it froths and can be stirred easily into a cream.

Sift the flour, salt and spice into a bowl. Cut the butter into small dice and rub it into the flour mixture, using your fingertips or a pastry blender, until the mixture resembles fine breadcrumbs. Add the remaining sugar and candied peel and toss lightly together.

Make a well in the flour mixture and drop in the egg. Add the yeast and the remaining warm water and mix with a fork to a soft dough. Turn the dough onto a well-floured surface and knead it for about five minutes, or until it is springy and elastic. Drain the raisins and currants and knead them lightly into the dough. Form the dough into a ball and put it in an oiled bowl. Cover with a plastic bag or film and leave it in a warm place until it has doubled in bulk.

Punch down the risen dough to knock the air out of it and knead it briefly on a floured surface. Form it into a ball and put it in a well-greased 23 cm (9 in) round cake tin with deep sides. Cover the dough and leave it to rise again until it has almost doubled in bulk.

Bake it in the centre of a preheated moderately hot oven (200°C/400°F, gas mark 6) for about one hour. The loaf should be well risen and sound hollow when rapped on the base. Turn it out to cool on a wire rack.

The better the flour the better the loaf. Nothing makes better tasting bread than freshly milled wholewheat flour.

Wholemeal Soda Bread

MAKES 2 SMALL LOAVES

450 g (1 lb) 100 per cent
wholewheat flour
2 teaspoons salt
1 teaspoon bicarbonate of soda
300 ml (½ pint) cultured
buttermilk

Sift together into a bowl the flour, salt and bicarbonate of soda and mix well together. Add the buttermilk and mix quickly and lightly, adding a little warm water if it is needed to make a soft but manageable dough.

Divide the dough into two equal pieces and shape each into a slightly flattened loaf. Cut a bold cross in the top of each loaf. Position the loaves on a floured baking sheet so that each can be covered with an inverted cake tin – deep-sided 15 cm (6 in) tins are ideal. Bake in a pre-heated moderately hot oven (200°C/400°F, gas mark 6) for about 40 minutes, removing the tins to allow the loaves to brown lightly for the last 15 minutes of baking. The loaves are ready if they sound hollow when tapped. Cool them on a wire rack.

Soda breads are at their best as soon as they have cooled after baking.

The texture of baking powder breads is light and moist, more cake-like than traditional yeast-raised mixtures. They may, of course, be made with wholemeal flour, but the loaves will rise less and the texture will be more dense. The 900 ml (1½ pint) loaf tin specified in the following recipes is the standard small loaf tin with sides that slope outwards a little from the base. It measures about 15 × 10 cm (6 × 4 in) × 7 cm (3 in) deep.

Ham and Cheese Loaf

MAKES 1 LOAF

170 g (6 oz) plain flour
2 teaspoons baking powder
½ teaspoon freshly ground black
pepper
pinch of freshly grated nutmeg
85 g (3 oz) butter, chilled
110 g (4 oz) cooked ham, finely
chopped
55 g (2 oz) Gruyère cheese, grated
1 large egg
4 tablespoons milk

Sift the flour, baking powder, pepper and nutmeg into a bowl. Cut the butter into small dice and rub it into the flour mixture, using your fingertips or a pastry blender, until the mixture resembles fine breadcrumbs. Add the ham and cheese and mix lightly with a fork. Mix the egg with the milk, add the liquid to the flour mixture and blend to a soft dough.

Turn the dough into a well-buttered 900 ml (1½ pint) loaf tin and level the top. Bake it in the centre of a pre-heated moderate oven (180°C/350°F, gas mark 4) for about one hour 10 minutes, or until a skewer plunged into the centre of the loaf comes out clean. Rest the newly baked loaf in its tin for about five minutes before turning it onto a wire rack to cool. Serve ham and cheese loaf warm or cold with unsalted butter.

Date and Walnut Loaf

MAKES 1 LOAF

170 g (6 oz) plain flour
2 teaspoons baking powder
¼ teaspoon salt
85 g (3 oz) butter, chilled
55 g (2 oz) chopped dates
55 g (2 oz) chopped walnuts
55 g (2 oz) dark brown sugar
1 tablespoon finely grated orange
  zest
1 large egg
4 tablespoons milk

Sift the flour, baking powder and salt into a bowl. Cut the butter into small dice and rub it into the flour mixture, using your fingertips or a pastry blender, until the mixture resembles fine breadcrumbs. Add the dates, walnuts, sugar and orange zest and mix thoroughly. Mix the egg with the milk, add the liquid to the flour mixture and blend to a soft dough.

Turn the dough into a well-buttered 900 ml (1½ pint) loaf tin and level the top. Bake it in the centre of a pre-heated moderate oven (180°C/350°F, gas mark 4) for about one hour 10 minutes, or until a skewer plunged into the centre of the loaf comes out clean. Rest the newly baked loaf in its tin for about five minutes before turning it onto a wire rack to cool. This bread tastes even better the day after it is made.

Pumpkin Tea Bread

MAKES 1 LOAF

200 g (7 oz) pumpkin
2 large eggs
6 tablespoons peanut oil
200 g (7 oz) plain flour
110 g (4 oz) light brown sugar
1½ teaspoons baking powder
½ teaspoon bicarbonate of soda
½ teaspoon ground cinnamon
85 g (3 oz) shelled hazelnuts or
  walnuts, finely chopped
1 tablespoon finely grated orange
  zest

Cook the peeled and seeded pumpkin in boiling water (as potatoes) until tender. Drain well then purée it by pressing it through a sieve or *mouli légumes*, or processing it briefly. Add the eggs and oil and whisk together until well blended.

Sift the flour, sugar, baking powder, bicarbonate of soda and cinnamon into a bowl and stir in the nuts and orange zest. Add the pumpkin mixture and stir well to form a soft dough.

Turn the mixture into a 900 ml (1½ pint) non-stick loaf tin, or a standard tin lined with buttered greaseproof paper, and level the top. Bake in the centre of a preheated moderate oven (180°C/350°F, gas mark 4) for about 1½ hours, or until a skewer plunged into the centre of the loaf comes out clean. Rest the newly baked loaf in its tin for about five minutes before turning it onto a wire rack to cool. Serve pumpkin tea bread sliced and lightly buttered.

Farmhouse Fruit Loaf

225 g (8 oz) plain flour
110 g (4 oz) butter
110 g (4 oz) stoned muscatels or
* seedless raisins*
110 g (4 oz) dates or figs, chopped
110 g (4 oz) crisp apple, peeled and
* chopped*
55 g (2 oz) shelled walnuts,
* chopped*
55 g (2 oz) soft brown sugar
1 teaspoon baking powder
1 teaspoon bicarbonate of soda
150 ml (¼ pint) milk
3 tablespoons runny honey or syrup

Sift the flour into a large bowl and cut the butter into small dice. Rub the butter into the flour, using your fingertips or a pastry blender, until the mixture resembles fine breadcrumbs. Add the muscatels or raisins, dates or figs, apple, walnuts and sugar and mix well.

Mix the baking powder, bicarbonate of soda, milk and honey or syrup and stir into the dry ingredients. The mixture should have a stiff dropping consistency and may need a little more milk. Spoon the mixture into a loaf tin about 20 × 10 cm (8 × 4 in) which has been well greased and lined with greaseproof paper. Bake in the centre of a moderate oven (180°C/350°F, gas mark 4) for 1¼–1½ hours, or until the loaf is well risen and firm to the touch. Turn it onto a wire rack to cool. When it is quite cold, store in an airtight container.

Shop pancakes are no substitute for the real thing. Pancakes warm from the pan are light and fragrant, very distant relations indeed of their clammy store-bought lookalikes.

Scotch Pancakes

225 g (8 oz) plain flour
½ teaspoon salt
2 teaspoons cream of tartar
1 teaspoon bicarbonate of soda
30 g (1 oz) caster sugar
1 tablespoon runny honey
1 large egg
about 300 ml (½ pint) milk

Sift the flour, salt, cream of tartar, bicarbonate of soda and sugar into a bowl and make a well in the centre. Add the honey and egg and gradually beat in the milk to make a thick, smooth batter.

A heavy cast iron griddle is best for cooking pancakes, but a good thick frying pan with a flat bottom will do very well. Heat it slowly and thoroughly before beginning to cook the pancakes. Grease the surface lightly with a ball of kitchen paper wiped on a piece of lard.

Drop tablespoonfuls of the batter onto the griddle, spacing them well apart. When bubbles rise to the surface and the underside is pale golden brown, turn the pancakes over and cook them briefly on the other side.

With trial and error you will find the best heat for cooking pancakes. They should be cooked in the middle but still no darker than golden brown on the outside. Grease the griddle sparingly between each batch of pancakes.

Serve them straight from the pan, or as freshly made as possible, with lightly salted butter and honey or jam.

Cinnamon Toast

Cinnamon toast is simpler still. It can be made in dainty fingers or crunchy chunks, and with white or brown bread. Toast the bread lightly and butter it lavishly. Combine four or more parts of caster sugar to one of powdered cinnamon and shake them together in a jar. Sprinkle the buttered toast generously with the mixture and pop it under the grill again to melt the sugar. It should be just melted and not quite toffee. Serve immediately.

Whitsun has been variously marked at different times. Cheese rolling was a popular ceremony to establish grazing rights at Brockworth near Gloucester, and boisterous parties called Whitsun ales were held in the sixteenth and seventeenth centuries to raise funds for parishes all over the country.

Describing the Whitsun church ale of Kingston St Michael in Wiltshire, the seventeenth century diarist John Aubrey wrote: 'In every parish is (or was) a church-house to which belonged spits, crocks, etc., utensils for dressing provisions. Here the housekeepers met, and were merry and gave their charity. The young people were there too, and had dancing, bowling, shooting at butts, etc., the ancients sitting gravely by, and looking on. All things wer civil and without scandal.'

Whitsun cakes featured in various local festivals. At Woodstock in Oxfordshire they were like small Banbury cakes, and in Yorkshire, Whitsun curd tarts, also called cheesecakes, were traditionally served.

During the eighteenth century the custom of holding church ales died out in all but a few villages, but we can still make the cheesecakes. The Yorkshire baked cheesecake is larger and flatter than most we make nowadays.

Yorkshire Curd Tart

MAKES A 25 cm (10 in) TART

225 g (8 oz) plain flour
1 tablespoon caster sugar
1/4 teaspoon salt
110 g (4 oz) butter, chilled
1 egg yolk
iced water to mix

For the filling:
340 g (12 oz) curd, or sieved
    cottage cheese
85 g (3 oz) caster sugar
2 teaspoons grated lemon zest
3 large eggs, separated
2 tablespoons melted butter
3 tablespoons sultanas
freshly grated nutmeg

To make the pastry, sift the flour, sugar and salt into a bowl. Cut the butter into small dice and toss them lightly in the flour. Rub in the fat, using a pastry blender or your fingertips, until the mixture looks like fine breadcrumbs. Beat the egg yolk with two tablespoons of iced water and sprinkle over the flour mixture. Mix lightly together, adding a little more water if needed to make a firm dough. Press the dough lightly into a ball, cover and chill it for 30 minutes.

Lightly grease a 25 cm (10 in) shallow cake or flan tin. Roll out the pastry thinly and rest it for five minutes before lifting it on the rolling pin and laying it over the tin. Ease the pastry gently into shape without stretching it, trim the edges and chill for another 10 minutes.

Just before baking prick the pastry base with a fork, line the shell with greaseproof paper and weight it with rice or dried beans. Set on a baking sheet and bake in a pre-heated moderately hot oven (200°C/400°F, gas mark 6) for 10 minutes. Remove from the oven, take out the beans and lining paper, reduce the temperature to moderate (180°C/350°F, gas mark 4) and bake the shell for another 10 minutes before filling it.

To make the filling, mix the cheese, sugar, grated zest, egg yolks, butter, sultanas and nutmeg. Whisk the egg whites until they hold stiff peaks and fold them into the cheese mixture. Spoon the filling into the pastry case and spread the top flat. Return the tin to the oven and bake the tart for about 35 minutes, or until the filling has set. Serve cool or cold.

Hazelnut torte is a cake to taste before passing judgement on the success of the recipe. It is unexciting to look at – flattish and undecorated. What counts in this case is the nutty taste and moist texture. It is the better for being kept in an airtight tin for two or three days before filling.

If you do not have large sandwich tins, make half quantities of the recipe twice in standard 18 cm (7 in) tins and pile them up to make a smaller, deeper cake.

Hazelnut Torte

SERVES 10–12

225 g (8 oz) shelled hazelnuts, unblanched
8 large eggs, separated
285 g (10 oz) caster sugar

For the filling:
300 ml (½ pint) double cream
4 tablespoons chocolate and hazelnut spread
icing sugar to dust

Using a coffee grinder or liquidiser, grind the nuts as finely as possible without reducing them to a paste.

Whisk the egg whites until they are stiff. In another bowl, whisk the egg yolks with the sugar until the mixture falls from the whisk in ribbons.

Fold the meringue and nuts lightly into the egg yolk mixture and divide it between two lightly greased 25 cm (10 in) sandwich tins. Bake in a preheated moderate oven (180°C/350°F, gas mark 4) for about 35 minutes. Test by pressing gently with a finger. The cakes are ready when the pressure leaves no impression.

Cool the cakes in their tins for 10 minutes before turning them onto a wire rack.

When they are quite cold sandwich them together with the whipped cream mixed with the chocolate and hazelnut spread. Dust the top with the icing sugar just before serving.

Orange almond cake is another deliciously moist cake to serve as a pudding, as well as at tea time.

Orange Almond Cake

SERVES 6–8

3 juicy oranges
55 g (2 oz) fresh white
*   breadcrumbs*
110 g (4 oz) ground almonds
110 g (4 oz) caster sugar
4 large eggs, separated
½ teaspoon salt
1 tablespoon orange flower water

Finely grate the zest of one of the oranges and squeeze the juice from all three. Mix together the breadcrumbs, almonds and orange zest and stir in the orange juice.

In another bowl mix the sugar, egg yolks, salt and orange flower water. Beat the mixture until it is light and fluffy then fold it into the first mixture.

Whisk the egg whites until they hold a firm peak and fold them into the cake mixture. Pour it into a shallow loose-bottomed 25 cm (10 in) cake tin which has been well buttered and dusted with breadcrumbs. Bake it in a preheated moderate oven (180°C/350°F, gas mark 4) for about 50 minutes.

Allow the cake to cool in its tin for about 10 minutes before turning it onto a wire rack. To serve, dust the cake with sifted icing sugar, or spread it with a thick layer of whipped cream which may be plain, sweetened, or flavoured with an orange liqueur.

The Owl of the remove, assiduous feast seeker that he was, liked nothing better than a good tuck-in. It is doubtful if the unscholarly Bunter knew that the earliest form of the expression was tuck-out, or that it derived from the smoothing effect of excessive feasting on the tucks, or pleats, in a chap's waistcoat or trousers.

If the practice of taking tuckboxes to school is frowned on by today's Beaks, they cannot stamp out fruit cake and fudge. Tuck hampers may be dying out, but tuck lives on as a description of all victuals which are a schoolboy's idea of a treat.

Tuckbox Fruit Cake

MAKES A 23 cm (9 in) CAKE

225 g (8 oz) butter
170 g (6 oz) soft brown sugar
juice and finely grated zest of 1
*   orange*
juice of 1 lemon
4 large eggs, beaten
225 g (8 oz) currants
225 g (8 oz) raisins
110 g (4 oz) glacé cherries, halved
110 g (4 oz) glacé pineapple,
*   chopped*
55 g (2 oz) glacé ginger, chopped
225 g (8 oz) self-raising flour

Butter a 23 cm (9 in) cake tin and line it with greaseproof paper or baking parchment.

In a large bowl cream together the butter and sugar until the mixture is pale and fluffy. Beat in the orange and lemon juices, and add the eggs, a little at a time, beating vigorously. Fold in all the remaining ingredients and stir the mixture to distribute the fruit evenly. Spoon the mixture into the prepared tin and spread it to make a shallow depression in the centre. Bake the cake in a preheated moderate oven (180°C/350°F, gas mark 4) for one hour. Reduce the temperature to cool (150°C/300°F, gas mark 2) and bake it for a further 1½–2 hours.

Leave the cake in its tin for 10 minutes before turning it onto a wire rack to cool completely before storing in an airtight container.

Carrot Cake

225 g (8 oz) butter, softened
340 g (12 oz) soft brown sugar
1 teaspoon ground cinnamon
1/2 teaspoon ground mace or grated
  nutmeg
1 teaspoon grated orange zest
4 large eggs
285 g (10 oz) plain flour
170 g (6 oz) carrot, finely grated
85 g (3 oz) shelled walnuts,
  chopped
3 teaspoons baking powder
1/2 teaspoon salt
5 tablespoons warm water

Cream together the butter and sugar until the mixture is very pale and fluffy. Beat in the spices and orange zest. Add the eggs, a little at a time, beating very thoroughly between each addition, and adding a tablespoon of the flour with the last couple of additions of egg. Stir in the carrots and walnuts. Sift together the remaining flour, baking powder and salt and fold them into the creamed mixture together with the water.

Divide the mixture between two greased and floured loose-bottomed 20 cm (8 in) round cake tins and bake in a preheated moderate oven (180°C/350°F, gas mark 4) for about an hour. The cakes are cooked when they spring back when pressed lightly in the centre.

Leave the cakes to cool in their tins for about 10 minutes before turning them onto a wire cooling rack. Carrot cake tastes all the better for being kept a day or two before cutting. It can be eaten plain, or filled and iced. Sandwich the layers together with honey or apricot jam, or with the cream or butter icing you will be using for the topping.

This is a very old fashioned chocolate cake – substantial, moist and rich.

Chocolate Cake

110 g (4 oz) dark chocolate
150 ml (1/4 pint) boiling water
285 g (10 oz) plain flour
3/4 teaspoon baking powder
1 1/2 teaspoons bicarbonate of soda
170 g (6 oz) butter
285 g (10 oz) soft brown sugar
3 large eggs
150 ml (1/4 pint) natural yogurt or
  sour milk
1 teaspoon vanilla essence

For the filling:
4 tablespoons sieved apricot jam

For the icing:
170 g (6 oz) unsalted butter
340 g (12 oz) icing sugar
6 tablespoons cocoa powder
1–2 tablespoons strong black coffee

Break the chocolate into small pieces and put them in a bowl. Pour the boiling water over them and stir until smooth. Set the mixture aside to cool a little. Sift together the flour, baking powder and bicarbonate of soda.

Cream the butter in a large bowl. Add the sugar and beat until the mixture is light and fluffy. Beat in the eggs, one at a time, adding a spoonful of the flour mixture with each addition of egg. Pour in the melted chocolate and beat until well blended. Beat in the remaining flour, yogurt and vanilla essence.

Divide the mixture between two greased 23 cm (9 in) sandwich tins and bake in a preheated moderate oven (180°C/350°F, gas mark 4) for about 35 minutes, or until well risen and springy to touch. Leave the cakes to settle for five minutes after baking before turning them out onto a wire rack to cool.

Sandwich the cakes together with the apricot jam.

To make the butter icing, cream the butter. Sift the icing sugar and cocoa together and add to the butter. Beat the mixture to a stiff cream, adding sufficient coffee to obtain a workable consistency.

Wedding cakes reached an apogee of sugary elaboration during the reign of Queen Victoria. Her own cake, although pretty astonishing by modern standards, did not seem over the top at the time.

Reporting on the royal wedding cake in the Court Circular of *The Times* of February 6, 1840, a few days before the marriage, an anonymous witness tells us:

'A select few have been gratified with a sight of the Royal wedding cake at the apartments of the confectionery in St James's Palace. This important piece of the appliances of the Royal Nuptials is the result of the labours and taste of Mr John C. Mauditt, the yeoman confectioner of the Royal household, and it does great credit to the skill of the artist. If it be not quite so elaborate in its decorations as if a professed modeller had been employed, there is a simplicity and chasteness in the design of the ornamental parts well becoming the auspicious occasion, and highly to the credit of the yeoman confectioner.

'This Royal cake weighs nearly 300 lb. It is 3 yards in circumference, and about 14 inches in depth or thickness. It is covered with sugar of the purest white; on the top is seen the figure of Britannia in the act of blessing the illustrious bride and bridegroom, who are dressed somewhat incongruously in the costume of ancient Rome. These figures are not quite a foot in height; at the feet of his Serene Highness is the effigy of a dog, said to denote fidelity; and at the feet of the Queen is a pair of turtle doves, denoting the felicities of the marriage state.

'A Cupid is writing in a volume expanded on his knees the date of the day of the marriage, and various other Cupids are sporting and enjoying themselves as such interesting little individuals generally do. These little figures are well modelled. On the top of the cake are numerous bouquets of white flowers tied with true lovers' knots of white satin riband, intended for presents to the guests at the nuptial breakfast.'

Bride cake, as it is called in early cookery books, has changed little in the past 200 years. Elizabeth Raffald's recipe, first published in her book *The Experienced English Housekeeper* in 1769, would work as well today as it did in the eighteenth century when she baked it in a wooden hoop lined with three layers of buttered paper. Our eggs are bigger now, of course, so we would need fewer. And the candied peel, *sweetmeats*, that she sandwiched between layers of cake mixture, would need to be top quality – the kind still sold as large, recognisable pieces of orange, lemon and citron.

'To make a Bride Cake
Take four pounds of fine flour well dried, four pounds of fresh butter, two pounds of loaf sugar, pound and sift fine a quarter of an ounce of mace the same of nutmegs, to every pound of flour put eight eggs, wash four pounds of currants, pick them well and dry them before the fire, blanch a pound of sweet almonds, and cut them lengthwise very thin, a pound of citron, one pound of candied orange, the same of candied lemon, half a pint of brandy; first work the butter with your hand to a cream, then beat in your sugar a quarter of an hour.

'Beat the whites of your eggs to a very strong froth, mix them with your sugar and butter, beat your yolks half an hour at least, and mix them with your cake, then put in your flour, mace, and nutmeg, keep beating it well till your oven is ready, put in your brandy, and beat your currants and almonds lightly in, tie three sheets of paper round the bottom of your hoop to keep it from running out, rub it well with butter, put in your cake, and lay your sweetmeats in three lays, with cake betwixt every lay, after it is risen and coloured, cover it with paper before your oven is stopped up; it will take three hours baking.

'To make Almond-Icing for the Bride Cake
Beat the whites of three eggs to a strong froth, beat a pound of Jordan almonds very fine with rose-water, mix your almonds with the eggs lightly together, a pound of common loaf sugar beat fine, and put it by degrees; when your cake is enough, take it out, and lay your icing on, then put it in to brown.

'To make Sugar Icing for the Bride Cake
Beat two pounds of double refined sugar, with two ounces of fine white starch, sift it through a gauze sieve, then beat the whites of five eggs with a knife upon a pewter dish half an hour; beat in your sugar a little at a time, or it will make the eggs fall, and will not be so good a colour, when you have put in all your sugar, beat it half an hour longer, then lay it on your almond icing, and spread it even with a knife; if it be put on as soon as the cake comes out of the oven it will be hard by the time the cake is cold.'

There is no suggestion in Mrs Raffald's instructions that the cake was many-tiered. Yet this tradition appears to be older than the ingredients she specifies.

A children's encyclopaedia called *Everybody's Enquire Within* published in 1938 gives this convincing explanation for the shape of wedding cakes: 'For centuries in England small buns or cakes were provided at weddings, and these were piled up in one great heap. The bride and bridegroom used to kiss one another over this pile. If they succeeded without upsetting the pile they were supposed to be assured of lifelong happiness.

'It is said that the iced wedding cake as we know it today was the idea of a French cook travelling in England. He noticed the inconvenience of piling a large number of small spiced cakes in one heap and he thought of the idea of icing the mound into one mass.'

The same tradition is echoed in *croquembouche*, the airy pyramid of choux pastry buns that is the wedding cake of France.

My recipe is for a two-tier wedding cake which should be made at least two months before it is to be eaten so that it has time to mature. If the top tier is to be saved for an anniversary or christening, seal it in an airtight container. The smaller cake is slightly shallower than the large one so that the proportions are maintained when they are assembled.

Wedding Cake

TOP TIER: makes an 18 cm (7 in) round, or a 15 cm (6 in) square cake

170 g (6 oz) plain flour
1/2 teaspoon salt
1/2 teaspoon mixed spice
110 g (4 oz) butter
110 g (4 oz) soft brown sugar
3 large eggs
1 1/2 teaspoons black treacle
1 1/2 teaspoons grated lemon zest
110 g (4 oz) sultanas
110 g (4 oz) seedless raisins
225 g (8 oz) currants
55 g (2 oz) candied peel, minced

Sift together the flour, salt and mixed spice and set aside. In a large mixing bowl, cream together the butter and sugar until the mixture is very light and fluffy. In another bowl, lightly beat together the eggs, treacle and lemon zest. Gradually beat the egg mixture into the fat, adding a little of the flour with the last few additions of egg to stop the mixture separating.

Sift a few tablespoons of the flour over the prepared fruit, candied peel and almonds and toss them all together. Fold the remaining flour into the creamed mixture, then add the fruit and nut mixture, and lastly the brandy. Mix all the ingredients thoroughly together.

Turn the mixture into a tin which has been generously buttered and neatly lined with buttered greaseproof

55 g (2 oz) slivered almonds
2 tablespoons brandy

For the decoration:
450 g (1 lb) almond paste
55 g (2 oz) apricot jam
2 egg whites
450 g (1 lb) icing sugar
1½ teaspoons lemon juice
1 teaspoon glycerine

BOTTOM TIER: makes a 23 cm (9 in) round, or a 20 cm (8 in) square cake

340 g (12 oz) plain flour
1 teaspoon salt
1 teaspoon mixed spice
225 g (8 oz) butter
225 g (8 oz) soft brown sugar
5 large eggs
1 tablespoon black treacle
1 tablespoon grated lemon zest
225 g (8 oz) sultanas
225 g (8 oz) seedless raisins
450 g (1 lb) currants
110 g (4 oz) candied peel, minced
110 g (4 oz) slivered almonds
4 tablespoons brandy

For the decoration:
800 g (1¾ lb) almond paste
110 g (4 oz) apricot jam
3 egg whites
680 g (1½ lb) icing sugar
2 teaspoons lemon juice
1½ teaspoons glycerine

paper. Make a shallow depression in the centre of the cake so that when the mixture rises in the oven the top will be level.

Bake the small cake in a preheated cool oven (150°C/300°F, gas mark 2) for one hour. Reduce the temperature to 140°C/275°F, gas mark 1 and continue baking for about another two hours.

Bake the large cake in a preheated cool oven (150°C/300°F, gas mark 2) for 1½ hours. Reduce the temperature to 140°C/275°F, gas mark 1 and continue baking for about another 2½ hours.

The cakes are cooked when a warmed skewer plunged into the centre comes out clean. Check that they are not becoming too brown at least 30 minutes before they are due out of the oven. If the cakes are browning too fast, cover them loosely with foil.

Cool the cakes in their tins for 24 hours, before stripping off their papers and storing them in an airtight container until they are decorated, two or three weeks before the wedding.

To apply the almond paste, first measure round the outer edge of the cake with a piece of string. Take two-thirds of the almond paste and roll it out on a surface dredged with icing sugar to a rectangle half the length of the string and twice the depth of the cake in width. Trim and cut it in halves lengthwise. Knead the trimmings into the remaining paste and roll it out to fit the cake top.

Brush the sides of the cake with an apricot glaze made by heating the jam with a tablespoon or two of water, then sieving it. Put the two strips of almond paste round the cake and smooth over the joins. Brush the top of the cake with glaze and cover it with the remaining almond paste, cut to fit with the cake tin and a sharp knife. Roll lightly with a sugar-dusted rolling pin and make sure the joins are neat and well sealed. Cover the cake with a clean cloth and leave it in a cool place for about three days to dry the paste a little before icing.

To make the royal icing, whisk the egg whites until they are frothy. Stir in the sifted icing sugar, a spoonful at a time. When half the sugar is incorporated, add the lemon juice. Continue adding more sugar, beating well after each addition, until the mixture almost holds a peak. Lastly stir in the glycerine which helps to prevent the icing becoming too hard.

To ice the cake smoothly as a base for piped decorations, coat the top and sides on consecutive days so that a clean edge can harden after the first application. A second coat of thinner icing may be applied after the first has been left to dry for 48 hours. Leave the second coat to dry for 48 hours too before applying piped decorations. Royal icing remains workable for several days if stored in an airtight container.

At one time simnel cakes were made for Mothering Sunday. That was when the day was a celebration of the Mother Church and not a sentimentally commercialised occasion for floral offerings to maternal parents. So it might be seen as no bad thing that simnel cake is now associated firmly with Easter, as are the plainest of the cake's traditional decorations, 11 small balls of marzipan to symbolise the apostles who remained faithful to Christ.

Simnel Cake

MAKES 1 CAKE

170 g (6 oz) ground almonds
170 g (6 oz) caster sugar
1 large egg, beaten
a few drops of almond essence
110 g (4 oz) butter
110 g (4 oz) granulated or soft
   brown sugar
170 g (6 oz) plain flour
1/4 teaspoon salt
1/2 teaspoon ground mixed spice
3 large eggs, beaten
110 g (4 oz) currants
110 g (4 oz) raisins
110 g (4 oz) sultanas
1 tablespoon finely grated orange
   zest
1 tablespoon apricot jam
1 egg, beaten to glaze

Line an 18 cm (7 in) deep cake tin with buttered grease-proof paper or baking parchment.

To make the marzipan, mix the almonds and caster sugar with enough beaten egg to form a soft dough. Add the almond essence and knead the mixture until it is smooth. Divide the marzipan in halves and roll out one piece to make an 18 cm (7 in) circle. Wrap the remainder and set it aside for decorating the cake.

To make the cake, cream the butter and granulated or soft brown sugar in a large bowl until the mixture is pale and fluffy. Sift together the flour, salt and mixed spice and beat a spoonful into the creamed mixture. Beat in the eggs, a little at a time, adding a spoonful of the flour from time to time to make sure the mixture does not curdle. Fold in the remaining flour, currants, raisins, sultanas and orange zest. Mix them well together.

Turn half the cake mixture into the prepared tin and spread the top flat. Place the circle of marzipan on top and cover it with the remaining cake mixture. Smooth the top and make a shallow depression in the centre. Bake in a preheated cool oven (160°C/325°F, gas mark 3) for about 1 3/4 hours. Cool the cake in its tin.

When the cake is quite cold, remove it from the tin and strip off the papers. Brush the top with the apricot jam. Make 11 small balls with a little of the remaining marzipan and roll out the rest to top the cake. Place the marzipan circle on the cake and arrange the balls evenly round the edge. Brush the marzipan with the beaten egg and brown the glaze by baking the cake in a preheated moderate oven (180°C/350°F, gas mark 4) for about 10 minutes.

When the cake is completely cold store it in an airtight container.

Feeding a Christmas cake with a few tablespoons of brandy after it has been baked and cooled helps the maturing process but is never quite, alas, a substitute for making it early. Finish the cake with marzipan and royal icing. Or give it a marzipan lid only and decorate the top with a closely packed pattern of glacé fruit and a variety of nuts, and cover the sides with a wide ribbon or cake frill.

MAKES A 1.8 kg (4 lb) CAKE

Christmas Cake

285 g (10 oz) plain flour
1 teaspoon salt
1 teaspoon ground cinnamon
1/2 teaspoon freshly grated nutmeg
1/4 teaspoon ground cloves
225 g (8 oz) butter, softened
225 g (8 oz) soft brown sugar
4 large eggs
1 tablespoon honey
finely grated zest of 1 lemon or 1
*   orange*
225 g (8 oz) sultanas
225 g (8 oz) currants
225 g (8 oz) seedless raisins
110 g (4 oz) glacé cherries, halved
110 g (4 oz) dried apricots, finely
*   chopped*
110 g (4 oz) slivered almonds
120 ml (4 fl oz) brandy, whisky or
*   dark rum*

Sift together the flour, salt, cinnamon, nutmeg and cloves and set them aside. In a large bowl cream together the butter and sugar until the mixture is very light and fluffy. In another bowl lightly beat together the eggs, honey and lemon or orange zest. Gradually beat the egg mixture into the fat, adding a little of the flour with the last few additions of egg to prevent the mixture separating.

Sift a few tablespoons of the flour over the prepared fruit and nuts and toss them all together. Fold the remaining flour into the creamed mixture, then add the fruit and nuts. Lastly stir in the spirits and mix very thoroughly.

Turn the mixture into a well-greased 20 cm (8 in) round cake tin at least 7.5 cm (3 in) deep, which has been neatly lined with baking parchment or buttered grease-proof paper. Make a shallow depression in the centre of the cake so that when the mixture rises in the oven the top will be level.

Bake the cake in a preheated cool oven (150°C/300°F, gas mark 2) for 1½ hours. Reduce the temperature to 140°C/275°F, gas mark 1 and continue baking for another three hours. The cake is cooked when a warmed skewer plunged into the centre comes out clean. If it is browning too fast, cover the top loosely with foil.

Edinburgh gingerbread, a traditional Hallowe'en cake, includes dates and walnuts and is baked in a square or rectangular tin.

Edinburgh Gingerbread

MAKES 1 LARGE CAKE

450 g (1 lb) plain flour
1/4 teaspoon salt
1 1/2 teaspoons ground ginger
1 1/2 teaspoons ground cinnamon
1 1/2 teaspoons mixed spice
1/2 teaspoon ground cloves
225 g (8 oz) stoned dates
110 g (4 oz) shelled walnuts
225 g (8 oz) butter
340 g (12 oz) black treacle
200 g (7 oz) dark brown sugar
4 large eggs, beaten
1 teaspoon bicarbonate of soda
a little warm milk

Sift the flour, salt, ginger, cinnamon, mixed spice and cloves into a large bowl. Chop the dates and walnuts coarsely and add them to the flour.

In a small saucepan melt together the butter, treacle and sugar on a low heat. Pour this mixture gradually into the flour, stirring constantly. Add the eggs and the bicarbonate of soda dissolved in a tablespoon of the warm milk. Stir well, adding a little more milk if needed to make a mixture which will just drop from the spoon.

Turn the mixture into a well-greased baking tin about 20 cm (8 in) square and at least 6.5 cm (2½ in) deep, which has been lined with greaseproof paper or baking parchment. Spread the top even and bake in a preheated moderate oven (180°C/350°F, gas mark 4) for about 20 minutes. Reduce the temperature to cool (150°C/300°F, gas mark 2) and continue baking for another two hours, or until a warmed skewer inserted in the centre of the cake comes out clean.

Cool the gingerbread on a wire rack, then strip off the papers. When it is completely cold store it in an airtight container.

Like pastry, shortbread should be handled as little as possible because too much messing about with the dough toughens it. Carved wooden moulds are sometimes used to pattern shortbread, but plain circles with hand-crimped edges are more usual.

Shortbread

MAKES 8 PIECES

110 g (4 oz) plain flour
55 g (2 oz) rice flour
1/4 teaspoon salt
110 g (4 oz) butter, chilled
55 g (2 oz) caster sugar
1 egg yolk

Sift the flour, rice flour and salt into a large bowl. Cut the butter into small dice and toss them lightly in the flour. Rub in the fat, using your fingertips or a pastry blender, until the mixture resembles fine breadcrumbs. Mix in the sugar lightly and bind the mixture with the egg yolk to form a stiff dough.

Press the dough lightly into a shallow 18 cm (7 in) round tart tin lined with baking parchment or greaseproof paper. Pinch the edges all round using your finger and thumb, mark into eight wedges and prick all over with a fork.

Bake it in a preheated moderate oven (180°C/350°F, gas mark 4) for 40 minutes, or until it is a light, golden brown. Allow the shortbread, which will still be soft, to cool a little before turning it onto a wire rack. When it is quite cold and crisp dredge it with caster sugar and store in an airtight container.

Oat and Maple Syrup Biscuits

MAKES ABOUT 30

110 g (4 oz) butter
175 ml (6 fl oz) maple syrup
1 teaspoon vanilla essence
½ teaspoon salt
½ teaspoon bicarbonate of soda
170 g (6 oz) rolled oats
55 g (2 oz) wholewheat flour

Beat the butter in a bowl until it is light and fluffy. Add the syrup and vanilla essence and beat until smooth. Stir in the salt, bicarbonate of soda, oats and flour.

Drop teaspoonfuls of the mixture onto well-buttered baking sheets, leaving plenty of room for the biscuits to spread out.

Bake them in a preheated moderate oven (160°C/325°F, gas mark 3) for about 15 minutes, or until the biscuits are golden brown. Allow them to cool on the baking sheets for a few minutes before lifting them carefully onto a wire rack to cool. When quite cold, store them in an airtight container.

Traditional ratafias, tiny almond meringue biscuits, are a useful standby and keep well in an airtight container. Use them in trifle or to accompany ice creams. Almonds are traditional, but the recipe works equally well with ground hazelnuts.

Ratafias

MAKES ABOUT 50

2 egg whites
110 g (4 oz) ground almonds
170 g (6 oz) caster sugar
½ teaspoon almond or ratafia essence
flaked almonds to decorate (optional)

Whisk the egg whites in a large bowl until they form stiff peaks. Fold in the ground almonds, sugar and almond or ratafia essence. Mix well together to make a soft, sticky dough.

Line heavy baking sheets with baking parchment or rice paper and pipe the mixture onto this in small mounds of about 2 cm (¾ in) diameter. Use a plain nozzle and space them well apart. Top each mound with a sliver of almond, if using.

Bake the ratafias in a preheated cool oven (150°C/300°F, gas mark 2) for about 45 minutes, or until they are a pale, pinkish brown. Cool on a wire rack, and when they are quite cold trim off the excess rice paper or peel off the baking parchment.

Cornish Fairings

MAKES AT LEAST 30

450 g (1 lb) plain flour
4 teaspoons baking powder
2 teaspoons bicarbonate of soda
2 tablespoons ground ginger
1 tablespoon ground cinnamon
1 tablespoon ground mixed spice
1 teaspoon salt
225 g (8 oz) butter, chilled
225 g (8 oz) soft brown sugar
8 tablespoons golden syrup

Sift together into a bowl the flour, baking powder, bicarbonate of soda, ginger, cinnamon, mixed spice and salt. Cut the butter into small dice and toss them lightly in the flour. Rub in the fat, using your fingertips or a pastry blender, until the mixture looks like fine breadcrumbs. Stir in the sugar.

Heat the syrup until it is liquid then pour it over the dry ingredients. Mix well to make a firm dough.

With well-floured hands roll the dough into walnut-sized balls. Set them well apart on greased baking sheets and bake in a preheated moderately hot oven (200°C/400°F, gas mark 6) for 10–15 minutes. Leave the biscuits on the baking sheets for a few minutes more before sliding them onto a wire rack to cool. As soon as they are quite cold, store them in an airtight tin.

Parmesan Biscuits

MAKES ABOUT 10

110 g (4 oz) plain flour
2 teaspoons salt
1 teaspoon cayenne pepper
110 g (4 oz) butter, chilled
110 g (4 oz) fine oatmeal
110 g (4 oz) Parmesan cheese,
   finely grated
1 large egg

Sift the flour, salt and cayenne into a bowl. Cut the butter into small dice over it and rub in the fat, using your fingertips or a pastry blender, until the mixture resembles fine breadcrumbs. Stir in the oatmeal and cheese.

Beat the egg with two tablespoons of cold water and stir the liquid into the dry ingredients. Add more liquid only if it is needed to make a firm dough.

On a lightly floured surface, roll out the dough thickly. It should be about 1 cm (⅓ in) thick. Cut into 7.5 cm (3 in) diameter rounds and arrange them on a well-greased baking sheet.

Bake the biscuits in a preheated moderate oven (160°C/325°F, gas mark 3) for about 25 minutes. Turn them onto a wire rack to cool. Store in an airtight tin.

15

Basic Batters, Butters, Stocks and Sauces

If nothing succeeds like success, then nothing so encourages failure as its anticipation. It is perfectly reasonable that dogs should sense when people are scared of them, and not unbelievable that plants should thrive on kind words. But egg yolks and olive oil, I ask you. How could they possibly have guessed that my expectation of beating them into mayonnaise was once a matter of unfounded optimism?

The fork and soup plate method, a flashy skill this one, produced nothing better than a runny mess. With a bowl and a wooden spoon it still declined to 'take'. With a balloon whisk it was coming on but never quite made the grade.

Now some people have this kind of trouble with their soufflés. But mayonnaise does not even need cooking, darn it, and my pride was beginning to hurt. In the end it was a food processor that showed me how. By watching the machine, which can do the whole job in seconds, I saw what the stuff was supposed to look like in the early stages and copied its efforts laboriously by hand. More elbow grease and more patience were the tricks.

The right olive oil for mayonnaise is the one you like the taste of best. Strong, fruity oils are fine, if you like them, especially for the robustly garlic flavoured version of mayonnaise, *aïoli*. Though for a classic mayonnaise to serve with fish or anything else which is delicately flavoured, a less pungent oil is usually preferable.

Mayonnaise

2 egg yolks
½–1 teaspoon hot mustard
salt and freshly ground black
  pepper
fresh lemon juice
300 ml (½ pint) olive oil

The first step in making an emulsion of egg yolks and oil is to ensure that all the ingredients are at room temperature. After that, it is a matter of patience and energy if a blender or food processor is not available.

Put the egg yolks in a bowl that is big enough to wield a wire whisk in, and add the mustard, a pinch of salt and pepper, and a tablespoon of the lemon juice. Whisk the mixture to a very smooth paste. Now start adding the oil, literally a drop at a time, whisking in each drop very thoroughly indeed. When a quarter of the oil has been incorporated, pour it into the sauce in a thin, steady trickle, whisking vigorously all the time.

The only thing that can go wrong with mayonnaise is that it curdles, either because the oil is added too quickly and the mixture is not being whisked thoroughly enough, or because it has become too thick and simply won't accept any more oil.

If it curdles because the oil has been added too quickly, start again with another egg yolk and a clean bowl, and gradually beat the curdled mixture into the new base.

If the mayonnaise is in danger of separating because it is becoming too thick before all the oil has been added, thin it down with more lemon juice or a little cold water before adding the rest of the oil.

To finish the mayonnaise, check the seasoning and add more salt, pepper and lemon juice to taste.

Hollandaise sauce is so rich in egg yolks and butter that a decent-sized dollop on a low calorie artichoke or asparagus seems something of a contradiction. A lighter, slightly tart version which still tastes buttery enough to complement delicate vegetable and fish flavours, can be made by substituting fresh natural yogurt for half the usual amount of butter.

A food processor is a boon for making emulsion sauces of all kinds, and especially for hot ones because they can be whizzed together at the last moment without one's guests being deafened by prolonged whisking or imagining one has nipped out for some forgotten ingredient.

SERVES 4–6

Less Fattening Hollandaise Sauce

1 tablespoon lemon juice
salt and freshly ground black
  pepper
110 g (4 oz) butter, softened
4 egg yolks
120 ml (4 fl oz) natural yogurt

To make the sauce by hand, mix the lemon juice with a little salt and pepper in the top of a double boiler. The water in the base should be just below boiling point. Add two tablespoons of the butter and the egg yolks, and whisk together until the mixture thickens. Whisking briskly, gradually add the remaining butter followed by the yogurt. Whisk the mixture until the sauce is thick and light, being careful that the water underneath does not boil and cause the sauce to curdle.

To make the sauce in a food processor, first warm the goblet in hot water, and heat the butter to boiling, but not browning, in a heavy saucepan. Put the lemon juice, salt, pepper and egg yolks in the goblet and process lightly. Keep the machine on and pour in the boiling butter and, when the sauce has thickened, the yogurt. If necessary, which is by no means always, return the sauce to the butter pan on a very low heat and whisk it as it thickens a little more.

Serve immediately.

Bread sauce is quite literally medieval and must be one of the recipes that has changed least in more than 500 years.

Bread Sauce

SERVES 4

1 small onion, peeled
2 whole cloves
1 bay leaf
175 ml (6 fl oz) milk
45 g (1½ oz) fresh white
    breadcrumbs
salt and freshly ground black
    pepper
single cream (optional)

Stick the onion with the cloves and put it in a small saucepan with the bay leaf and milk. Bring to the boil and remove it from the heat immediately. Set the milk aside for at least 15 minutes, then strain it and return the liquid only to the pan.

Add the breadcrumbs and bring slowly to the boil, stirring constantly, to make a thick, smooth sauce. Season it to taste with salt and pepper and cook on a very low heat for a minute or two longer. Add a little single cream if you prefer a thinner, creamier sauce. Serve very hot.

Bechamel is the most useful of basic sauces, and the basis for innumerable variations from everyday cheese to party thermidor.

Bechamel Sauce

MAKES ABOUT 600 ml (1 pint)

1 small onion, quartered
1 bay leaf
a few celery leaves (optional)
a sprig of parsley
750 ml (1¼ pints) milk
55 g (2 oz) butter
3 tablespoons plain flour
salt and cayenne pepper
nutmeg (optional)

Put the onion, bay leaf, celery leaves if you have them, and parsley in a small pan with the milk and bring to the boil. Remove it from the heat immediately and leave the milk to infuse for 30 minutes or longer. Strain.

In a clean pan heat the butter until it froths. Stir in the flour and cook on a low heat for a minute or two, stirring the *roux* to prevent it sticking. Gradually add the strained milk, stirring constantly on a low heat to make a smooth sauce. Cook the sauce for three or four minutes to cook out the taste of raw flour, then season to taste with salt, cayenne and, if appropriate, nutmeg.

Basil, tarragon and oregano are flavours which go particularly well with tomato. Use any of these herbs, preferably fresh, to make a real tomato sauce. Serve it with meatballs (see page 121), or with freshly boiled spaghetti or noodles and a little grated Parmesan cheese.

Fresh Tomato Sauce

SERVES 4

3 tablespoons olive oil
1 small onion, finely chopped
1 clove garlic, finely chopped
900 g (2 lb) tomatoes, peeled and
    chopped
salt and freshly ground black
    pepper
4 fresh basil leaves, chopped
1 bay leaf

(To peel the tomatoes, drop them into boiling water for about 30 seconds, then drain immediately and the skins will slip off easily.)

Heat the oil in a saucepan on a medium heat, add the onion and garlic and cook until the onion is soft and just beginning to brown. Add the tomatoes, salt and pepper and simmer gently, uncovered, for about 30 minutes. Add the basil and bay leaf and cook the sauce for 10 minutes more. Fish out the bay leaf and serve the sauce very hot.

Fresh herbs are the essence of summer, their scents evoking other summers, other places. Thyme is picnics on the South Downs sprawling on springy turf under blue skies. It is an idle search for four-leafed clover to the sound of skylarks. Fennel brings back Brittany where it is a tall roadside weed between hydrangeas. Rosemary captures the resinous heat of the south of France, and basil, peppery and pungent, will set any table talking of sunlit Mediterranean pleasures.

Bunches of fresh sorrel are a dream for window-box gardeners who snip a leaf or two at a time for salads, but lots of other herbs provide an ample flowerpot harvest. Use them first in those dishes for which dried herbs are no substitute.

Fresh herb butters are child's play to make and provide the simplest of finishing touches to speedily cooked grills or steamed fresh vegetables. As with the cream cheese mixtures (see page 66) you can vary the herbs to suit your purpose, but instead of lemon juice, try fresh lime or orange juice sometimes to add another new dimension. Lime juice is particularly good in butters intended for fish.

Herb Butter

MAKES 110 g (4 oz)

110 g (4 oz) butter, softened
1–2 tablespoons lemon, lime or
    orange juice
about 8 tablespoons finely chopped
    parsley, chives, chervil,
    tarragon, basil, dill, mint,
    thyme or marjoram
salt and freshly ground black
    pepper

Cream the butter then beat in the juice and herbs. Season the butter to taste with salt and pepper. Firm the butter in the refrigerator, then shape it into a cylinder of about 2.5 cm (1 in) diameter. Wrap it in greaseproof paper or foil and keep chilled until needed.

Cut off fairly thick slices of herb butter to top grilled meat or fish, or freshly cooked vegetables just before serving so that it melts on the food in front of the diners.

If clarified butter were renamed non-stick butter more cooks might acknowledge its merits because it is easily made and keeps for months in the fridge. Clarifying butter involves removing its milky protein residues and this process allows the fat to be heated to high temperatures without burning. In terms of flavour, clarified butter is the ideal fat for sautéing. The alternative is to use oil, or a combination of butter and oil.

Clarified Butter

MAKES ABOUT 680 g (1½ lb)

900 g (2 lb) unsalted butter

Melt the butter on a low heat in your heaviest pan or casserole. Bring it to the gentlest of simmers and hold it at this temperature, without stirring, until all the sediment has fallen to the bottom of the pan and the liquid butter is clear. This will take between 30 minutes and one hour.

Line a fine sieve with a double layer of muslin and strain the butter into a warm bowl or jar, leaving the sediment in the pan. Allow the butter to cool completely before covering it and storing in a cool place.

Crème fraîche is another classy ingredient which it is not at all difficult to make at home. As when making yogurt, a culture is introduced into the cream which sharpens its flavour. It can then be used in almost any savoury recipe which calls for double cream, and the slightly tart taste of *crème fraîche* is excellent too with sweet pies and tarts.

Crème Fraîche

MAKES 450 ml (¾ pint)

300 ml (½ pint) double cream
150 ml (¼ pint) cultured
 buttermilk

Mix the cream and buttermilk in a saucepan and heat them to about 25°C/75°F. This is below body temperature, barely lukewarm, and can be measured with a dairy or photographic thermometer. Transfer the cream to a warm bowl and keep it at this temperature for about eight hours, or until the cream has thickened and its flavour has become very slightly tart. My airing cupboard is about the right temperature for this process. Stir the cream, cover and store it in the refrigerator for up to two weeks. Use your own home-made *crème fraîche* as a starter for the next batch in place of the buttermilk.

As everyone knows pancakes are delicious eaten straight from the pan with a sprinkling of lemon juice and sugar. Jam or honey toppings are quick and easy, too. Add a blob of whipped cream or ice cream and the simplest pancake becomes a feast. More flamboyantly, make crêpes Suzette serving the pancakes in a flaming sauce of sugar, butter, tangerine juice and brandy (see page 182).

With savoury fillings, pancakes make popular lunch or supper dishes. And as deep frozen pancakes take only minutes to thaw, they are a particularly useful home-made standby.

My favourite batter includes oil or melted butter, an addition which makes the crêpes tender and seems to improve their freezing qualities. I have to admit that it also makes them fragile and tricky to turn without tearing. Brandy adds a definite something to the taste.

Basic Crêpe Batter

MAKES 15–20

55 g (2 oz) plain flour
1/2 teaspoon salt
2 large eggs
450 ml (3/4 pint) milk
2 tablespoons vegetable oil,
    preferably peanut, or melted
    butter
2 tablespoons brandy (optional)

Sift the flour and salt into a bowl. Beat the eggs, add them to the flour with a little of the milk and beat lightly together until the mixture is smooth. Gradually add the remaining milk, with the oil or melted butter and brandy, if you are adding it. Strain the batter, which should be no thicker than single cream, into a large jug. If it is thicker add a little water.

Heat a small, heavy crêpe or omelette pan on a medium heat and grease it very lightly with a piece of crumpled kitchen paper wiped on a knob of butter. Pour in just enough batter to coat the base of the pan (usually about two tablespoons), swirl it to cover the base of the pan and cook until the underside of the pancake is golden. Run a knife or spatula round the edge of the pancake to loosen it, and turn it over carefully. Cook until the second side is lightly coloured. Cook the remaining batter in the same way.

To keep the pancakes warm, stack them on a plate over a pan of simmering water with a leaf of greaseproof paper between each one. To freeze the crêpes, simply wrap the stack loosely in foil and freeze in the usual way.

Breakfast pancakes, the kind that Americans slosh with maple syrup, are delicious with grilled bacon and fried eggs. They are little more trouble than fried bread.

Breakfast Pancakes

MAKES ABOUT 12

285 g (10 oz) plain flour
1 tablespoon caster sugar
2 teaspoons cream of tartar
1 teaspoon bicarbonate of soda
1 teaspoon salt
2 large eggs

Sift the flour, sugar, cream of tartar, bicarbonate of soda and salt into a mixing bowl. In another bowl mix the eggs, fat and milk and beat lightly together. Tip the liquid into the flour mixture all at once and beat well to make a thick batter.

Heat a frying pan on a medium heat and grease it

*2 tablespoons melted butter or
    bacon fat
450 ml (¾ pint) sour milk, or half
    and half fresh milk and natural
    yogurt*

lightly with butter or bacon fat. To make two or three pancakes at a time drop about four tablespoon portions of batter into the pan, spacing them well apart. Cook until bubbles appear on the surface of the pancakes, then flip them over to cook on the other side until brown. Continue until all the batter is used up.

A really light fritter batter is an invaluable culinary asset, especially when the basic technique of deep frying has been mastered.

Fritter Batter

MAKES ABOUT 450 ml (¾ pint)

*110 g (4 oz) plain flour
¼ teaspoon salt
2 tablespoons vegetable oil
120 ml (4 fl oz) water
2 egg whites*

Sift the flour and salt into a bowl and make a well in the centre. Pour in the oil and water and mix from the centre, gradually drawing in the flour to make a smooth batter. Rest the batter for at least 30 minutes. Just before using it, whisk the egg whites until stiff and fold the meringue into the batter until well mixed.

Fat for deep frying must be able to withstand the high temperatures used. Lard is particularly good for frying sweet fritters. Olive oil gives its own characteristically nutty flavour to foods cooked in it – marvellous for shallow fried vegetable fritters, but it cannot take the high temperatures needed for deep frying. Peanut oil is excellent for deep frying. Corn oil too works well, although its taste is one I do not find pleasing.

To test the temperature of fat without a thermometer use the 2.5 cm (1 in) cube of day-old bread test. At the following temperatures it will take approximately the times listed to fry to a crisp golden brown.

180°C/350°F . . . 90 seconds
190°C/375°F . . . 60 seconds
220°C/425°F . . . 30 seconds

Look after the fat or oil by filtering it carefully after use.

Using a pan of fat on top of the stove, the following safety rules should be followed to avoid fires or accidents.

★ Never leave a pan of fat or oil unattended while the heat is switched on.

★ Keep nearby a lid which fits the pan tightly to cover the pan quickly should it catch fire.

★ There should always be at least 7.5 cm (3 in) space between the rim of the pan and the top of the fat. This allows room for the fat to froth when a new batch of fritters is added without bubbling over the sides of the pan.

Apple fritters demonstrate the technique of deep frying.

Apple Fritters

SERVES 4–6

4 crisp eating apples (about
450 g/1 lb)
1 tablespoon lemon juice
1 recipe fritter batter (see page 229)
lard or oil for deep frying
sugar to dust

Core the apples, peel them whole and cut the flesh into rings about 2 cm (¾ in) thick. Drop them into a bowl of water acidulated with the lemon juice.

Finish the fritter batter by folding in the beaten egg whites. Heat the lard or oil to 190°C/375°F.

Dry the apple slices carefully, dip them in the batter to coat all sides and deep fry them, a few at a time, until golden brown, turning once. Drain the fritters on absorbent paper and dust them with the sugar. Serve immediately.

Numerous variations on the basic apple fritter are possible. Dust the fritters with brown, white or icing sugar, plain or flavoured with ground cinnamon or cardamom, or with dried citrus zest. Marinate the apple slices in Calvados or brandy for 30 minutes before cooking. Keep the used booze for chocolate mousse, or a pâté, or flaming something. Halves of ripe apricot or short lengths of banana make excellent fritters too. Plumped prunes filled with walnut halves are another choice.

Grilling, whether over a barbecue or in the kitchen, tends to dry the meat or fish cooked by this direct heat method. Marinating the food to be grilled can make all the difference not only to its taste, but also to the texture. Yogurt, lemon juice or wine are acid ingredients which help to tenderise meat and fish as well as adding flavour. Oil in a marinade, or pieces of fat bacon on kebabs, baste the meat and prevent it drying too much.

For flavour and texture thread bay leaves, button mushrooms, pieces of red or green pepper and onion slices on the skewers. Blanch the pieces of pepper or onion in boiling water for a minute or two and they will be tender by the time the meat is cooked.

The following yogurt marinade is particularly suitable for lamb kebabs made with cubes of lean meat. Serve them hot with pitta bread, or French bread, and a big green salad.

Yogurt Marinade

150 ml (¼ pint) natural yogurt
3 tablespoons olive oil
2 cloves garlic, crushed
2 tablespoons chopped parsley
1 teaspoon salt
½ teaspoon freshly ground black
pepper

Put all the ingredients in a large bowl and mix thoroughly. Soak the meat in the marinade for at least four hours before cooking.

For chicken or pork a marinade which includes soy sauce is good. Use it to soak joints or smaller pieces of chicken, or cubes or chops of pork.

Soy Marinade

4 tablespoons olive or vegetable oil
4 tablespoons dry sherry or white
  wine
1 tablespoon soy sauce
1 clove garlic, crushed (optional)
½ teaspoon salt
½ teaspoon freshly ground black
  pepper

Put all the ingredients in a large bowl and mix thoroughly. Soak the meat in the marinade for at least four hours before cooking.

An authentic tasting tandoori recipe is invaluable for summer barbecues and this is a really excellent one. Use it to marinate skinned joints of chicken, bite-sized pieces of chicken or lamb, and raw peeled jumbo prawns or any firm-fleshed white fish. Cook over charcoal for a real tandoori taste.

Tandoori Marinade

1 medium onion
4 large cloves garlic
30 g (1 oz) fresh green ginger
250 ml (8 fl oz) natural yogurt
4 tablespoons fresh lemon juice
4 tablespoons vegetable oil
1 tablespoon ground coriander
1 tablespoon ground turmeric
1 teaspoon ground cumin
½ teaspoon grated nutmeg
½ teaspoon ground cinnamon
½ teaspoon freshly ground black
  pepper
¼ teaspoon ground cloves
¼ teaspoon cayenne pepper
2 teaspoons salt
2 teaspoons orange Indian food
  colouring (optional)

Peel and roughly chop the onion, garlic and ginger. Using a food processor or pestle and mortar, reduce them to a smooth paste before stirring in all the remaining ingredients.

Serve extra lemon wedges to squeeze on the food when it is cooked.

Herb marinades can complement almost any kind of meat or poultry. A little tarragon, thyme or rosemary for chicken or lamb; bay, parsley and chives for beef.

Herb Marinade

4 tablespoons olive oil
4 tablespoons dry red or white
  wine, or lemon juice
1 clove garlic, crushed (optional)
1–2 tablespoons fresh herbs,
  chopped, or 1 teaspoon dried
  herbs
$1/2$ teaspoon salt
$1/2$ teaspoon freshly ground black
  pepper

Put all the ingredients in a large bowl and mix thoroughly. Soak the poultry or meat in the marinade for at least two hours before cooking.

Home-made stocks need not cost much in either ingredients or time. Butchers and fishmongers will always produce bits and bones for stock provided you ask for them really early in the day, or give them warning. Make sure there are plenty of gelatine-rich ingredients like chicken bones and feet, veal bones and calves' feet or pigs' trotters if a jellied stock is required to add smoothness to sauces or to set well. For stocks which will be used in a reduced, strongly flavoured form use only a little salt. Some salt is needed to draw the flavour from the ingredients, but too much would make the final stock over-salty.

Stock freezes well and can be stored in large or small quantities, depending on which you find more useful. I find small portions of well-reduced stock invaluable for gravies and sauces.

Fish stock is the quickest and simplest to make.

Fish Stock

MAKES ABOUT 1.2 litres (2 pints)

340 g (12 oz) fish bones and
  trimmings
1 medium onion, quartered
2 carrots, quartered
a handful of parsley stalks or
  parsley
a small piece of lemon peel
salt and freshly ground black
  pepper

Put the fish bones and trimmings in a large saucepan with the onion, carrots, parsley, lemon peel, salt and pepper. Cover with 1.5 litres (2½ pints) of cold water and bring to the boil. Skim, cover the pan and simmer for about 20 minutes. Strain the stock and use immediately or, if you have time, allow it to cool before straining. Use as directed.

For poaching fish to be served hot or cold a splash of dry white wine is a rewarding addition to the stock.

Chicken stock is the most useful and versatile of the basic stocks. A chicken carcass, raw or the remains of a roast, is the ideal basis. Giblets go in too, of course, and any trimmings or leftovers.

Chicken Stock

MAKES ABOUT 1.5 litres
(2½ pints)

1 chicken carcass, giblets, etc.
2 onions, quartered
1 carrot, roughly chopped
2 sticks of celery, roughly chopped
plenty of parsley
1 bay leaf
salt and freshly ground black
*   pepper*

Put the chicken in a deep pan and add about 2 litres (3½ pints) of cold water. Bring to the boil slowly, then skim off all the froth very thoroughly. Add the onions, carrot, celery, parsley, bay leaf, a little salt and a generous quantity of the pepper and reduce the heat to a gentle simmer. (Cooking stock at a rolling boil produces a cloudy liquid which the Chinese call cream stock and make deliberately.)

Simmer the stock for two or three hours, then strain it into a bowl. Cover and cool well before skimming off the fat.

For a light beef or veal stock, as opposed to a dark stock which is made with browned ingredients, there must be plenty of bones and some good meat. If there are not enough trimmings or leftovers to flavour the stock well, and the bones have no meat on them, there is nothing for it but to buy 450–900 g (1–2 lb) shin of beef or something similar.

Light Meat Stock

MAKES ABOUT 1.5 litres
(2½ pints)

2 kg (4–5 lb) beef or veal bones
225–450 g (½–1 lb) fresh beef or
*   veal*
3 onions, quartered
1 carrot, roughly chopped
2 sticks of celery, roughly chopped
plenty of parsley
1 bay leaf
salt and freshly ground black
*   pepper*

Put the bones and meat, roughly chopped, in a deep pan and cover them with about 3 litres (5½ pints) of cold water. Bring to the boil slowly, then skim very thoroughly. Add the onions, carrot, celery, parsley, bay leaf, a little salt and a generous amount of the pepper and reduce the heat to a gentle simmer. Cook the stock for at least three hours, or longer if you have time. Strain it into a bowl, and allow to cool before skimming off the fat.

Dark or brown beef stock is a great standby for gravy making and for adding to rich stews and casseroles.

Dark or Brown Stock

MAKES ABOUT 1.5 litres
(2½ pints)

30 g (1 oz) dripping or lard
2 kg (4–5 lb) meaty beef or veal
  bones
225–450 g (½–1 lb) shin of beef
3 onions, quartered
2 leeks, roughly chopped
2 carrots, roughly chopped
2 sticks of celery, roughly chopped
plenty of parsley
1 sprig of thyme
1 bay leaf
salt and freshly ground black
  pepper

The colour and flavour of brown stock comes from browning the bones and meat well. Have them chopped into fairly large chunks and brown them in the dripping or lard in the stockpot, if it has a heavy base, or in a hot oven if that is more convenient. Brown the onions, leeks, carrots and celery and put them with the meat and bones in a deep pot. Add about 3 litres (5½ pints) of cold water and bring slowly to the boil, then skim thoroughly. Reduce the heat to a simmer, add the parsley, thyme, bay leaf, salt and pepper and simmer for a minimum of three hours. Strain the stock into a bowl, cover and allow to cool before skimming off the fat.

16

Preserves

Before the Exeter by-pass and motorways, when a blue and rusting bucket with a starfish shape in the bottom was a treasured possession, holidays started at four in the morning. The neighbours slept tight as we spun out of London at dawn. The high Hogsback ridge of the North Downs was the first stop on the long, long drive to Cornwall, and we breakfasted there with a primus. The cat got out and ran amuck for an hour one year which let the late starters catch up a bit.

Polperro in those days was a place where children could run wild. We lived in a pinkwashed cottage up I cannot remember how many hydrangea-shaded steps which had the grown ups puffing for the first few days. I learned to swim out of my depth in a chilly tide-filled rock pool at Polperro, and caught my first snatching mackerel with a spinner just outside the harbour. But it is the pearly morning mist I remember best, when my brother and I would creep out of the house and down to the quay.

Arkie – if he had been christened Noah we never knew – who had lobster pots thereabouts and a wealth of patience, had been up and about for hours. Back with his haul of blue-black lobsters and fat crabs he gave us a grin and the time of day, and we were honoured by our association with his weathered person. By mid-morning those crabs we had seen before breakfast would be boiled and on sale in the town.

Potted crab is a traditional seaside delicacy. Like potted shrimps, it keeps for up to two weeks in a cold place or the refrigerator. The crab must, of course, be freshly boiled. It should taste sweet, without a hint of the ammonia-like smell that characterises ageing specimens.

Spider crabs are just as delicious as the kind usually sold by fishmongers, though their flesh is admittedly more difficult to extract. Hairpins are good for picking the meat out of their long legs.

Potted Crab

SERVES 4–6

450 g (1 lb) fresh crab meat, white and brown, or white only
1/4 teaspoon ground mace
salt and freshly ground black pepper
110 g (4 oz) butter, softened
110 g (4 oz) clarified butter (see page 227)

Make sure that the crab meat is completely free of small chips of shell and pieces of the hard white blades inside the claws. Shred the meat roughly with a fork and season it with the mace, salt and pepper. Divide the crab meat between four or six ovenproof ramekins or cocotte dishes and spread the softened butter on the surface.

Cover the dishes loosely with foil and bake in a pre-heated moderate oven (180°C/350°F, gas mark 4) for 30 minutes. Remove the dishes from the oven and leave them to cool until the butter has solidified.

Heat the clarified butter until it has just melted and pour it over the crab to make an airtight seal. Chill the potted crab for a day or two to allow the flavours to blend and develop. Serve it at room temperature with freshly made toast.

Shrimping is an engrossing, as well as a rewarding holiday pastime, especially when the harvest is a bumper one. Throw the live shrimps into boiling salted water and cook them for only one or two minutes. Then when they are cool, enrol as many hands as possible to peel them. Eat them just as they are, or with salad, or if there are plenty, pot them in butter.

Potted Shrimps

SERVES 4–6

450 g (1 lb) peeled shrimps, preferably the small brown shrimps called crevettes grises
1/2 teaspoon ground mace
1/4 teaspoon cayenne pepper
salt
225 g (8 oz) clarified butter (see page 227)

Dry the peeled shrimps and put them in a saucepan with the mace, cayenne, a little salt and two-thirds of the clarified butter. Heat gently together for a minute or two without allowing the mixture to boil which would toughen the shrimps. Add more salt to taste.

Divide the shrimps and butter mixture between four or six ramekins or cocotte dishes, pressing the shrimps lightly to pack them well and exclude air bubbles. Set the dishes aside until the butter is firm and set.

Heat the remaining clarified butter until it has just melted and pour it over the shrimps to make an airtight seal. Chill the potted shrimps for at least 48 hours to allow the flavours to blend and develop. Bring them to room temperature before serving with fresh toast or lightly buttered brown bread.

It would be a pity if freezers were to kill off too many of the older methods of preserving food. In the case of most vegetables, of course, freezing beats bottling any day. And pickles, chutneys, jams and marmalades, all of which were contrived to store summer's bounty against winter privation, are too well established to become the endangered species of this domestic ice age.

Many cooks who grew up with refrigeration have never attempted any of the marvellous old ways of preserving meat or fish. Indeed few people have any need or reason now to prepare their own hams or bacon. But there are less widely available preserves which are well worth the little trouble they take to prepare at home.

Some, like *confit d'oie*, the succulent chunks of preserved goose which are such a speciality of south-west France, are almost impossible to find here, and costly on either side of the Channel. Fresh geese are not cheap either and usually have to be ordered. But *confit* works so well with duck and pork too, and the flavour makes such an enjoyable change from the fresh meat, that the recipes have much to recommend them.

Confit, whether of goose, duck or pork, is a key ingredient of *cassoulet*, the poshest and most delicious of the baked bean dishes. *Cassoulet* is the ideal vehicle for leftovers of Christmas poultry as well as a splendid method of serving a crowd from one big pot. A jar of *confit* is also the kind of gift that goes down well.

Confit of Goose

MAKES 12 OR MORE PORTIONS

*1 fat goose weighing about 9 kg
(20 lb)*
225 g (8 oz) sea salt
1 teaspoon saltpetre (optional)
8 bay leaves, crumbled
2 teaspoons dried thyme
goose fat and lard (see method)

Cut the goose into large serving portions, leaving the skin and underlying fat intact. Save any loose lumps of fat to render down, and cut away the wing tips and carcass for stock.

Mix together the sea salt (pounded if it is very coarse), saltpetre, if using, bay leaves and thyme and rub this mixture into the pieces of goose. Pack them closely into a large bowl and sprinkle with the remaining salt mixture. Cover loosely and leave the bowl in a cool place or the refrigerator for 24–48 hours, turning the pieces of goose once or twice. (If the goose is freshly killed it should be salted for 48 hours longer than a bought bird.)

Render down the reserved goose fat by cooking it very slowly until all the fat has melted and only golden crackling remains. Strain the fat and set it aside.

Wipe the excess salt and moisture from the goose pieces with kitchen paper and pack them into a large casserole. Add the reserved goose fat and enough melted lard to cover the goose completely. Cover the casserole and cook in a preheated cool oven (150°C/300°F, gas mark 2) for about 3½ hours, or until the goose is very tender. When the meat is ready, most of the fat under the skin will have melted and if the meat is pierced with a skewer no juices will run out.

Prepare one or more large preserving jars or crocks by washing them very thoroughly and scalding them. Make sure they are completely dry. Pour a ladle of hot goose fat into each jar and pack them with pieces of goose to within 5 cm (2 in) of the top. Pour in hot goose fat to cover them completely. Tap the jars firmly on a solid surface to release any air bubbles trapped with the meat, and leave them in a cool place until quite cold. Top up the jars with a good layer of hot fat or melted lard. Seal with lids if using preserving jars, or with foil pressed down on top of the fat and store in a cool, dark and dry place for at least a week to mellow the flavours. Provided it is stored in cool, dry conditions, *confit* will keep well for six months or more.

When you want to retrieve one or more pieces of the *confit*, heat the jar gently in a pan of hot water or a very low oven and fish out the quantity you need, making sure that the remaining pieces stay covered with fat. (Cool and reseal the remainder for later use.) Regardless of how you serve the *confit* – on its own, in *cassoulet* or another recipe – it should be very well heated for at least five minutes to disarm any bacteria which may be present.

Confit of duck is made in exactly the same way as *confit* of goose except, of course, that the bird is smaller and the quantities are reduced accordingly. *Confit* of pork may also be made with the same recipe, but it is even more delicious if the pieces of pork are spiked with slivers of garlic before it is cooked. Shoulder of pork is the ideal cut for the purpose. It should be boned, then cut into large chunks, skin and all. A 3 kg (7 lb) shoulder takes about 110 g (4 oz) sea salt, ½ teaspoon saltpetre (optional), 4 bay leaves, 1 teaspoon dried thyme and 3 peeled cloves of garlic. It is then cooked for about 3½ hours in pure lard or pork fat.

A storecupboard purée of cooked garlic is a particularly useful preserve. Because it is less pungent and more digestible than raw garlic, it is handy for salad dressings as well as for any number of other recipes.

Garlic Purée

MAKES ABOUT 250 ml (8 fl oz)

340 g (12 oz) whole heads of garlic
3 tablespoons olive oil
salt

Wrap the whole garlic heads (do not peel them or separate them into individual cloves) in a loose parcel of kitchen foil and bake in a preheated moderately hot oven (190°C/375°F, gas mark 5) for one hour.

Leave them in the foil until they are cool enough to handle, then separate the heads into cloves. Place a sieve over a bowl and squeeze each clove into the sieve, discarding the skin. Rub the cooked garlic through the sieve and stir to a smooth purée with one tablespoon of olive oil and salt to taste. Transfer the purée to a storage jar and cover it with the remaining oil.

The purée is ready for use immediately or it can be stored for up to three months in the refrigerator.

Marmalade as we know it today is the much modified descendant of a medieval confection based on quinces. The original, which took its name from the Portuguese for quince, was a strongly spiced sweetmeat; a paste not a spread. An early English version was called charedequynce, of which one version included wine, honey, ginger, galingale, cinnamon and wardens as well as quinces. By the sixteenth century medlars, berries called services and checkers, damsons, plums, apples, pears and strawberries were all used to make stiff, sugar-sweetened marmalades.

Marmalade of bitter oranges and lemons was probably first made in the sixteenth century. Including chips of the peel was a seventeenth century innovation, and spreadable marmalade as we know it now seems not to have been made, except perhaps by accident, until the late eighteenth century.

Today marmalade is made from citrus fruits of every kind. Limes, lemons, grapefruit, sweet oranges, tangerines and many of the newly introduced crossbreeds make splendid marmalades. But for my money, the bitter orange, the incomparable orange of Seville, makes the finest marmalade of all. Thick, dark, chunky marmalade with chewy bits of peel to savour is a handy preference because it is also the easiest sort to make.

A really sharp knife is the essential piece of equipment for marmalade making. An old fashioned brass preserving pan is pleasing but by no means essential. Its shape, with outward sloping sides, is ideal because it allows rapid evaporation of the liquid when boiling the mixture for a set. The briefest possible boiling is more important to the appearance and taste of soft fruit jams than to marmalade which is an altogether more robust preserve. New preserving pans are usually made of aluminium, and a very large pan or flameproof casserole will do the job perfectly well. For success every time the following points are useful.

★ Scrub citrus fruit well with a stiff brush to remove dirt and chemicals.

★ Make sure the jars, whether new or recycled, are very thoroughly washed and dried. Heat them in a very cool oven (110°C/225°F, gas mark ¼) before filling.

★ Simmer the peel until it is very tender before adding the sugar. It will not become any softer after the sugar has been added; in fact, it seems to toughen a little.

★ Warm sugar dissolves more quickly when added to the fruit so heat it in a very cool oven (110°C/225°F, gas mark ¼) for about 15 minutes.

★ Ensure that the sugar has dissolved completely before boiling for a set or it may crystallise later in the preserve.

★ To test whether setting point has been reached, usually after 10–20 minutes of rapid boiling, drop a little of the marmalade or jelly onto a cold plate. If it stiffens and forms a skin almost immediately, it will set. A sugar thermometer will register about 104°C/220°F when setting point is reached.

★ As soon as setting point has been reached, remove the pan from the heat and skim off any froth and scum immediately.

★ To prevent the peel or fruit rising to the top of the jars allow the marmalade to stand off the heat for 10–15 minutes, then stir well before potting.

★ To improvise a jelly bag, line a large sieve with a well-boiled and still damp tea cloth. Tip in the pulp, then gather up and knot the corners.

★ Packets of jam pot covers include discs of waxed paper. Put these, wax side down, on the surface of the marmalade or jelly as soon as the jars are filled. When they are cold, apply the covers.

Dark, Thick Cut Marmalade

900 g (2 lb) Seville oranges
2 lemons
2.25 litres (4 pints) water
900 g (2 lb) granulated or
  preserving sugar
900 g (2 lb) Demerara sugar
2 tablespoons treacle

Line a sieve with a square of muslin (or a well-boiled handkerchief) and set it over a bowl. Cut the oranges and lemons in halves, squeeze out the juice and strain it into the bowl. Using a teaspoon, scoop out the pips and ragged pieces of pith into the sieve. Tie up the muslin into a bag and put it in the preserving pan with the juice.

Cut the orange peel only into short, thick strips and add them to the pan with the water. Bring to the boil, reduce the heat and simmer gently until the peel is very tender and the liquid is well reduced – this usually takes at least two hours.

Lift the muslin bag out of the liquid and squeeze as much as possible of its pectin-rich juice back into the pan. Now add all the sugar and the treacle and stir the mixture on a low heat until the sugar has dissolved completely. Increase the heat and boil the marmalade rapidly. After 10 minutes test for setting (see page 239), and repeat the test every minute or two until a set is reached. Remove the pan from the heat and skim immediately. Allow the marmalade to cool a little, stir well and pour it into hot jars.

To transform this or the following recipe into the master's special reserve, add two tablespoons of whisky to each 600 ml (1 pint) of finished marmalade just before potting.

Oxford Marmalade

900 g (2 lb) Seville oranges
1 lemon
2.25 litres (4 pints) water
1.8 kg (4 lb) granulated or
  preserving sugar

Line a sieve with a square of muslin (or a well-boiled handkerchief) and set it over a bowl. Cut the oranges and lemon in halves, squeeze out the juice and strain it into the bowl. Using a teaspoon, scoop out the pips and ragged pieces of pith into the sieve. Tie up the muslin into a bag and put it in the preserving pan with the juice.

Cut the orange and lemon peel into short, thick strips and add them to the pan with the water. Bring to the boil, reduce the heat and simmer gently until the peel is very tender and the liquid is well reduced – this usually takes at least two hours.

Lift the muslin bag out of the liquid and squeeze as much as possible of its juice back into the pan. Now add the sugar and stir the mixture on a low heat until the sugar has dissolved completely. Simmer the marmalade slowly for about 1½ hours, or until it is dark in colour and has reached setting point (see page 239). Remove the pan from the heat and skim immediately. Allow the marmalade to cool a little before stirring well and potting.

Seville Orange Marmalade

MAKES ABOUT 3.2 kg (7 lb)

900 g (2 lb) Seville oranges
2 lemons
2.25 litres (4 pints) water
1.8 kg (4 lb) granulated or
*   preserving sugar*

Line a sieve with a square of muslin (or a well-boiled handkerchief) and set it over a bowl. Cut the oranges and lemons in halves, squeeze out the juice and strain it into the bowl. Using a teaspoon, scoop out the pips and ragged pieces of pith into the sieve. Tie up the muslin into a loose bag and put it in the preserving pan with the juice.

Cut the orange peel only into fine strips about 2.5 cm (1 in) long and add them to the pan with the water. Bring to the boil, reduce the heat and simmer gently until the peel is very tender and the liquid has reduced to about half its original volume – this usually takes at least two hours.

Lift the muslin bag out of the liquid and squeeze as much as possible of its juice back into the pan. Now add the warmed sugar and stir the mixture on a low heat until the sugar has dissolved completely. Increase the heat and boil the marmalade rapidly. After 10 minutes test for setting (see page 239), and repeat the test every minute or two until a set is reached. Remove the pan from the heat and skim off any froth immediately. Allow the marmalade to cool a little, stir well and pour it into hot jars.

Lemon and lime marmalade is especially good on very fresh dark rye bread. The recipe can, of course, be made with lemons only and I have included it here for anyone who cannot find Seville oranges, or wants to make marmalade outside their short season.

Lemon and Lime Marmalade

MAKES ABOUT 3.2 kg (7 lb)

450 g (1 lb) lemons
450 g (1 lb) limes
2.25 litres (4 pints) water
1.8 kg (4 lb) granulated sugar

Line a sieve with a square of muslin (or a well-boiled handkerchief) and set it over a bowl. Cut the lemons and limes in halves, squeeze out the juice and strain it into the bowl. Using a teaspoon, scoop out the pips and as much as possible of the pith into the sieve. Tie up the muslin into a loose bag and put it in the preserving pan with the juice.

Cut the lemon and lime peel into very fine strips about 2.5 cm (1 in) long and add them to the pan with the water. Proceed exactly as for Seville orange marmalade (see page 241).

Bitter orange jelly with no peel at all is not for breakfast but for dinner. Serve it with crisply roasted duck, or with roast game, lamb or pork.

Bitter Orange Jelly

MAKES ABOUT 900 g (2 lb)

900 g (2 lb) Seville oranges
2.25 litres (4 pints) water
preserving sugar (for amount see method)

Cut the oranges in halves and chop them coarsely, face down, on a board as for onions. Put them in a pan with the water and simmer for about two hours. Strain the pulp through a scalded jelly bag and leave it to drip overnight.

Measure the strained juice and return it to the pan. Heat it, and to every 600 ml (1 pint) of hot juice, add 450 g (1 lb) of preserving sugar.

Heat slowly until the sugar has dissolved completely, then increase the heat and boil briskly to obtain a set. After 10 minutes test for setting (see page 239), and repeat the test every minute or two until a set is reached. Remove the pan from the heat and skim immediately. Pot the jelly as quickly as possible.

Strawberry jam calls for small berries, ripe, but only just, which will keep their shape during cooking. Jelly needs fully ripe strawberries, but the good bits of bruised fruit serve as well as perfect berries.

Strawberry Jam

MAKES ABOUT 2.7 kg (6 lb)

1.8 kg (4 lb) small, just ripe strawberries
1.6 kg (3¹/₂ lb) granulated sugar
6 tablespoons fresh lemon juice

Hull and rinse the strawberries. Crush a handful of the berries and put them in the bottom of the preserving pan. Add the whole fruit, sugar and lemon juice.

Heat slowly, stirring occasionally, until the sugar has melted completely. This is important, because if the sugar is boiled before it has dissolved, it may revert to its crystal form in the finished jam.

As soon as the sugar has dissolved, bring the mixture quickly to the boil, then boil as rapidly as possible, until setting point is reached (see page 239).

Remove the pan from the heat and skim off the frothy pink scum. Set the jam aside until a skin begins to form on the surface, then stir it to distribute the fruit evenly and pour it into hot, very clean jars, filling them almost to the brim. Seal the jars immediately.

Strawberries and gooseberries ripen at about the same time which makes them ideal partners in a ravishingly pretty jelly. The high pectin content of the gooseberries ensures a good set, and the strawberries give the jelly its lovely flavour and colour. Use it to glaze strawberry or peach tarts or flans, or serve it as a summery accompaniment to cold meats like chicken, duck or pork.

Strawberry Jelly

MAKES ABOUT 1.8 kg (4 lb)

900 g (2 lb) ripe gooseberries
300 ml (¹/₂ pint) water
900 g (2 lb) ripe strawberries
juice of 2 large lemons
preserving or granulated sugar (for amount see method)

Do not bother to top and tail the gooseberries. Just wash them and put them in a preserving pan with the water. Bring to the boil, reduce the heat and simmer until the fruit is pulpy. Add the hulled and rinsed strawberries and continue simmering until the strawberries too are mushy. Tip the pulp into a scalded jelly bag and leave it to drip overnight.

Measure the strawberry and gooseberry juice, add the lemon juice and put it in the preserving pan. Add 450 g (1 lb) of sugar for every 600 ml (1 pint) of juice. Heat gently, stirring now and then until the sugar has dissolved completely, then boil as rapidly as possible to obtain a set (see page 239).

It is not necessary to skim the jelly as it boils, but when it is ready, strain it quickly through a sieve lined with muslin.

Pour the jelly immediately into hot, very clean jars, filling them almost to the brim. Fit a waxed paper disc, wax side down, on the surface of the jelly. When the jelly is quite cold, seal the jars with transparent jam pot covers, label the pots and store in a cool, dark place.

Tradition has a lot to say about the combination of gooseberries with elderflowers. If you have never tasted gooseberry and elderflower jelly it is hard to believe that a few lacy elderflower heads will give it such a remarkable flavour of muscat grapes. The same combination of fruit and flowers makes a lovely sorbet too (see page 196).

Transforming sour green gooseberries into a warm pink jelly is one of life's simpler pleasures. Eat it, like redcurrant jelly, with toast or roasts. And if you do not trust yourself to identify elderflowers, tarragon is another pleasant flavour to combine with gooseberries.

Gooseberry and Elderflower Jelly

MAKES ABOUT 1.6 kg (3½ lb)

1.8 kg (4 lb) green gooseberries
1 litre (1¾ pints) water
about 680 g (1½ lb) preserving or granulated sugar (see method)
4 elderflower heads, or a large handful of tarragon

There is no need to top and tail the gooseberries. Just wash them and put them in a preserving pan with the water. Bring to the boil, reduce the heat and simmer, uncovered, until the fruit is pulpy. Put the pulp in a scalded jelly bag and leave it to drip overnight.

Measure the juice and return it to the pan. Stir in 450 g (1 lb) of sugar for every 600 ml (1 pint) of juice. Tie the elderflower heads or tarragon loosely in muslin and add it to the pan. Heat the juice slowly until the sugar has dissolved completely, then boil rapidly to obtain a set (see page 239).

Remove the muslin and elderflowers, then pour the jelly into hot, immaculately clean jars, filling them almost to the brim. When they are quite cold, seal the jars with transparent jam pot covers, label the pots and store in a cool, dark place.

London pigeons put on an uncharacteristic display of agility when fat bunches of orange rowan berries dangle for the pecking. As soon as the fruit starts to ripen the blasted pigeons are out there practising a balancing act, flapping noisily to keep control. Every year it is a race with the birds to pick the berries first.

Rowans make a bitter jelly which in Scotland is traditionally served with venison. Mixed with apples they make a distinctively flavoured but less astringent preserve which goes beautifully with any roast game and roast pork.

Rowan Jelly

MAKES ABOUT 1.8 kg (4 lb)

900 g (2 lb) rowan berries
900 g (2 lb) cooking or crab apples
1 lemon
preserving or granulated sugar (for amount see method)

Pull the berries off their stalks and rinse them in cold water. Wash the apples. Chop them roughly without peeling or coring them, but do cut out any bruises or bad bits. Remove the lemon peel with a sharp knife or potato peeler and squeeze the juice from the flesh.

Put the rowans, apples, lemon peel and juice in a preserving pan and add enough cold water barely to cover the fruit. Bring to the boil, reduce the heat and simmer until the fruit is pulpy. Tip the pulp into a scalded jelly bag and leave it to drip overnight.

Measure the juice and return it to the pan. Stir in 450 g (1 lb) of sugar for every 600 ml (1 pint) of juice. Heat gently, stirring from time to time, until the sugar has dissolved completely, then boil rapidly to obtain a set (see page 239).

Quickly strain the jelly through a sieve lined with muslin and pour it into hot, very clean jars, filling them almost to the brim. Fit a waxed paper disc, wax side down, on the surface of the jelly. When the jelly is quite cold, seal the jars with transparent jam pot covers, label the pots and store in a cool, dark place.

Apple and tarragon jelly has a flavour which goes as well with grilled lamb chops as it does with hot buttered toast. Mint and thyme are alternative flavouring herbs.

Apple and Tarragon Jelly

MAKES ABOUT 1.8 kg (4 lb)

1.8 kg (4 lb) cooking apples
preserving or granulated sugar (for amount see method)
a handful of fresh tarragon, or 1 tablespoon dried tarragon

Wash the apples. Chop them roughly without peeling or coring them, but do cut out any bruises or bad bits. Put them in a preserving pan with 1.25 litres (2¼ pints) of cold water. Bring to the boil, reduce the heat and simmer until the fruit is pulpy. Tip the pulp into a scalded jelly bag and leave it to drip overnight.

Measure the juice and return it to the pan. Tie the tarragon loosely in a square of muslin, and put it in the pan. Stir in 450 g (1 lb) of sugar for every 600 ml (1 pint) of juice. Heat gently, stirring now and then, until the sugar has dissolved completely, then boil fast to obtain a set (see page 239).

Quickly strain the jelly through a sieve lined with muslin and pour it into hot, very clean jars, filling them almost to the brim. Fit a waxed paper disc, wax side down, on the surface of the jelly. When the jelly is quite cold, seal the jars with transparent jam pot covers, label the pots and store in a cool, dark place.

Spiced apple cheese is a really thick preserve which can be eaten as jam, or served like chutney with cheese, a cold roast pork or ham. It can take a couple of hours or more to simmer down to the required thickness, and be warned: the seething brew spits sticky gobbets all round the pan.

Spiced Apple Cheese

MAKES ABOUT 2.7 kg (6 lb)

cooked apple pulp left over from making apple and tarragon jelly (see page 245)
600 ml (1 pint) cider
150 ml (¹/4 pint) cider or wine vinegar
soft brown sugar (for amount see method)
1 teaspoon ground cinnamon
1 teaspoon ground ginger
¹/2 teaspoon ground cloves

Mix the apple pulp and the cider. Press the pulp through a sieve and discard the residue.

Measure the purée and put it in a stainless steel or enamel pan with the vinegar. Add 450 g (1 lb) of sugar for every 600 ml (1 pint) of purée, then add the cinnamon, ginger and cloves.

Bring slowly to the boil and simmer gently, stirring frequently, until the cheese is thick. When it is thick enough you can draw a wooden spoon across the cheese and the bottom of the pan will remain visible for a moment or two.

Pot the preserve in small jars or moulds prepared in the usual way, cover, label and store in a cool, dark place for a couple of months before using.

Spring rhubarb made delicious runny rhubarb and ginger jam which we spooned over Scotch pancakes as fast as my mother could make them on a black iron girdle. The rhubarb and ginger jam-maker was my grandmother who said that spring rhubarb made jam which never set as stiffly as jam made later in the year with full grown stalks.

You could use extra pectin from the chemist to firm it up but, for myself, I am not tempted. A bit runny is how it is supposed to be.

Rhubarb and Ginger Jam

MAKES ABOUT 2.3 kg (5 lb)

1.35 kg (3 lb) tender, young rhubarb
1.35 kg (3 lb) preserving or granulated sugar

Wash and dry the rhubarb, trim the ends and chop the stalks into 1.25 cm (¹/2 in) lengths. Put the rhubarb and sugar in alternate layers in a bowl, cover the bowl and leave overnight. The sugar will draw the juice from the fruit.

*30 g (1 oz) fresh green ginger,
  chopped, or dry root ginger,
  well-bruised*
3 large lemons

Tip the fruit and sugar into a preserving pan. Add the ginger, loosely tied in muslin, and the finely grated zest and strained juice of the lemons.

Bring the mixture slowly to the boil, reduce the heat and simmer until the rhubarb is almost pulpy. Remove the ginger bag, increase the heat and boil the jam very fast to a set (see page 239).

Pour the jam into hot, very clean jars, filling them almost to the brim. Fit a waxed paper disc, wax side down, on the surface of the jam and seal immediately with transparent jam pot covers. Store the jam in a cool, dark place.

Another old fashioned preserve is lemon curd. New-laid eggs, or at least very fresh eggs are needed for it. Even with refrigeration it seldom keeps longer than about three months, so make small quantities at a time.

MAKES ABOUT 1.35 kg (3 lb)

Lemon Curd

6 juicy lemons
225 g (8 oz) unsalted butter
570 g (1¼ lb) caster sugar
*6 large fresh eggs, newly laid if
  possible*

Wash and dry the lemons. Finely grate the zest and squeeze and strain the juice. Put the juice and grated zest into the top of a large double saucepan (or in a bowl over a pan of hot water) with the butter and sugar. Cook slowly over hot water until the butter has melted and the sugar has dissolved completely.

Beat the eggs lightly in a bowl and pour them into the lemon mixture through a fine sieve. Cook the mixture gently, stirring constantly, until the curd thickens enough to coat the back of a wooden spoon. On no account boil the mixture or it will curdle.

Pour the curd into spotlessly clean heated jars. Fit each jar with a waxed paper disc, wax side down, and pressing out any air bubbles. Cover and label the jars. As soon as they are cool, store them in the refrigerator.

Bears and honey have a well documented affinity. But have you heard tell about bears and blueberries?

My source for what follows was a mountain man who, in the manner of men of the American west, told the tale in a matter-of-fact drawl.

Bears, he declared, are mighty fond of blueberries which grow high in the Rockies. In late summer, when the fruit is ripe and sweet, the bears set to and eat themselves silly. Their muzzles turn blue with the juice of pawfuls of berries, and such is their gluttony, that so do their rumps.

The bears had holed up for the winter by the time I passed through their territory, so there was no chance of checking the story. But the picture of blue-tailed bears feasting on wild berries is so diverting that I dearly hope it is true.

Blueberries have a subtle flavour, not unlike blackberries. It is much less assertive than better known soft fruits like raspberries or blackcurrants. They are widely cultivated in the United States where the small low bush fruit of Maine is more highly prized than the bigger berries and more abundant high bush crops of other states.

Wild blueberries are not common in Britain, but their larger, cultivated cousins, plump berries about the size of small grapes with a dusty bloom on their blue-black skins, can be found in late summer. Serve them raw with sugar and cream or natural yogurt, or use them to make recipes like America's famous blueberry muffins.

Although there are over 100 varieties of the blueberry shrub *Vaccinium nitidum*, it should not be confused with the bilberry plant, *Vaccinium myrtillus*. Other British names for the bilberry are blaeberry, hurtleberry and whortleberry, and in France, where the fruit is used for jams and small tarts, the berries are called *myrtilles*. Bilberries can be used in the following recipe.

Blueberries make a subtly flavoured jam. Its colour is a really deep purple and it does not set stiffly. Like bilberry jam, the *confiture de myrtilles* of the French alps, it is particularly good with warm croissants and big cups of fresh breakfast coffee.

Blueberry Jam

MAKES ABOUT 3.2 kg (7 lb)

1.8 kg (4 lb) granulated or preserving sugar
1.8 kg (4 lb) fresh blueberries
3 lemons
½ teaspoon salt

Put the sugar in an ovenproof dish and set it in a preheated cool oven (150°C/300°F, gas mark 2) while you prepare the fruit.

Wash the blueberries and put them in a preserving pan or large saucepan with about 300 ml (½ pint) of water. Squeeze the juice from the lemons and add it to the pan with the salt. Bring the fruit slowly to the boil and simmer it gently for five minutes.

Add the warmed sugar to the blueberries and, keeping the heat low, stir gently until the sugar has dissolved completely. Now increase the heat and boil briskly, stirring from time to time, until the jam reaches a soft set (see page 239). Continued boiling will not make it set more firmly and will only spoil the flavour and appearance of the jam.

Skim the surface, and pour the jam into hot, spotlessly clean jars. Fit a disc of waxed paper, wax side down, on the surface of the jam, then cover and seal the jars. Store the jam in a cool, dark place.

Mincemeat is the one traditional Christmas recipe in which I still put candied peel, preferring freshly grated zests in cakes and puddings. Look for top quality candied peel in large pieces, rather than the diced tubs of mixed peels. Not only will it taste better, but you can avoid the green citron peel if you share my dislike of its flavour. Good grocers and wholefood shops are the likeliest hunting grounds. Mincemeat can be made with melted butter instead of the usual suet. Use it to stuff baked apples as well as in large or individual mince pies.

Mincemeat

MAKES 1.8 kg (4 lb)

340 g (12 oz) dessert apples
225 g (8 oz) currants
225 g (8 oz) stoned raisins
225 g (8 oz) sultanas
170 g (6 oz) candied orange peel
170 g (6 oz) candied lemon peel
170 g (6 oz) dark brown sugar
110 g (4 oz) chopped almonds
1 teaspoon finely grated orange zest
1 teaspoon mixed spice
¹/₂ teaspoon freshly grated nutmeg
¹/₂ teaspoon salt
2 tablespoons fresh lemon juice
225 g (8 oz) butter, melted
6 tablespoons cognac or whisky

Peel and core the apples. Pass them through the coarse blade of a mincer together with the currants, raisins, sultanas and candied peels. Alternatively, grate the apple and use a food processor to chip the candied peel very finely before mixing both with the fruit. Mix this in a bowl with the sugar, almonds, orange zest, mixed spice, nutmeg and salt. Add the lemon juice, butter and cognac or whisky and mix well. Pack the mincemeat into clean jars, seal tightly and store in a cool, dark place for four weeks or more before using.

Spiced prunes make an excellent sweet-sour accompaniment to serve with cold meats, especially pork and duck.

Spiced Prunes

MAKES ABOUT 1.8 kg (4 lb)

900 g (2 lb) large prunes
cold weak tea
450 g (1 lb) sugar
450 ml (³/₄ pint) cider or wine vinegar
1 stick of cinnamon, splintered
6 whole cloves
thinly pared zest of 1 small orange

Soak the prunes overnight in just enough cold tea to cover them.

Put the sugar in a large stainless steel or enamel saucepan with the vinegar and heat slowly until the sugar has dissolved completely. Add the cinnamon and cloves and the orange zest cut in thin strips. Add the prunes and tea, bring to the boil and simmer for about 15 minutes.

Remove the prunes from the liquid with a slotted spoon and pack them into hot, very clean jars, filling them almost to the top. Reduce the liquid to a thickish syrup by fast boiling, then strain it over the prunes to cover them. Seal the jars and store for a month or more before using. Glass-topped jars with rubber sealing washers are the best type to use for any preserve based on vinegar. On no account use unpainted metal lids which would corrode when in contact with the acid.

17

Drinks

Somewhere near the index of many a cookery book there is a brief entry on coffee. An especially memorable one appears in *The Frugal American Housewife* published in Boston in 1833 and 'dedicated to those who are not ashamed of economy'. The author is Mrs Child – Lydia Maria Child, writer and reformer – and her advice on coffee speaks eloquently of nineteenth century thrift.

'French coffee is so celebrated, that it may be worth while to tell how it is made; though no prudent housekeeper will make it, unless she has boarders, who are willing to pay for expensive cooking.

'The coffee should be roasted more than is common with us; it should not hang drying over the fire, but should be roasted quick; it should be ground soon after roasting, and used as soon as it is ground. Those who pride themselves on first-rate coffee, burn it and grind it every morning.

'As substitutes for coffee, some use dry brown bread crusts, and roast them; others soak rye grain in rum, and roast it, others roast peas in the same way as coffee. None of these is very good; and peas so used are considered unhealthy. Where there is a large family of apprentices and workmen, and coffee is very dear, it may be worthwhile to use the substitutes, or to mix them half and half with coffee; but, after all, the best economy is to go without.'

Going without is a virtue which has gone out of fashion. But stretching coffee with other substances, chicory or fig usually, is an economy measure still widely practised. It is a pity that the coffee used as a flavouring in recipes so often needs to be double or triple strength. It means that almost the only use for cold, leftover coffee is to serve it iced.

Camp coffee, cold milk and ice cubes smashed together in a blender make excellent instant iced coffee for those who take sugar. Simpler and more refreshing is fresh black coffee, double strength, poured over ice cubes. Spiced iced black coffee is a pleasing variation which can be laced with something stronger as the occasion demands. Rum is good.

Spiced Iced Coffee

SERVES 6

1 litre (1³/4 pints) freshly brewed
  strong black coffee
4 sticks of cinnamon
6 cloves
thinly pared zest of ¹/2 an orange
sugar, syrup or honey to taste

Stir into the hot coffee the cinnamon, cloves and orange zest, then allow it to cool. Chill for several hours before straining the spiced coffee into tall glasses filled with ice. Desperate caffeine addicts are strangers to moderation and make their ice cubes from black coffee too. Add the sugar, syrup or honey as required.

A less promising combination of ingredients than beer, wine, gin and eggs is hard to conceive. But *rumfustian* is such an irresistibly unruly sounding name for a drink that it had to be tried. One sip of this hot, creamy stunner and my husband had retitled it electric custard. After that he did not say very much at all for an hour or so, which may explain why rumfustian was a popular nineteenth century nightcap.

Hot and heady punches are certainly soporific, but there is no more festive or traditional welcome for winter travellers.

Rumfustian

SERVES ABOUT 12

12 egg yolks
170 g (6 oz) sugar
1.2 litres (2 pints) light beer
750 ml (1¹/4 pints) dry white wine
600 ml (1 pint) gin
1 teaspoon ground ginger
1 teaspoon freshly grated nutmeg
1 teaspoon ground cinnamon

Remove any stringy bits of white from the egg yolks and put them in a heavy-based saucepan with all the other ingredients. Whisk the mixture thoroughly, then set it on a low heat. Cook, stirring constantly and without allowing the mixture to come to the boil, until the rumfustian thickens slightly. Serve immediately.

Among the recipes for hot and cold punches and cups in *Modern Cookery*, 1845, Eliza Acton included this Oxford Receipt for Bishop.

'Make several incisions in the rind of a lemon, stick cloves in these, and roast the lemon by a slow fire. Put small but equal quantities of cinnamon, cloves, mace, and allspice, with a race of ginger, into a saucepan with half a pint of water: let it boil until it is reduced by one-half. Boil one bottle of port wine, burn a portion of the spirit out of it by applying a lighted taper to the saucepan; put the roasted lemon and spice into the wine; stir it up well, and let it stand near the fire ten minutes. Rub a few knobs of sugar on the rind of a lemon, put the sugar into a bowl or jug, with the juice of half a lemon (not roasted), pour the wine into it, grate in some nutmeg, sweeten it to taste, and serve it up with the lemon and spice floating in it.

'*Obs*. Bishop is frequently made with a Seville orange stuck with cloves and slowly roasted, and its flavour to many tastes infinitely finer than that of the lemon.'

Mulled Wine

SERVES ABOUT 12

2 litres (3¹/₂ pints) red wine
1 orange, thinly sliced
1 lemon, thinly sliced
sugar to taste
2 sticks of cinnamon
6 cloves
350 ml (12 fl oz) orange flavoured
    liqueur (optional)

Stir together 600 ml (1 pint) of the wine, the orange and lemon slices, 110 g (4 oz) of sugar, the cinnamon and cloves. Bring to the boil, remove from the heat and leave to stand for an hour or more so that the flavours of the fruit and spice permeate the wine. Add the remaining wine and heat the mixture almost to boiling point, adjusting the sweetness to taste.

Pour one or two tablespoons of orange liqueur – orange Curaçao, Cointreau or Grand Marnier – into each glass and top up with hot spiced wine. Fresh slices of fruit may be added as a garnish.

Lambswool

SERVES ABOUT 12

900 g (2 lb) eating or cooking
    apples
225 g (8 oz) light brown sugar
2 teaspoons freshly grated nutmeg
2 teaspoons ground cinnamon
1 teaspoon ground ginger
2.75 litres (5 pints) light beer

Wash and core the apples and bake them in a preheated moderately hot oven (190°C/375°F, gas mark 5) until the skins burst and the flesh is soft and fluffy. Discard the skins and put the apple pulp in a large warmed bowl. Add the sugar, nutmeg, cinnamon and ginger and mix well.

Heat the beer until it is hot, but not boiling, and pour it over the apples. Stir and serve.

Hot Toddy

FOR EACH SERVING:

1–3 teaspoons Demerara sugar or
    runny honey
1 tablespoon fresh lemon juice
small piece of cinnamon stick
1 clove
2 tablespoons, or more, whisky,
    whiskey or rum
boiling water

Put the sugar or honey, lemon juice, cinnamon, clove and spirits into a tumbler and top up with the boiling water. Stir and serve.

Index